Programming

Common to Computer Science and Information Technology

R. Vinston Raja
Assistant Professor
Information Technology
Panimalar Institute of Technology
Chennai

K. Hemapriya
Assistant Professor
Computer Science and Engineering
Panimalar Institute of Technology
Chennai

Dr.A. Joshi
Professor and Head
Information Technology
Panimalar Institute of Technology
Chennai

Dr.V. Subedha
Professor and Head
Computer Science and Engineering
Panimalar Institute of Technology
Chennai

Dr.D. Srinath
Professor
Computer Science and Engineering
Panimalar Institute of Technology
Chennai

Published by

BONFRING®
intellectual integrity

Programming and Data Structures I(Common to Computer Science and Information Technology)
Copyright © 2017 by Bonfring

All rights reserved. Authorized reprint of the edition published by Bonfring. No part of this book may be reproduced in any form without the written permission of the publisher.

Limits of Liability/Disclaimer of Warranty: The authors are solely responsible for the contents of the paper in this volume. The publishers or editors do not take any responsibility for the same in any manner. Errors, if any, are purely unintentional and readers are required to communicate such errors to the editors or publishers to avoid discrepancies in future. No warranty may be created or extended by sales or promotional materials. The advice and strategies contained herein may not be suitable for every situation. This work is sold with the understanding that the publisher is not engaged in rendering legal, accounting, or other professional services. If professional assistance is required, the services of a competent professional person should be sought. Further, reader should be aware that internet website listed in this work may have changed or disappeared between when this was written and when it is read.

Bonfring also publishes its books in a variety of electronic formats. Some content that appears in print may not be available in electronic books.

ISBN 978-93-86638-28-1

Authors

R. Vinston Raja

K. Hemapriya

Dr.A. Joshi

Dr.V. Subedha

Dr.D. Srinath

Bonfring

309, 2nd Floor, 5th Street Extension, Gandhipuram,

Coimbatore-641 012.

Tamilnadu, India.

E-mail: info@bonfring.org | Website: www.bonfring.org

Phone: 0422 4213231

Preface

This book titled "Programming and Data Structures I" is written to provide a significant amount of flexibility in the order in which the material is covered, as illustrated in the accompanying programs. Selected material from:

Chapters 1 through 8 can serve as a quick review of the basics of **C programming**, followed by **advanced features of C programming** in Chapters 9 and 10. Care has been taken throughout to include sets of exercises to have an in depth idea about **C programming**. Also included are suggested **sample programs** that incorporate the essential concepts of each chapter.

Chapters 11 through 15 cover the concepts of **linear data structures**. Systematic care has been taken to support the topics with necessary routines and relevant diagrams about Linear Data structure concepts like **List, Stack, Queue, Circular Queue and Double Ended Queue**.

Chapters 16 through 18 cover the concepts of **Sorting, Searching and Hashing Techniques**. These topics are explained with necessary routines and relevant diagrams.

This book includes review **questions with solution** for each Part. University question papers are enclosed at the end of the book.

This book explains and demonstrates the tools needed to craft good programs and to solve substantial problems. This book emphasizes the entire program development process; readers will learn how to write well-designed programs and how to recognize them. They will, at the same time, develop insight into program analysis and learn how to analyse programs in order to determine their correctness and efficiency.

R. Vinston Raja
K. Hemapriya
Dr.A. Joshi
Dr.V. Subedha
Dr.D. Srinath

Acknowledgement

We sincerely thank the almighty God, who is the source of life and strength of knowledge and wisdom.

Special acknowledgement to our **Honorable Chairman Dr. Jeppiaar, M.A., B.L., Ph.D.**, Chancellor, Sathyabama University, **Esteemed Secretary and Correspondent Dr.P. Chinnadurai, M.A., Ph.D.**, and respected Directors **Tmt. C. Vijayarajeswari, Thiru C. Sakthikumar, M.E., Tmt. Saranya Sree Sakthikumar, B.E.**, of "Panimalar Group of Institutions" for their continuous support for the successful completion and publication of this book.

We thank our **principal, Dr.T. Jayanthy M.E., Ph.D.**, Panimalar Institute of Technology. We like to extend our thanks to our HOD's Dr.A. Joshi M.Tech., Ph.D., and Dr.V. Subedha M.Tech., Ph.D for their continuous support for the publication.

I would like to thank my family for standing beside me throughout my career and writing this book. Their motivation continued me to improve my knowledge towards the development of my career.

We also thank all our **friends and colleagues** for their constant source of encouragement and help in various stages of writing this book. Our sincere thanks to our Publisher, for their help and co-operation in publishing this book.

R. Vinston Raja
K. Hemapriya
Dr.A. Joshi
Dr.V. Subedha
Dr.D. Srinath

Author's Profile

R. Vinston raja, currently working as Assistant Professor in the Department of Information Technology. He has completed his M.Tech IT in Sathiyabama University in 2012. His area of interest is in Networks, Robotics and Artificial intelligence. He has published more than 20 papers in international journal and conference proceedings. He is also a recipient of Best Teacher Award in the academic year 2017-2018. He has experience in guiding student development projects.

K. Hema Priya, currently working as Assistant Professor in the Department of Computer Science and Engineering. She has completed her M.Tech in SRM University in 2013. Her area of interest is in Computer Networks, Data Structures, Database Management System and Programming Languages. She has published around 10 papers in international journal and conference proceedings. She has experience in guiding student development projects.

Dr.A. Joshi currently working as Professor and Head in the Department of Information Technology. She has completed her Ph.D from Mother Teresa Women's university in 2010, M.E from Sathiyabama University in 2012 and perusing her PhD in computer Science and Engineering in St.Peter's University. Her Research interest is in Graph Theory and networks, Theory of computation, data structures and network security. She has published more than 25 papers in international journal and conference proceedings. She is also a recipient of Best Teacher Award in the academic year 2007-2008. She is a reviewer for reputed journals. She has vast experience in guiding student and working on the research and development projects.

Dr.V. Subedha currently working as Professor and Head in the Department of Computer Science and Engineering. She has completed her M.Tech from Dr.MGR University in 2007 and Ph.D from Sathyabama University in 2013. Her Research interest are in Image Processing, Web Services, Computer Networks and security and Neural Networks. She has published more than 40 papers in international journal and conference proceedings. She is also a recipient of Best Teacher Award in the academic year 2009-2010.She is a reviewer and editorial board member for reputed journals. She has vast experience in guiding student and working on the research and development projects.

Dr.D. Srinath received his B.Tech degree from the University of Madras, India in 2004, the M.E degree from Anna University, India, in 2006 and the PhD degree from St.Peter's University, Chennai, India, in 2014. He worked at different levels in various reputed engineering colleges across India and Abroad. Currently, he is working has Professor in the Department of Computer Science and Engineering at Panimalar Institute of Technology, India. His research interests are in Network Security, Cloud computing, Mobile Adhoc Networks. He has published more than 28 research articles in various international journals and conference proceedings. He is reviewer for reputed international journals and conferences.

Chapter	Contents	Page No
Part I	**C Programming Fundamentals–A Review**	**1**
1	C Programming Fundamentals - A Review	2
	1.1. Introduction	2
	1.2. Basic Structure of C Programming	3
	1.3. C Tokens	5
	1.3.1. C Identifiers	5
	1.3.2. C - Reserved Keywords	5
	1.3.3. C - Basic Data Types	5
	1.3.4. C Modifiers	6
	1.3.5. C Qualifiers	6
	1.3.6. C - Variable	7
	1.3.7. C - Storage Classes	7
	1.3.8. C Constants	10
	1.3.9. C Escape Sequences	11
	1.4. Operators in C	12
2	**Conditional and Control Statements in C**	**16**
	2.1. Introduction	16
	2.1.1. Simple if Statement	16
	2.1.2. if else Statement in C	17
	2.1.3. Nested if in C	17
	2.1.4. If else Ladder	18
	2.1.5. Switch Statement in C	19
	2.1.6. Goto Statement in C	20
	2.1.7. Break Statement in C	21
	2.1.8. Continue Statement in C	22
	2.2. Introduction to Control Statements in C	22
	2.2.1. While Loop	23
	2.2.2. Do...While Loop	23
	2.2.3. For Loop	24
	2.3. Sample Programs Using Conditional and Control Statements	25
3	**Functions**	**34**
	3.1. Introduction	34
	3.2. Types of C Functions	34
	3.2.1. C – Library Functions	34
	3.2.2. Sample Program Using Library Functions	36

		3.2.3. C - User Defined Function	37
		3.2.4. Function Declarations	38
		3.2.5. Function Call	38
		3.2.6. Defining a Function	38
		3.2.7. Sample Program Using User Defined Functions	39
	3.3.	Parameter Passing Methods	39
		3.3.1. Function - Call by Value in C	40
		3.3.2. Function - Call by Reference in C	40
	3.4.	Function Prototypes	41
		3.4.1. Function with No Arguments and No Return Value	42
		3.4.2. Function with No Arguments but Return Value	42
		3.4.3. Function with Arguments and No Return Value	44
		3.4.4. Function with Argument and a Return Value	44
	3.5.	C-Recursion	45
	3.6.	Sample Programs for Functions	47
4	**Arrays**		**53**
	4.1.	Introduction	53
	4.2.	Types of Array	53
	4.3.	Declaring One Dimensional Array	53
	4.4.	Initializing One Dimensional Arrays	53
	4.5.	Accessing Array Elements	54
	4.6.	Passing Arrays as Function Arguments in C	56
	4.7.	Sample Program for Arrays	59
5	**String**		**68**
	5.1.	Introduction	68
	5.2.	Declaration of Strings	68
	5.3.	Initialization of String	68
	5.4.	Reading String	69
	5.5.	Passing Strings to Functions	69
	5.6.	String Manipulations Using Library Functions	70
	5.7.	Sample Programs for String Manipulations	71
6	**Preprocessor**		**77**
	6.1.	Introduction	77
	6.2.	Preprocessor Directives in C	77
	6.3.	Preprocessors Examples	77
	6.4.	Predefined Macros	78

	6.5. Preprocessor Operators	78
	6.5.1. Macro Continuation (\)	79
	6.5.2. Stringize (#)	79
	6.5.3. Token Pasting (##)	79
	6.5.4. The defined() Operator	80
	6.5.5. Parameterized Macros	80
7	**Pointers**	**82**
	7.1. Introduction	82
	7.2. Reference Operator(&)	82
	7.3. Working of Pointers in C	82
	7.4. Variation in Pointer Declarations	83
	7.4.1. NULL Pointers in C	83
	7.4.2. Void Pointers in C	84
	7.4.3. Dereferencing Operator (*)	84
	7.5. Function Pointers	84
	7.5.1. Function Pointer Without Argument	85
	7.5.2. Function Pointer with Argument	86
	7.5.3. C - Pointer to Pointer	86
	7.5.4. Pointer Arithmetic	87
	7.5.5. Pointer and Array	87
8	**Function with Variable Number of Arguments**	**89**
	8.1. Introduction	89
	8.2. Sample Program	90
	Review Questions	91
Part II	**C Programming Advanced Features**	**100**
9	**Structure and Union**	**101**
	9.1. Introduction	101
	9.2. Defining a Structure	101
	9.3. Accessing Structure Members	101
	9.4. Structure as Function Argument	102
	9.5. Structure and Pointer	103
	9.6. Array of Structure	104
	9.7. Self-Referential Structure	105
	9.8. Union	105
	9.9. Accessing Union Members	106
	9.10. Difference between Structure and Union	107

	9.11. Type Def in C		107
	9.12. Sample Programs Using Structure and Union		108
10	**File Handling Concepts**		112
	10.1. Introduction		112
	10.2. Need for a File		112
	10.3. File Operations		112
	10.4. Types of File		112
	10.4.1. Text File		112
	10.4.1.1. File Open		112
	10.4.1.2. File Close		113
	10.4.1.3. Writing a File		113
	10.4.1.4. Reading a File		114
	10.4.2. Binary File		115
	10.4.2.1. Binary File Modes		116
	10.4.2.2. Binary I/O Functions		116
	Review Questions with Solution		123
Part III	**Linear Data Structures-List**		**129**
11	**Overview of Linear Data Structure-List**		130
	11.1. Introduction to Data Structures		130
	11.2. Application of Data Structures		130
	11.3. Classification of Data Structure		131
	11.4. Abstract Data Type(ADT)		131
	11.5. List ADT		132
	11.5.1. Methods to Implement a List		132
	11.5.2. Array Implementation of List		132
	11.5.3. Linked List Implementation of List		139
	11.5.4. Singly Linked List (SLL)		139
	11.5.5. Doubly Linked List (DLL)		145
	11.5.6. Circular Linked List		149
	11.6. Applications of Linked List		153
	11.7. Sample Programs		156
	Review Questions with Solutions		166
Part IV	**Linear Data Structures-Stack, Queue**		**172**
12	**Linear Data Structures-Stack**		173
	12.1. Introduction		173
	12.2. Stack Model		173

		12.3. Operations on Stack(Stack ADT)	173
		12.4. Implementation of Stack	174
		12.4.1. Array Implementation of Stack	174
		12.4.2. Linked List Implementation of Stack	179
		12.5. Applications of Stack	186
		12.5.1. Evaluating the Arithmetic Expression	186
		12.5.2. Towers of Hanoi	195
		12.5.3. Function Calls	198
		12.5.4. Balancing the Symbols	198
	13	**Queue**	**201**
		13.1. Introduction	201
		13.2. Queue Model	201
		13.3. Operations on Queue	201
		13.4. Implementation of Queue	202
		13.4.1. Array Implementation of Queue	202
		13.4.2. Linked List Implementation of Queue	207
		13.5. Applications of Queue	212
		13.6. Drawbacks of Queue (Linear Queue)	213
	14	**Circular Queue**	214
		14.1. Introduction	214
		14.2. Operations on Circular Queue	214
	15	**Double-Ended Queue (DEQUE)**	219
		15.1. Introduction	219
		15.2. Exceptional Condition of DEQUE	219
		15.3. Operations on DEQUE	220
		Review Questions with Solution	224
Part V		**Sorting, Searching and Hash Techniques**	**228**
	16	**Sorting**	229
		16.1. Introduction	229
		16.2. Types of Sorting	229
		16.3. Sorting Algorithms	229
		16.3.1. Insertion Sort	230
		16.3.2. Selection Sort	232
		16.3.3. Shell Sort	234
		16.3.4. Bubble Sort	236
		16.3.5. Quick Sort	239

	16.3.6. Merge Sort	242
	16.3.7. Radix Sort	246
17	**Searching**	249
	17.1. Introduction	249
	17.2. Types of Searching	249
	17.2.1. Linear Search	249
	17.2.2. Binary Search	250
	17.3. Working Principle	251
18	**Hashing**	253
	18.1. Introduction	253
	18.2. Types of Hash Functions	254
	18.3. Collision	256
	18.4. Collision Resolution Strategies/Techniques (CRT)	256
	18.4.1. Separate Chaining (Open Hashing)	256
	18.4.2. Open Addressing	261
	18.4.3. Linear Probing	261
	18.4.4. Quadratic Probing	263
	18.4.5. Double Hashing	264
	18.5. Rehashing	265
	18.6. Extendible Hashing	266
	18.7. Applications of Hashing	266
	Review Questions with Solution	267
	Sample Question Papers	270
	Index	

PART I

- C programming fundamentals-a review
- Conditional and Control statements in C
- Functions
- Arrays
- String
- Preprocessor
- Pointers
- Function with variable number of arguments
- Review Questions

CHAPTER 1

C PROGRAMMING FUNDAMENTALS-A REVIEW

1.1. Introduction

C is a general-purpose high level language that was originally developed by Dennis Ritchie for the UNIX operating system. It was first implemented on the Digital Equipment Corporation PDP-11 computer in 1972. The UNIX operating system and virtually all UNIX applications are written in the C language. C has now become a widely used professional language for various reasons.

- Easy to learn.
- Structured language.
- It produces efficient programs.
- It can handle low-level activities.
- It can be compiled on a variety of computers.

Facts about C

- C was invented to write an operating system called UNIX.
- C is a successor of B language which was introduced around 1970.
- The language was formalized in 1988 by the American National Standard Institute (ANSI).
- By 1973 UNIX OS almost totally written in C.
- Today C is the most widely used System Programming Language.
- Most of the state of the art software have been implemented using C.

Why to Use C?

C was initially used for system development work, in particular the programs that make-up the operating system. C was adopted as a system development language because it produces code that runs nearly as fast as code written in assembly language. Some examples of the use of C might be:

- Operating Systems.
- Language Compilers.
- Assemblers.
- Text Editors.

- Print Spoolers.
- Network Drivers.
- Modern Programs.
- Data Bases.
- Language Interpreters.

C Program File

All the C programs are written into text files with extension ".c" for example ***hello.c***.

C Compilers

When you write any program in C language then to run that program you need to compile that program using a C Compiler which converts your program into a language understandable by a computer. This is called machine language (i.e. binary format).

1.2. Basic Structure of C Programming

A C program is segmented to many sections as shown in the Figure 1.1.

Documentation section

Link section
Definition section
Global declaration section

main() function section
{
        Declaration part
        Executable part
}

Subprogram section	
Function 1	
Function 2	
. . Function n	

Figure 1.1: Basic Structure of a C Program

The following program is written in the C programming language. Open a text file **hello.c**

| /* My first program */ Comment Line |
| #include <stdio.h>   Preprocessor |
| int main() |
| { |
| printf("Hello, World! \n"); |
| return 0; |
| } |

(i) Comments

Comments are used to give additional useful information inside a C Program. All the comments will be put inside /*...*/ as given in the example above. A comment can span through multiple lines.

(ii) Preprocessor Commands

These commands tell the compiler to do preprocessing before doing actual compilation. Like *#include <stdio.h>* is a preprocessor command which tells a C compiler to include stdio.h file before going to actual compilation.

(iii)   Functions

Functionsare main building blocks of C Program. Every C Program will have one or more functions and there is one mandatory function which is called *main()* function. This function is prefixed with keyword *int* which means this function returns an integer value when it exits. This integer value is returned using *return* statement. The C Programming language provides a set of built-in functions. In the above example *printf()* is a C built-in function which is used to print anything on the screen.

(iv) Statements & Expressions

Expressions combine variables and constants to create new values. Statements are expressions, assignments, function calls, or control flow statements which make up C programs.

Note
- C is a case sensitive programming language. It means in C, *printf* and *Printf* will have different meanings.
- C has a free-form line structure. End of each C statement must be marked with a semicolon.
- Multiple statements can be one the same line.
- White Spaces (i.e. tab space and space bar) are ignored.
- Statements can continue over multiple lines.

1.3. C Tokens

Tokens are the smallest individual unit of a C program.

Tokens in C includes identifiers, keywords, constants, string, operators.

1.3.1. C Identifiers

Identifiers are the names given to the program elements like variables, arrays and functions. They are sequence of letters(both uppercase and lowercase), numbers and underscore. Rules for naming identifiers:

- Keywords cannot be used as identifiers.
- Identifiers cannot contain special characters(#, $, ?, etc).
- Identifiers can begin with a letter or a underscore (e.g.) int _total, int total.
- Identifiers can be of any length but the compiler looks at only the first 31 characters.

1.3.2. C - Reserved Keywords

C has a set of reserved words known as keywords which cannot be used as an identifier. All the keywords are sequence of characters that have a fixed meaning. Keywords are always written in lower case letters. The following names are reserved by the C language. Their meaning is already defined, and they cannot be re-defined to mean anything else.

auto	else	long	switch
break	enum	register	typedef
case	extern	return	union
char	float	short	unsigned
const	for	signed	void
continue	goto	sizeof	volatile
default	if	static	while
do	int	struct	_Packed
double			

While naming your functions and variables, other than these names, you can choose any names of reasonable length for variables, functions etc.

1.3.3. C - Basic Data Types

C has a concept of 'data types' which are used to define a variable before its use. The definition of a variable will assign storage for the variable and define the type of data that will be held in the location. The value of a variable can be changed any time.

Basic built-in data types in C

Data Type	Size in Byte	Range
int	2	-32768 to 32767
float	4	3.4E -38 to 3.4E +38
char	1	-128 to 127
double	8	1.7E -308 to 1.7E +308

1.3.4. C Modifiers

C supports four modifiers to modify the default nature of a data type.

(i) Signed

By default all data types are declared as signed. Signed means that the data type is capable of storing negative values.

(ii) unsigned

To modify a data types behavior so that it can only store positive values, we require to use the data type unsigned.

unsignedint age;

(iii) long

Many times in our programs we would want to store values beyond the storage capacity of the basic data types. In such cases we use the data type modifier long. This doubles the storage capacity of the data type being used.

long int annualsalary;

(iv) short

If long data type modifier doubles the size, short on the other hand reduces the size of the data type to half.

short int age;

1.3.5. C Qualifiers

A type qualifier is used to refine the declaration of a variable, a function, and parameters specifying whether. C language supports the following two qualifiers:

- const.
- volatile.

(i) *const qualifier* is used to tell the compiler that the variable value cannot change after initialization.

const float pi=3.14159;

(ii) *volatile qualifier* declares a data type that can have its value changed in ways outside the control or detection of the compiler. This prevents the compiler from optimizing code referring to the object by storing the object's value in a register and re-reading it from there, rather than from memory, where it may have changed.

1.3.6. C - Variable

A variable is just a named area of storage that can hold a single value (numeric or character).

The Programming language C has two main variable types.

- Local Variables.
- Global Variables.

(i) Local Variables

- Local variables scope is confined within the block or function where it is defined. Local variables must always be defined at the top of a block.
- When a local variable is defined - it is not initialized by the system, you must initialize it yourself.
- When execution of the block starts, the variable is available and when the block ends the variable 'dies'.

(ii) Global Variables

Global variable is defined at the top of the program file and it can be visible and modified by any function that may reference it.

Data Type	Initialed
int	0
char	'\0'
float	0
pointer	NULL

1.3.7. C - Storage Classes

Every variable in a C program has memory associated with it. Memory requirement of variables is different for different types of variables. In C, memory is allocated and released at different places. C supports 4 types of storage classes and these are used to specify the scope of different variables defined within function blocks and programs.

(i) auto

- Variables without any storage class specification are considered as automatic variables.
- 'auto' keyword is used to explicitly declare the variable. All the variables declared are of type 'auto' by default.
- These are called as automatic because their memory space is automatically allocated as the variable is declared.
- These variables are given only temporary memory space and after the execution all the variables are disposed.

Syntax: storage_class_type data_type var1, var2, ………,varn;

Example: auto int a, b;

Program Using auto Storage Class

```
#include<stdio.h>
void inc();
void main()
{
        inc();
        inc();
        inc();
        getch();
}
void inc()
{
        auto int i=1;
        printf("%d\n",i);
        i++;
}
```

Output
1
1
1

(ii) Static

- Static variables are variables for which the contents of the variables will be retained throughout the program.
- These are permanent within the function in which they are declared.
- These are capable of retaining their latest values, when the function is invoked again.

Syntax: storage_class_type data_type var1, var2, ………,varn;

Example: static int a, b;

Program Using Static Storage Class

```
#include<stdio.h>
static int i=1;
void inc();
void main()
{
    inc();
    inc();
    inc();
    getch();
}
void inc()
{
    printf("%d\n",i);
    i++;
}
```

Output
1
2
3

(iii) Extern

- Extern variables are declared out of the main() function.
- The availability of these variables are throughout the program ie) both in main function and inside the user defined functions.
- The external declaration of the variables makes the variables available even for the external functions that are called during program execution.

Syntax: storage_class_type data_type var1, var2, ...,varn;

Example: extern int a, b;

Program Using Extern Storage Class

```
#include<stdio.h>
extern int v=10;
void call1();
void call2();
void main()
{
    call1();
    call2();
    printf("%d\n",v);
}
void call1()
{
    int v=20;
    printf("%d\n",v);
}
void call2()
{
    printf("%d\n",v);
}
```

Output
10
20
30

(iv) Register

- Registers are special storage areas within CPU.
- The actual arithmetic and logical operation that comprise a program are carried out within these registers.

Syntax: storage_class_type data_type var1, var2, ...,varn;
Example: register int a, b;

Here, a and b values will be stored within the registers of the computer CPU rather than in RAM.

Note

- For faster access of a variable, it is better to go for register specifiers rather than auto specifiers.
- Because, register variables are stored in register memory where as auto variables are stored in main memory.

Difference between Storage Class

Storage Specifier	Storage place	Initial / default value	Scope	Life
auto	Main Memory	Garbage value	local	Within the function only.
extern	Main memory	Zero	Global	Till the end of the main program. Variable definition might be anywhere in the C program
static	Main memory	Zero	local	Retains the value of the variable between different function calls.
register	CPU Register memory	Garbage value	local	Within the function

1.3.8. C Constants

Constants are the terms that cannot be changed during the execution of a program. In C, constants can be classified as:

(i) Integer Constants

Integer constants are the numeric constants (constant associated with number) without any fractional part or exponential part. There are three types of integer constants in C language: decimal constant (base 10), octal constant (base 8) and hexadecimal constant (base 16).

For Example

Decimal constants: 0, -9, 22 etc

Octal constants: 021, 077, 033 etc

Hexadecimal constants: 0x7f, 0x2a, 0x521 etc..

Notes

1. Use small caps *a, b, c, d, e, f* instead of uppercase letters while writing a hexadecimal constant.
2. Every octal constant starts with 0 and hexadecimal constant starts with 0x in C programming.

(ii) Floating-Point Constants

Floating point constants are the numeric constants that have either fractional form or exponent form. For example:

-2.0

0.0000234

(iii)   Character Constants

Character constants are the constants which are enclosed in a pair of single-quotation.

For Example

char a= 'S';

(iv) String Constants

String constants are the constants which are enclosed in a pair of double-quote marks.

For Example

char a[ ]="Good";

1.3.9.   C Escape Sequences

Sometimes, it is necessary to use newline(enter), tab, quotation mark etc. in the program which either cannot be typed or has special meaning in C programming. In such cases, escape sequence are used.

For example: \n is used for newline. The backslash (\ ) causes "escape" from the normal way the characters are interpreted by the compiler.

Escape Sequences	Character
\b	Backspace
\f	Form feed
\n	Newline
\r	Return
\t	Horizontal tab
\v	Vertical tab
\\	Backslash
\'	Single quotation mark
\"	Double quotation mark
\?	Question mark
\0	Null character

1.4. Operators in C

What is Operator?

Simple answer can be given using expression *4 + 5 is equal to 9*. Here 4 and 5 are called operands and + is called operator. C language supports following type of operators.

- Arithmetic Operators.
- Logical (or Relational) Operators.
- Bitwise Operators.
- Assignment Operators.
- Misc. Operators.

Let's have a look on all operators one by one.

(i) Arithmetic Operators

There are following arithmetic operators supported by C language:

Assume variable A holds 10 and variable B holds 20 then:

Operator	Description	Example
+	Adds two operands	A + B will give 30
-	Subtracts second operand from the first	A - B will give -10
*	Multiply both operands	A * B will give 200
/	Divide numerator by denumerator	B / A will give 2
%	Modulus Operator and remainder of after an integer division	B % A will give 0
++	Increment operator, increases integer value by one	A++ will give 11
--	Decrement operator, decreases integer value by one	A-- will give 9

(ii) Logical (or Relational) Operators

Following are the logical operators supported by C language.

Assume variable A holds 10 and variable B holds 20 then:

Operator	Description	Example
==	Checks if the value of two operands is equal or not, if yes then condition becomes true.	(A == B) is not true.
!=	Checks if the value of two operands is equal or not, if values are not equal then condition becomes true.	(A != B) is true.
>	Checks if the value of left operand is greater than the value of right operand, if yes then condition becomes true.	(A > B) is not true.
<	Checks if the value of left operand is less than the value of right operand, if yes then condition becomes true.	(A < B) is true.
>=	Checks if the value of left operand is greater than or equal to the value of right operand, if yes then condition becomes true.	(A >= B) is not true.
<=	Checks if the value of left operand is less than or equal to the value of right operand, if yes then condition becomes true.	(A <= B) is true.
&&	Called Logical AND operator. If both the operands are non-zero then then condition becomes true.	(A && B) is true.
||	Called Logical OR Operator. If any of the two operands is non-zero then then condition becomes true.	(A || B) is true.
!	Called Logical NOT Operator. Use to reverses the logical state of its operand. If a condition is true then Logical NOT operator will make false.	!(A && B) is false.

(iii) *Bitwise Operators*

Bitwise operator works on bits and performs bit by bit operation.

Assume A = 60 and B = 13. Now in binary format they will be as follows:

A = 0011 1100 (60)

B = 0000 1101 (13)

A&B = 0000 1100

A|B = 0011 1101

A^B = 0011 0001

~A = 1100 0011

Operator	Description	Example
&	Binary AND Operator copies a bit to the result if it exists in both operands.	(A & B) will give 12 which is 0000 1100
|	Binary OR Operator copies a bit if it exists in either operand.	(A | B) will give 61 which is 0011 1101
^	Binary XOR Operator copies the bit if it is set in one operand but not both.	(A ^ B) will give 49 which is 0011 0001
~	Binary Ones Complement Operator is unary and has the effect of 'flipping' bits.	(~A) will give -60 which is 1100 0011
<<	Binary Left Shift Operator. The left operands value is moved left by the number of bits specified by the right operand.	A << 2 will give 240 which is 1111 0000
>>	Binary Right Shift Operator. The left operands value is moved right by the number of bits specified by the right operand.	A >> 2 will give 15 which is 0000 1111

(iv) Assignment Operators

The assignment operators supported by C language:

Operator	Description	Example
=	Simple assignment operator, Assigns values from right side operands to left side operand	C = A + B will assign value of A + B into C
+=	Add AND assignment operator, It adds right operand to the left operand and assign the result to left operand	C += A is equivalent to C = C + A
-=	Subtract AND assignment operator, It subtracts right operand from the left operand and assign the result to left operand	C -= A is equivalent to C = C - A
*=	Multiply AND assignment operator, It multiplies right operand with the left operand and assign the result to left operand	C *= A is equivalent to C = C * A
/=	Divide AND assignment operator, It divides left operand with the right operand and assign the result to left operand	C /= A is equivalent to C = C / A
%=	Modulus AND assignment operator, It takes modulus using two operands and assign the result to left operand	C %= A is equivalent to C = C % A
<<=	Left shift AND assignment operator	C <<= 2 is same as C = C << 2
>>=	Right shift AND assignment operator	C >>= 2 is same as C = C >> 2
&=	Bitwise AND assignment operator	C &= 2 is same as C = C & 2
^=	bitwise exclusive OR and assignment operator	C ^= 2 is same as C = C ^ 2
|=	bitwise inclusive OR and assignment operator	C |= 2 is same as C = C | 2

(v) Miscellaneous Operators

There are few other operators supported by C Language.

Operator	Description	Example
sizeof()	Returns the size of an variable.	sizeof(a), where a is interger, will return 4.
&	Returns the address of an variable.	&a; will give actaul address of the variable.
*	Pointer to a variable.	*a; will pointer to a variable.
? :	Conditional Expression	If Condition is true ? Then value X : Otherwise value Y

(vi) Precedence of C Operators

Operator precedence determines the grouping of terms in an expression. This affects how an expression is evaluated.

Certain operators have higher precedence than others. Here operators with the highest precedence appear at the top of the table, those with the lowest appear at the bottom. Within an expression, higher precedence operators will be evaluated first.

Category	Operator	Associativity
Postfix	() [] -> . ++ - -	Left to right
Unary	+ - ! ~ ++ - - (type) * & sizeof	Right to left
Multiplicative	* / %	Left to right
Additive	+ -	Left to right
Shift	<<>>	Left to right
Relational	<<= >>=	Left to right
Equality	== !=	Left to right
Bitwise AND	&	Left to right
Bitwise XOR	^	Left to right
Bitwise OR	|	Left to right
Logical AND	&&	Left to right
Logical OR	||	Left to right
Conditional	?:	Right to left
Assignment	= += -= *= /= %= >>= <<= &= ^= |=	Right to left
Comma	,	Left to right

CHAPTER 2

CONDITIONAL AND CONTROL STATEMENTS IN C

2.1. Introduction

Statements in C usually get executed in sequential order (i.e.) starting from the first statement till last statement in the program. This is generally referred as "Top down Approach".

There are cases where a selected group of statements to be executed. This is achieved with the use of conditional statements.

Following are the conditional statements in C.

1. Simple if statement.
2. if else statement.
3. nested if else statement.
4. else if ladder statement.
5. switch statement.
6. goto.
7. break.
8. continue.

2.1.1. Simple if Statement

If the condition is true then the statement block1 gets executed otherwise these statements are skipped.

Syntax

| if (condition) |
| { |
| Statement block 1; |
| } |
| statements; |

Note: If the statement block contains only one statement then parenthesis { } is optional.

Sample Program

```
#include < stdio.h >
void main( )
{
    int a = 10 , b = 5 ;
    if ( a > b )
    {
        printf ( " a is greater " ) ;
    }
}
```

Output
a is greater

2.1.2. if else Statement in C

Statement block1 gets executed when condition is true. If condition is false, then else part statements are executed.

Syntax for if else

```
if ( condition )
{
        Statement Block1;
}
else
{
        Statement Block2;
}
Statements;
```

Sample Program

```
#include < stdio.h >
void main( )
{
    int a , b ;
    printf ( " Enter a value for a : " ) ;
    scanf ( " %d " , & a ) ;
    printf ( " \n Enter a value for b : " ) ;
    scanf ( " %d " , & b ) ;
    if ( a > b )
        printf ( " \n a is greater " ) ;
    else
        printf ( " \n b is greater " ) ;
}
```

Output :
Enter a value for a:12
Enter a value for b:16
b is greater

2.1.3. Nested if in C

Nested if else statment is same like if else statement, where new block of if else statement is defined in existing if or else block statment.

Syntax

The syntax for a **nested if** statement is as follows:

```
if ( condition 1 )
{
if ( condition 2 )
{
Statement Block 1 ;
}
else
{
Statement Bloack 2 ;
}
}
Statements ;
```

Example

```
#include <stdio.h>
int main ( )
{
    int a = 100;
    int b = 200;
    if ( a = = 100 )
{
if ( b = = 200 )
{
    printf("Value of a is 100 and b is 200\n" );
}
}
    printf("Exact value of a is : %d\n", a );
    printf("Exact value of b is : %d\n", b );
    return 0;
}
```

Result:
Value of a is 100 and b is 200
Exact value of a is : 100
Exact value of b is : 200

2.1.4. If else Ladder

The conditionns are evaluated from the top to bottom. As soon as a true condition is found, the statement associated with it is executed, and the rest of the ladder is bypassed. If non of the conditions is true, then the final else statement will be executed.

Syntax

```
if(condition1)
        statements;
    else if(condition2)
        statements;
        else if(condition)
            statements;
    else
        statements;
```

Example

```
#include<stdio.h>
#include<conio.h>
void main()
{
    int a, b;
    printf("Enter a value for a:");
    scanf("%d",&a);
    printf("\nEnter a value for b:");
    scanf("%d",&b);
    if(a>b)
            {
                    printf("\n a is greater than b");
            }
            else if(b>a)
                    {
                            printf("\n b is greater than a");
                    }
                    else
                            {
                                    printf("\n Both a and b are equal");
                            }
}
```

Output:
Enter a value for a:3
Enter a value for b:6
b is greater than a

2.1.5. Switch Statement in C

Switch case checks the value of expression/variable against the list of case values and when the match is found, the block of statement associated with that case is executed. Expression should be Integer Expression/Character.

Break statement takes control out of the case. Break Statement is Optional.

Syntax

```
switch(variable)
{
case 1:
Statements;
break;
case n:
Statements;
break;
default:
Statements;
break;
}
```

Example

```
#include<stdio.h>
void main( )
{
    int a;
    printf("Enter a no between 1 and 5 : ");
    scanf ( "%d",&a);
    switch(a)
    {
        case 1:
                printf("You choosed One");
                break;
        case 2:
                printf("You choosed Two");
                break;
        case 3:
                printf("You choosed Three");
                break;
        case 4:
                printf("You choosed Four");
                break;
        case 5:
                printf("You choosed Five");
                break;
        default :
                printf("Wrong Choice. Enter a no between 1 and 5");
                break;
    }
}
```

Output :
Enter a no between 1 and 5 : 4
You Choosed Four

2.1.6. goto Statement in C

goto is a unconditional jump statement.

Syntax

goto label;

Example

```
#include<stdio.h>
#include<conio.h>
void main()
{
    int a,b;
    printf("Enter 2 nos A and B one by one : ");
    scanf("%d%d",&a,&b);
    if(a>b)
        {
```

Output :
Enter 2 nos A and B one by one : 12
34
B is greater..

20

```
            goto first;
            }
    else
            {
            goto second;
            }
    first:
            printf("\n A is greater..");
    goto g;
    second:
            printf("\n B is greater..");
        g:
  getch();
}
```

2.1.7. Break Statement in C

Break is used to terminate the loop immediately after it is encountered. The break statement is used with conditional statements and looping statements.

Syntax of Break Statement

> break;

Example

/* C program to demonstrate the working of break statement by terminating a loop, if user inputs negative number*/

```
# include <stdio.h>
int main()
{
            float num,average,sum;
            int i,n;
            printf("Maximum no. of inputs\n");
            scanf("%d",&n);
            for(i=1;i<=n;++i)
            {
                    printf("Enter n%d: ",i);
                    scanf("%f",&num);
                    if(num<0.0)
                            break;
                    sum=sum+num;
            }
            average=sum/(i-1);
            printf("Average=%.2f",average);
    return 0; }
```

Output:
Maximum no. of inputs
4
Enter n1: 1.5
Enter n2: 12.5
Enter n3: 7.2
Enter n4: -1
Average=7.07

2.1.8. Continue Statement in C

To skip some statements inside the loop, continue statement is used.

Syntax of Continue Statement

> continue;

Continue statement is used with conditional statements and looping statements.

Example

C program to find the product of 4 integers entered by a user. If user enters 0 skip it.

```
# include <stdio.h>
int main()
{
    int i,num,product;
    for(i=1,product=1;i<=4;++i)
    {
        printf("Enter num%d:",i);
        scanf("%d",&num);
        if(num==0)
            continue;
        product*=num;
    }
    printf("product=%d",product);
    return 0;
}
```

Output:
Enter num1:3
Enter num2:0
Enter num3:-5
Enter num4:2
product = -30

2.2. Introduction to Control Statements in C

Loops causes program to execute the certain block of code repeatedly until some conditions are satisfied, i.e., loops are used in performing repetitive work in programming. There are 3 types of control statements in C programming:

1. while loop.
2. do...while loop.
3. for loop.

2.2.1. While Loop

While loop is an entry check looping statement. The while loop checks the test expression. If it is true, code inside the body of the loop gets executed. Again the test expression is checked. This process continues until the test expression becomes false.

Syntax of While Loop

```
while (test expression)
{
    Body of the loop;
}
```

Example

C Program to Find the Factorial of a Number

```
#include <stdio.h>
int main()
{
    int number,factorial = 1;
    printf("Enter a number.\n");
    scanf("%d",&number);
    while (number>0)
    {
        factorial=factorial*number;
        --number;
    }
    printf("Factorial=%d",factorial);
    return 0;
}
```

```
Output
Enter a number.
5
Factorial=120
```

2.2.2. do...while Loop

Do...while loop is very similar to while loop. Only difference between these two loops is that, in while loop, test expression is checked at first but, in do...while loop code is executed first and then the condition is checked. So, the code is executed at least once in do...while loop though the condition is false.

Syntax of do...while Loops

```
do
{
    Body of the loop;
}
while (test expression);
```

Example

C program to add all the numbers entered by a user until user enters 0.

```
#include <stdio.h>
void main()
{
    int sum=0,num;
    do
    {
        printf("Enter a number\n");
        scanf("%d",&num);
        sum+=num;
    }while(num!=0);
    printf("sum=%d",sum);
}
```

Output
Enter a number
3
Enter a number
-2
Enter a number
0
sum=1

Difference between While and Do-While Statements

while loop	do-while loop
1. Entry controlled loop	1. Exit controlled loop
2. Condition is tested first, if the condition is true then body of the loop will be executed, until the condition fails.	2. Body of the loop is executed at least once and then the condition is tested. If the condition is true then body of the loop will be executed, until the condition fails.
3. If the condition fails control comes out of the looping statements	3. If the condition fails control comes out of the looping statements

4. while (test expression)
{
    Body of the loop;
}
	4. do
	{
	    Body of the loop;
	}
	while (test expression);

2.2.3. for Loop

For loop is used to execute a set of statements repeatedly until a particular condition is satisfied. It is an open ended loop. The for loop can have more than one initialization or increment/decrement, separated using comma operator.

Syntax

```
for(initialization statement; test expression; Increment/Decrement)
{
    Body of the loop;
}
```

Example

Program to Find the Sum of First n Natural Numbers

```
#include <stdio.h>
int main()
{
    int n, count, sum=0;
    printf("Enter the value of n.\n");
    scanf("%d",&n);
    for(count=1;count<=n;++count)
    {
        sum+=count;
    }
    printf("Sum=%d",sum);
    return 0;
}
```

Output
Enter the value of n.
19
Sum=190

2.3. Sample Programs Using Conditional and Control Statements

Program 1: Area and Circumference of Circle	Output

`#include<stdio.h>`
`#include<conio.h>`
`#define PI 3.14`
`void main()`
`{`
`    int r;`
`    float area,circum;`
`    clrscr();`
`    printf("Enter the radius of the circle:\t");`
`    scanf("%d",&r);`
`    area=PI*r*r;`
`    circum=2*PI*r;`
`    printf("\n Area of the circle:\t%f\n",area);`
`    printf("\n circumference of the circle:\t%f\n",circum);`
`    getch();`
`}`
	Enter the radius of the circle:
	3
	
	Area of the circle:
	28.260000
	
	circumference of the circle:
	18.840000

Program 2: Numbers Divisible By 2 But Not By 3 and 5	Output

`#include<stdio.h>`
`#include<conio.h>`
`void main()`
`{`
`    int i;`
`    clrscr();`
`    printf("The Numbers Divisible By 2 But Not By 3 and 5 \n");`
`    for(i=20;i<=100;i++)`
`    {`
`        if(i%2==0 && i%3!=0 && i%5!=0)`
`            printf("\t\t%d\n",i);`
`    }`
`    getch();`
`}`
	The Numbers Divisible
	By 2 But Not By 3 and 5
	22 26 28 32 34 38 44 46 52 56 58 62
	64 68 74 76 82 86 88 92 94 98

Program 3: Roots of the Quadratic Equation	Output
| ```c
#include<stdio.h>
#include<conio.h>
#include<math.h>
void main()
{
    float a, b, c, d, root1, root2;
    clrscr();
    printf("Enter the values of a, b, c\n");
    scanf("%f%f%f", &a, &b, &c);
    if(a == 0 || b == 0 || c == 0)
    {
        printf("Error: Roots can't be determined");
    }
    else
    {
        d = (b * b) - (4.0 * a * c);
        if(d > 0.00)
        {
            printf("Roots are real and distinct \n");
            root1 = -b + sqrt(d) / (2.0 * a);
            root2 = -b - sqrt(d) / (2.0 * a);
            printf("Root1 = %f \nRoot2 = %f", root1, root2);
        }
        else if (d < 0.00)
        {
            printf("Roots are imaginary");
            root1 = -b / (2.0 * a) ;
            root2 = sqrt(abs(d)) / (2.0 * a);
            printf("Root1 = %f +i %f\n", root1, root2);
            printf("Root2 = %f -i %f\n", root1, root2);
        }
        else if (d == 0.00)
        {
            printf("Roots are real and equal\n");
            root1 = -b / (2.0 * a);
            root2 = root1;
            printf("Root1 = %f\n", root1);
            printf("Root2 = %f\n", root2);
        }
    }
}
``` | Enter the values of a, b, c<br><br>2<br><br>4<br><br>8<br><br>Roots are imaginary<br><br>Root1 = -1.000000 +i 1.732051<br><br>Root2 = -1.000000 -i 1.732051 |
```

Program 4 : Prime Number	Output
| ```
#include<stdio.h>
#include<conio.h>
void main()
{
    int n;
    int i;
    clrscr();
    printf("Enter a number\n\n");
    scanf("%d",&n);
    for(i=2;i<n;i++)
    {
        if(n%i==0)
        {
            printf("not prime\n");
            break;
        }
    }
    if(n==i)
        printf("prime");
    getch();
}
``` | Enter a number<br><br>5<br><br>Prime |

Program 5 : Reverse of the Number	Output
| ```
#include<stdio.h>
#include<conio.h>
void main()
{
    int sum=0,n,d;
    clrscr();
    printf("Enter the number\n\n");
    scanf("%d",&n);
    while(n>0)
    {
        d=n%10;
        sum=(sum*10)+d;
        n=n/10;
    }
    printf("Reversed number is %d",sum);
    getch();
}
``` | Enter the number<br><br>253<br><br>Reversed number is 352 |

Program 6: printing 10 10 times, 9 9 times and so on	Output
| ```
#include<stdio.h>
#include<conio.h>
void main()
{
    int a=10,i;
    clrscr();
    while(a)
    {
        for(i=a;i>=1;i--)
        {
            printf("%d\t",a);
        }
        printf("\n");
        a--;
    }
    getch();
}
``` | 10 10 10 10 10 10 10 10 10 10<br>9 9 9 9 9 9 9 9 9<br>8 8 8 8 8 8 8 8<br>7 7 7 7 7 7 7<br>6 6 6 6 6 6<br>5 5 5 5 5<br>4 4 4 4<br>3 3 3<br>2 2<br>1 |

Program 7 : Fibonacci Series	Output
| ```
#include<stdio.h>
#include<conio.h>
int main()
{
    int k,a=0,b=1,c,n;
    clrscr();
    printf("Enter the number range:");
    scanf("%d",&n);
    printf("Fibonacci Series: ");
    printf("%d %d",a,b);
    for(k=2;k<n;k++)
    {
        c=a+b;
        a=b;
        b=c;
        printf(" %d",b);
    }
    getch();
    return 0;
}
``` | Enter the number range:<br><br>5<br><br>Fibonacci Series: 0 1 1 2 3 |

Program 8 : Floyd's triangle	Output
| ```
#include <stdio.h>
int main()
{
    int n,i,j,a=1;
    clrscr();
    printf("Enter the number of rows \n");
    scanf("%d",&n);
    for (i = 1; i <= n; i++)
    {
        for (j = 1; j<=i; j++)
        {
            printf("%d ",a);
            a++;
        }
        printf("\n");
    }
    getch();
    return 0;
}
``` | Enter the number of rows<br>5<br>1<br>2 3<br>4 5 6<br>7 8 9 10<br>11 12 13 14 15 |
```

Program 9 : Leap Year	Output
| ```
#include<stdio.h>
#include<conio.h>
void main()
{
    int year;
    clrscr();
    printf("Enter a year\n\n");
    scanf("%d",&year);
    if(year%4==0)
        printf("The year %d is a leap year\n",year);
    else
        printf("The year %d is not a leap year\n",year);
    getch();
}
``` | Enter a year<br><br>1996<br><br>The year 1996 is a leap year |

Program 10 : Even or Odd	Output
| ```
#include<stdio.h>
#include<conio.h>
void main()
{
    int a;
    clrscr();
    printf("Enter a number\n");
    scanf("%d",&a);
    if(a%2==0)
        printf("The given number %d is even number\n",a);
    else
        printf("The given number %d is odd number\n",a);
    getch();
}
``` | Enter a number<br>50<br>The given number 50 is even number<br><br>Enter a number<br>11<br>The given number 11 is odd number |

Program 11 : Square Root of number	Output
| ```
#include<stdio.h>
#include<conio.h>
#include<math.h>
void main()
{
    int n;
    clrscr();
    printf("Enter a number\n\n");
    scanf("%d",&n);
    printf("Square root of %d = %0.2f \n",n, sqrt(n));
    getch();
}
``` | Enter a number<br>5<br>Square root 5 = 2.24 |
```

Program 12 : Sum of the given numbers	Output

#include<stdio.h>
#include<conio.h>
void main()
{
int n,sum=0;
clrscr();
printf("\n Enter the numbers \n");
/* (press 0 to stop giving inputs) */
do
{
scanf("%d",&n);
sum+=n;
}while(n!=0);
printf("\nsum = %d",sum);
getch();
}
	Enter the numbers
	3
	8
	5
	10
	-2
	0
	
	sum = 24

Program 13 : Swap 2 numbers	Output

#include<stdio.h>
#include<conio.h>
void main()
{
int a,b;
clrscr();
printf("Enter the value of a and b\n\n");
scanf("%d%d",&a,&b);
printf("\n\nBefore swapping\n\n");
printf("a = %d \n \nb = %d\n\n",a,b);
printf("\n\nAfter swapping\n\n");
//   a=a+b;
//   b=a-b;
//   a=a-b;
b=a+b-(a=b);
printf("a = %d \n \nb = %d\n\n",a,b);
    getch();
}
	Enter the value of a and b
	
	100
	300
	
	Before swapping
	
	a = 100
	b = 300
	
	After swapping
	
	a = 300
	b = 100

Program 14 : Sum of the digits of given number	**Output**

#include<stdio.h>
#include<conio.h>
void main()
{
int n;
int m,r,sum=0;
clrscr();
printf("Enter a number\n\n");
scanf("%d",&n);
m=n;
while(n>0)
{
r=n%10;
sum+=r;
n=n/10;
}
printf("Sum of the digits of %d is %d",m,sum);
    getch();
}
	Enter a number
	
	256
	
	Sum of the digits of 256 is 13

Program 15: Greatest of 2 number using Ternary Operator	Output

#include<stdio.h>
#include<conio.h>
void main()
{
int a,b,big;
clrscr();
printf("Enter the values of a and b\t");
scanf("%d%d",&a,&b);
big=(a>b)?a:b;
printf("\n\n The greatest among %d and %d is\t%d",a,b,big);
getch();
}
	Enter the values of a and b
	3
	7
	
	The greatest among 3 and 7 is 7

Program 16 : Combination of 4 Digit Number	Output

#include<stdio.h>
#include<conio.h>
int main()
{
int a,b,c,d;
clrscr();
printf("Combination of 4 Digit Number\n\n\n");
for(a=1; a<5; a++)
{
for(b=1; b<5; b++)
{
for(c=1; c<5; c++)
{
for(d=1; d<5; d++)
{
if(!(a==b || a==c || a==d || b==c || b==d || c==d))
printf("%d %d %d %d\n",a,b,c,d);
}
}
}
}
getch();
return 0;
}
	Combination of 4 Digit Number
	1 2 3 4
	1 2 4 3
	1 3 2 4
	1 3 4 2
	1 4 2 3
	1 4 3 2
	2 1 3 4
	2 1 4 3
	2 3 1 4
	2 3 4 1
	2 4 1 3
	2 4 3 1
	3 1 2 4
	3 1 4 2
	3 2 1 4
	3 2 4 1
	3 4 1 2
	3 4 2 1
	4 1 2 3
	4 1 3 2
	4 2 1 3
	4 2 3 1
	4 3 1 2
	4 3 2 1

Program 17 : Temperature Conversion	Output
| ```c
#include<stdio.h>
int main()
{
float fah,cel;
int choice;
clrscr();
printf("1. celsius to fahrenheit\n");
printf("2. Fahrenheit to celsius \n");
printf("3.Exit\n");
printf("Enter your choice\n\n");
scanf("%d",&choice);
switch(choice)
{
case 1:
        printf("Enter celsius value\n");
        scanf("%f",&cel);
        fah=cel*1.8+32;
        printf("%0.2f degrees celsius = %0.2f
        degrees fahrenheit\n\n",cel,fah);
        break;
case 2:
        printf("Enter fahrenheit value\n");
        scanf("%f",&fah);
        cel= (fah-32)/1.8;
        printf("%0.2f degrees fahrenheit = %0.2f
                    degrees celsius\n\n",fah,cel);
        break;
case 3:
        exit(1);
}
getch();
return 0;
}
``` | 1. celsius to fahrenheit<br>2. Fahrenheit to celsius<br>3.Exit<br><br>Enter your choice<br><br>1<br>Enter celsius value<br>32<br>32.00 degrees celsius = 89.60 degrees fahrenheit |

Program 18 : Sum of N natural numbers	Output
| ```c
#include<stdio.h>
#include<conio.h>
void main()
{
int n,i,sum=0;
clrscr();
printf("Enter the value of n:");
scanf("%d",&n);
for(i=1;i<=n;++i)
{
printf("%d\n",i);
sum+=i;
}
printf("\n Sum of n natural numbers is:%d",sum);
getch();
}
``` | Enter the value of n:5<br>1<br>2<br>3<br>4<br>5<br><br>Sum of first n natural numbers is:15 |

32

Program 19 : Simple example for Switch Case	Output
| ```c
#include<stdio.h>
#include<conio.h>
void main( )
{
int n;
clrscr( );
printf("enter a number :");
scanf("%d",&n);
switch(n)
{
case 0: printf("ZERO");
break;
case 1: printf("ONE");
break;
case 2: printf("TWO");
break;
case 3: printf("THREE");
break;
case 4: printf("FOUR");
break;
case 5: printf("FIVE");
break;
case 6: printf("SIX");
break;
case 7: printf("SEVEN");
break;
case 8: printf("EIGHT");
break;
case 9: printf("NINE");
break;
default:
printf("please enter the number between 0 and 9");
}
}
``` | enter a number : <br> 1 <br> ONE <br><br><br><br> enter a number : <br> 14 <br> please enter the number between 0 and 9 |

Program 20 : Largest digit of given number	Output
| ```c
#include<stdio.h>
#include<conio.h>
void main()
{
int d,n,large=1;
clrscr();
printf("Enter the number\n");
scanf("%d",&n);
while(n>0)
{
d=n%10;
if(d>=large)
large=d;
n=n/10;
}
printf("Largest digit : %d",large);
getch();
}
``` | Enter the number <br><br> 3458 <br><br> Largest digit : 8 |

CHAPTER 3

FUNCTIONS

3.1. Introduction

A function is a group of statements that together perform a task. Every C program has at least one function, which is main( ), and all the most trivial programs can define additional functions. A function **declaration** tells the compiler about a function's name, return type, and parameters. A function **definition** provides the actual body of the function.

3.2. Types of C Functions

Basically, there are two types of functions in C on basis of whether it is defined by user or not.

- Library function.
- User defined function.

3.2.1. C – Library Functions

- Library functions in C language are inbuilt functions which are grouped together and placed in a common place called library.
- Each library function in C performs specific operation.

(i) C – Stdio.h Library Functions

All C inbuilt functions which are declared in stdio.h header file are given below. The source code for stdio.h header file is also given below for your reference.

Function	Description
printf()	This function is used to print the character, string, float, integer, octal and hexadecimal values onto the output screen
scanf()	This function is used to read a character, string, numeric data from keyboard.
getc()	It reads character from file
gets()	It reads line from keyboard
getchar()	It reads character from keyboard
puts()	It writes line to o/p screen
putchar()	It writes a character to screen
clearerr()	This function clears the error indicators
f open()	All file handling functions are defined in stdio.h header file
f close()	closes an opened file
getw()	reads an integer from file
putw()	writes an integer to file
f getc()	reads a character from file

putc()	writes a character to file
f putc()	writes a character to file
f gets()	reads string from a file, one line at a time
f puts()	writes string to a file
f eof()	finds end of file
f getchar	reads a character from keyboard
f getc()	reads a character from file
f printf()	writes formatted data to a file
f scanf()	reads formatted data from a file
f getchar	reads a character from keyboard
f putchar	writes a character from keyboard
f seek()	moves file pointer position to given location
SEEK_SET	moves file pointer position to the beginning of the file
SEEK_CUR	moves file pointer position to given location
SEEK_END	moves file pointer position to the end of file.
f tell()	gives current position of file pointer
rewind()	moves file pointer position to the beginning of the file
putc()	writes a character to file
sprint()	writes formatted output to string
sscanf()	Reads formatted input from a string
remove()	deletes a file
fflush()	flushes a file

(ii) List of Inbuilt C Functions in string.h File

string functions	Description
strcat(str1, str2)	Concatenates str2 at the end of str1.
strcpy(str1, str2)	Copies str2 into str1
strlen(strl)	gives the length of str1.
strcmp(str1, str2)	Returns 0 if str1 is same as str2. Returns <0 if strl < str2. Returns >0 if str1 > str2.
strchr(str1,char)	Returns pointer to first occurrence of char in str1.
strstr(str1, str2)	Returns pointer to first occurrence of str2 in str1.
strcmpi(str1,str2)	Same as strcmp() function. But, this function negotiates case. "A" and "a" are treated as same.
strdup()	duplicates the string
strlwr()	converts string to lowercase
strncat()	appends a portion of string to another
strncpy()	copies given number of characters of one string to another
strrchr()	last occurrence of given character in a string is found
strrev()	reverses the given string
strset()	sets all character in a string to given character
strupr()	converts string to uppercase
memset()	It is used to initialize a specified number of bytes to null or any other value in the buffer
memcpy()	It is used to copy a specified number of bytes from one memory to another
memcmp()	It is used to compare specified number of characters from two buffers

3.2.2. Sample Program Using Library Functions

Write a C Program to Illustrate how to Read String from Terminal

```
#include <stdio.h>
void main()
{
    char name[20];
    printf("Enter name: ");
    scanf("%s",name);
    printf("Your name is %s.",name);
}
```

Output
Enter name: Dennis Ritchie
Your name is Dennis.

Example of strlen()

```
#include <stdio.h>
#include <string.h>
void main()
{
    char a[20]="Program";
    char b[20]={'P','r','o','g','r','a','m','\0'};
    char c[20];
    printf("Enter string: ");
    gets(c);
    printf("Length of string a=%d \n",strlen(a));
    printf("Length of string b=%d \n",strlen(b));
    printf("Length of string c=%d \n",strlen(c));
}
```

Output
Enter string: String
Length of string a=7
Length of string b=7
Length of string c=6

Example of strcpy()

```
#include <stdio.h>
#include <string.h>
void main()
{
    char a[10],b[10];
    printf("Enter string: ");
    gets(a);
    strcpy(b,a);   //Content of string a is copied to string b.
    printf("Copied string: ");
    puts(b);
}
```

Output
Enter string: Programming Tutorial
Copied string: Programming Tutorial

Example of strcat()

```
#include <stdio.h>
#include <string.h>
void main()
{
    char str1[]="This is ", str2[]="programiz.com";
    strcat(str1,str2);  //concatenates str1 and str2 and resultant string is stored in str1.
    puts(str1);
    puts(str2);
}
```

Output
This is programiz.com
programiz.com

Example of strcmp()

```
#include <stdio.h>
#include <string.h>
int main()
{
    char str1[30],str2[30];
    printf("Enter first string: ");
    gets(str1);
    printf("Enter second string: ");
    gets(str2);
    if(strcmp(str1,str2)==0)
        printf("Both strings are equal");
    else
        printf("Strings are unequal");
    return 0;
}
```

Output
Enter first string: Apple
Enter second string: Apple
Both strings are equal.

Use of Library Function to Find Square Root

```
#include <stdio.h>
#include <math.h>
int main()
{
    float num,root;
    printf("Enter a number to find square root.");
    scanf("%f",&num);
    root=sqrt(num);
    printf("Square root of %.2f=%.2f",num,root);
    return 0;
}
```

Output
Enter a number to find square root.25
Square root of 25.00=5.00

3.2.3. C - User Defined Function

C allows programmer to define their own function according to their requirement. These types of functions are known as user-defined functions.

Advantages of User Defined Functions

1. User defined functions helps to decompose the large program into small segments which makes programmer easy to understand, maintain and debug.
2. If repeated code occurs in a program. Function can be used to include those codes and execute when needed by calling that function.
3. Programmer working on large project can divide the workload by making different functions.

3.2.4. Function Declarations

A function **declaration** tells the compiler about a function name and how to call the function. The actual body of the function can be defined separately. A function declaration has the following parts:

> return_type function_name(parameter list);

Eg: int max(int num1, int num2);

3.2.5. Function Call

When a program calls a function, program control is transferred to the called function. A called function performs defined task and when its return statement is executed or when its function-ending closing brace is reached, it returns program control back to the main program. To call a function, simply pass the required parameters along with function name.

Eg: ret = max(a, b);

3.2.6. Defining a Function

The general form of a function definition in C programming language is as follows:

> returntype functionname(parameter list)
> {
>   body of the function
> }

A function definition in C programming language consists of a *function header* and a *function body*. Here are all the parts of a function:

- **Return Type:** A function may return a value. The **returntype** is the data type of the value the function returns. Some functions perform the desired operations without returning a value. In this case, the returntype is the keyword **void**.
- **Function Name:** This is the actual name of the function. The function name and the parameter list together constitute the function signature.

- **Parameters**

    Actual arguments: The arguments that are passed in a function call are called actual arguments. These arguments are defined in the calling function.

    Formal arguments: The formal arguments are the parameters/arguments in a function declaration. The scope of formal arguments is local to the function definition in which they are used. Formal arguments belong to the called function. Formal arguments are a copy of the actual arguments. A change in formal arguments would not be reflected in the actual arguments.

- **Function Body:** The function body contains a collection of statements that define what the function does.

3.2.7. Sample Program Using User Defined Functions

```
#include <stdio.h>
int max(int num1, int num2);
void main ( )
{
    int a = 100;
    int b = 200;
    int ret;
    ret = max(a, b);
    printf( "Max value is : %d\n", ret );
}
int max (int num1, int num2)
{
    int result;
    if (num1 > num2)
            result = num1;
    else
            result = num2;
    return result;
}
```

Output:
Max value is : 200

3.3. Parameter Passing Methods

While calling a function, there are two ways that arguments can be passed to a function:

Call Type	Description
Call by value	This method copies the actual value of an argument into the formal parameter of the function. In this case, changes made to the parameter inside the function have no effect on the argument.
Call by reference	This method copies the address of an argument into the formal parameter. Inside the function, the address is used to access the actual argument used in the call. This means that changes made to the parameter affect the argument.

By default, C uses **call by value** to pass arguments.

3.3.1. Function - Call by Value in C

The **call by value** method of passing arguments to a function copies the actual value of an argument into the formal parameter of the function. In this case, changes made to the parameter inside the function have no effect on the argument.

By default, C programming language uses *call by value* method to pass arguments.

In general, this means that code within a function cannot alter the arguments used to call the function. Consider the function **swap()** definition as follows.

Sample Program

```
#include <stdio.h>
void swap(int x, int y);
int main ()
{
    int a = 100;
    int b = 200;
    printf("Before swap, value of a : %d\n", a );
    printf("Before swap, value of b : %d\n", b );
    swap(a, b);
    printf("After swap, value of a : %d\n", a );
    printf("After swap, value of b : %d\n", b );
    return 0;
}
void swap(int x, int y)
{
    int temp;
    temp = x;
    x = y;
    y = temp;
}
```

Output:
Before swap, value of a :100
Before swap, value of b :200
After swap, value of a :100
After swap, value of b :200

3.3.2. Function - Call by Reference in C

The **call by reference** method of passing arguments to a function copies the address of an argument into the formal parameter.

Inside the function, the address is used to access the actual argument used in the call. This means that changes made to the parameter affect the passed argument.

Sample Program

```
#include <stdio.h>
void swap(int *x, int *y);
int main ( )
{
    int a = 100;
    int b = 200;
    printf("Before swap, value of a : %d\n", a );
    printf("Before swap, value of b : %d\n", b );
    swap(&a, &b);
    printf("After swap, value of a : %d\n", a );
    printf("After swap, value of b : %d\n", b );
    return 0;
}
void swap(int *x, int *y)
{
    int temp;
    temp = *x;
    *x = *y;
    *y = temp;
}
```

Output:
Before swap, value of a :100
Before swap, value of b :200
After swap, value of a :200
After swap, value of b :100

3.4. Function Prototypes

For better understanding of arguments and return type in functions, user-defined functions can be categorized as:

1. Function with no arguments and no return value
2. Function with no arguments and with return value
3. Function with arguments but no return value
4. Function with arguments and with return value.

3.4.1. Function with No Arguments and No Return Value

/*C program to check whether a number entered by user is prime or not using function with no arguments and no return value*/

Sample Program

```
#include <stdio.h>
void prime( );
int main()
{
    prime( );    //No argument is passed to prime().
    return 0;
}
void prime()
{
    int num,i,flag=0;
    printf("Enter positive integer enter to check:\n");
    scanf("%d",&num);
for(i=2;i<num;++i)
    {
    if(num%i==0)
    {
        flag=1;
    }
    }
    if (flag= =1)
        printf("%d is not prime",num);
    else
        printf("%d is prime",num);
}
```

Output:
Enter positive integer enter to check:
11
11 is prime

Function prime() is used for asking user a input, check for whether it is prime of not and display it accordingly. No argument is passed and returned form prime() function.

3.4.2. Function with No Arguments but Return Value

/*C program to check whether a number entered by user is prime or not using function with no arguments but having return value */

Sample Program

```
#include <stdio.h>
int input();
int main()
{
    int num,i,flag = 0;
    num=input( );   /* No argument is passed to input() */
    for(i=2; i<num; ++i)
    {
        if(num%i==0)
        {
            flag = 1;
            break;
        }
    }
    if(flag = = 1)
        printf("%d is not prime",num);
    else
        printf("%d is prime", num);
    return 0;
}
int input( )
{
    /* Integer value is returned from input() to calling function */
    int n;
    printf("Enter positive integer to check:\n");
    scanf("%d",&n);
    return n;
}
```

Output:
Enter positive integer enter to check:
11
11 is prime

There is no argument passed to input() function But, the value of n is returned from input() to main() function.

3.4.3. Function with Arguments and No Return Value

/*Program to check whether a number entered by user is prime or not using function with arguments and no return value */

Sample Program

```
#include <stdio.h>
void check_display(int n);
int main()
{
        int num;
        printf("Enter positive enter to check:\n");
        scanf("%d",&num);
        check_display(num);      /* Argument num is passed to function. */
        return 0;
}
void check_display(int n)
{
/* There is no return value to calling function. Hence, return type of function is void. */
int i, flag = 0;
for(i=2; i<n; ++i)
        {
                if(n%i==0)
                {
                flag = 1;
                break;
                }
        }
        if(flag == 1)
        printf("%d is not prime",n);
        else
        printf("%d is prime", n);
}
```

Output:
Enter positive integer enter to check:
11
11 is prime

Here, check_display() function is used for check whether it is prime or not and display it accordingly. Here, argument is passed to user-defined function but, value is not returned from it to calling function.

3.4.4. Function with Argument and a Return Value

/* Program to check whether a number entered by user is prime or not using function with argument and return value */

44

Sample Program

```
#include <stdio.h>
int check(int n);
int main()
{
int num,num_check=0;
    printf("Enter positive enter to check:\n");
    scanf("%d",&num);
num_check=check(num); /* Argument num is passed to check() function. */
if(num_check==1)
    printf("%d is not prime",num);
else
    printf("%d is prime",num);
return 0;
}
int check(int n)
{
/* Integer value is returned from function check() */
int i;
for(i=2;i<n;++i)
{
if(n%i==0)
    return 1;
}
    return 0;
}
```

Output:
Enter positive integer enter to check:
11
11 is prime

Here, check() function is used for checking whether a number is prime or not. In this program, input from user is passed to function check() and integer value is returned from it. If input the number is prime, 0 is returned and if number is not prime, 1 is returned.

3.5. C-Recursion

A function that calls itself is known as recursive function and this technique is known as recursion in C programming.

```
void recursion( )
{
        recursion(); /* function calls itself */
}
 int main( )
 {
        recursion( );
}
```

45

Advantage of Recursion

- Code reusability.
- It reduces the length of the source program.
- Recursion is more elegant and requires few variables which make program clean.
- Recursion can be used to replace complex nesting code by dividing the problem into same problem of its sub-type.

Sample Program for Recursion

(i) Fibonacci Series Using Recursive Function

```
#include<stdio.h>
int Fibonacci(int);
int main()
{
    int n, i = 0, c;
    scanf("%d",&n);
    printf("Fibonacci series\n");
    for ( c = 1 ; c <= n ; c++ )
    {
        printf("%d\n", Fibonacci(i));
        i++;
    }
    return 0;
}
int Fibonacci(int n)
{
if ( n == 0 )
    return 0;
else if ( n == 1 )
    return 1;
else
    return ( Fibonacci(n-1) + Fibonacci(n-2) );
}
```

Output:
Enter Fibonacci series limit
5
Fibonacci series
0
1
1
2
3

(ii) Calculate Factorial Using Recursion

```
#include<stdio.h>
int factorial(int n);
int main()
{
    int n;
    printf("Enter an positive integer: ");
    scanf("%d",&n);
    printf("Factorial of %d = %ld", n, factorial(n));
    return 0;
}
int factorial(int n)
{
    if(n= = 0)
        return 0;
    else if(n = = 1)
        return 1;
    else
        return (n*factorial(n-1));
}
```

Output:
Enter an positive integer: 5
Factorial of 5 = 120

3.6. Sample Programs for Functions

Program 1 : Calculator Using Function	Output
#include<stdio.h>	Enter two numbers
#include<conio.h>	5
#include<stdlib.h>	3
void add(int,int);	
void sub(int,int);	1.ADD
void mul(int,int);	2.SUBTRACT
void division(int,int);	3.MULTIPLY
void mod(int,int);	4.DIVIDE
void main()	5.MODULO
{	6.EXIT
int n,a,b;	Enter your choice
clrscr();	1
printf("Enter two numbers\n");	sum = 8
scanf("%d%d",&a,&b);	

```
do
{
printf("\n1.ADD\n"
printf("\n2.SUBTRACT");
printf("\n3.MULTIPLY");
printf("\n4.DIVIDE");
printf("\n5.MODULO");
printf("\n6.EXIT\n");
printf("Enter your choice \n");
scanf("%d",&n);
switch(n)
{
case 1:
        add(a,b);
        break;
case 2:
        sub(a,b);
        break;
case 3:
        mul(a,b);
        break;
case 4:
        division(a,b);
        break;
case 5:
        mod(a,b);
        break;
case 6:
        exit(1);
default:
        printf("Enter number between 1 - 6\n");
}
}while(n!=6);
getch();
}
void add(int x,int y)
{
printf("sum = %d\n",x+y);
}
void sub(int x,int y)
{
printf("difference = %d\n",x-y);
}
```

```
1.ADD
2.SUBTRACT
3.MULTIPLY
4.DIVIDE
5.MODULO
6.EXIT
Enter your choice
2
difference = 2

1.ADD
2.SUBTRACT
3.MULTIPLY
4.DIVIDE
5.MODULO
6.EXIT
Enter your choice
3
product = 15

1.ADD
2.SUBTRACT
3.MULTIPLY
4.DIVIDE
5.MODULO
6.EXIT
Enter your choice
4
division = 1

1.ADD
2.SUBTRACT
3.MULTIPLY
4.DIVIDE
5.MODULO
6.EXIT
Enter your choice
5
mod = 2

1.ADD
2.SUBTRACT
3.MULTIPLY
```

void mul(int x,int y)
{
printf("product = %d\n",x*y);
}
void division(int x,int y)
{
printf("division = %d\n",x/y);
}
void mod(int x,int y)
{
printf("mod = %d\n",x%y);
}
	4.DIVIDE
	5.MODULO
	6.EXIT
	Enter your choice

Program 2 : Armstrong Number using Function	Output

#include<stdio.h>
#include<conio.h>
void arms();
void main()
{
  clrscr();
      arms();
      getch();
}
void arms()
{
int n,m,r,sum=0;
printf("Enter a number\n");
scanf("%d",&n);
m=n;
while(n>0)
{
r=n%10;
sum=sum+(r*r*r);
n=n/10;
}
if(m==sum)
printf("%d is a Armstrong number\n",m);
else
printf("%d is not a Armstrong number\n",m);
}
	Enter a number
	
	153
	
	153 is a Armstrong number

Program 3 : Armstrong Number between 1 to 1000 using Function	Output
| ```
#include<stdio.h>
#include<conio.h>
void arms();
void main()
{
        arms();
}
void arms()
{
    int i,n,m,r,sum;
    for(i=1;i<=1000;i++)
    {
        sum=0,n=i;
        while(n>0)
        {
            r=n%10;
            sum=sum+(r*r*r);
            n=n/10;
        }
        if(i==sum)
            printf("%d is a Armstrong number\n",i);
    }
}
``` | 1 is a Armstrong number<br><br>153 is a Armstrong number<br><br>370 is a Armstrong number<br><br>371 is a Armstrong number<br><br>407 is a Armstrong number |

Program 4 : Square and Cube of number	Output
| ```
#include<stdio.h>
#include<conio.h>
int square(int);
int cube(int);
void main()
{
int n,sq,cub;
clrscr();
printf("Enter a number\n");
scanf("%d",&n);
sq=square(n);
cub=cube(n);
printf("square of %d is %d\n",n,sq);
printf("cube of %d is %d\n",n,cub);
getch();
}
int square(int a)
{
return(a*a);
}
int cube(int a)
{
return(a*a*a);
}
``` | Enter a number<br><br>5<br><br>square of 5 is 25<br><br>cube of 5 is 125 |

Program 5 : Factorial using Recursion	Output
| ```
#include<stdio.h>
int fact(int);
int main()
{
        int num,f;
        clrscr();
        printf("\nEnter a number: ");
        scanf("%d",&num);
        f=fact(num);
        printf("\nFactorial of %d is: %d",num,f);
        getch();
        return 0;
}

int fact(int n)
{
if(n==1)
              return 1;
else
              return(n*fact(n-1));
}
``` | Enter a number:<br><br>5<br><br>Factorial of 5 is: 120 |

Program 6 : Fibonacci series using Recursion	Output
| ```
#include<stdio.h>
#include<conio.h>
int Fibonacci(int);
void main()
{
        int n,fib=0,i;
        clrscr();
        printf("Enter the limit\n");
        scanf("%d",&n);
        printf("Fibonacci series\n");

        for ( i = 0 ; i < n ; i++ )
        {
                printf("%d\t", Fibonacci(fib));
                fib++;
        }
        getch();
}

int Fibonacci(int num)
{
        if ( num == 0 )
           return 0;
        else if ( num == 1 )
           return 1;
        else
           return ( Fibonacci(num-1) + Fibonacci(num-2) );
}
``` | Enter the limit<br><br>5<br><br>Fibonacci series<br><br>0   1   1   2   3 |

51

Program 7 : Call by value & Call by reference	Output

#include<stdio.h>
#include<conio.h>
void value(int,int);
void reference(int *,int *);
void main()
{
int a,b;
clrscr();
printf("\nEnter a :\t");
scanf("%d",&a);
printf("\nEnter b :\t");
scanf("%d",&b);
printf("\nBefore swapping\n");
printf("a = %d\nb = %d\n",a,b);
value(a,b);
printf("\nAfter call by value \n");
printf("a = %d\nb = %d\n",a,b);
reference(&a,&b);
printf("\nAfter call by reference \n");
printf("a = %d\nb = %d\n",a,b);
getch();
}
void value(int x,int y)
{
int temp;
temp = x;
x = y;
y = temp;
}
void reference(int *x,int *y)
{
int temp;
temp = *x;
*x = *y;
*y = temp;
}
	Enter a : 100
	
	Enter b : 200
	
	Before swapping
	a = 100
	b = 200
	
	After call by value
	a = 100
	b = 200
	
	After call by reference
	a = 200
	b = 100

52

CHAPTER 4

ARRAYS

4.1. Introduction

C programming language provides a data structure called **array**. Array is a collection of similar data items.

A specific element in an array is accessed by an index. Array index starts from 0 to n-1, where n represents the total number of elements in an array. All array elements occupy contiguous memory locations. The lowest address corresponds to the first element and the highest address to the last element.

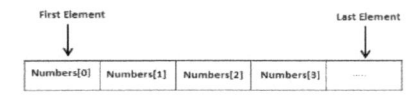

4.2. Types of Array

There are 3 types of array
1. Single dimensional array(1-dimensional array).
2. 2-dimensional array(Matrix).
3. Multi-dimensional array.

4.3. Declaring One Dimensional Array

To declare one dimentional array in C, a programmer specifies the type of the elements and the number of elements required by an array as follows:

type arrayName [arraySize];

This is called a single-*dimensional* array. The **arraySize** must be an integer constant greater than zero and **type** can be any valid C data type.

Example

double balance[10];

4.4. Initializing One Dimensional Arrays

One dimentional array can be initialized as follows:

double balance[5] = {1000.0, 2.0, 3.4, 7.0, 50.0};

The number of values between braces { } cannot be larger than the number of elements that we declare for the array between square brackets [ ].

	0	1	2	3	4
balance	1000.0	2.0	3.4	7.0	50.0

Declaring Two Dimentional Array

To declare two dimentional array in C, a programmer specifies the type of the elements and the number of rows and columns required by an array as follows:

type arrayName [RowSize][Colomn size];

Two dimentional array is also called as **matrix**.

Initialization of 2D Array

There are many ways to initialize two Dimensional arrays –

int disp[2][4] = {
    {10, 11, 12, 13},
    {14, 15, 16, 17}
};

OR

int disp[2][4] = { 10, 11, 12, 13, 14, 15, 16, 17};

4.5. Accessing Array Elements

Array elements are accessed with the help of index or subscript.

Sample Program

/* C program to find the sum of all the marks of a studentusing arrays */

```
#include <stdio.h>
int main()
{
    int marks[10],i,n,sum=0;
    printf("Enter number of marks: ");
    scanf("%d",&n);
    for(i=0;i<n;++i)
    {
        printf("Enter marks of marks %d: ",i+1);
        scanf("%d",&marks[i]);
        sum+=marks[i];
    }
    printf("Sum= %d",sum);
    return 0;
}
```

Output
Enter number of students: 3
Enter marks of student 1: 12
Enter marks of student 2: 31
Enter marks of student 3: 2
sum=45

Sample Program

Matrix Multiplication in c Language

```c
#include <stdio.h>
int main()
{
int m, n, p, q, c, d, k, sum = 0;
int first[10][10], second[10][10], multiply[10][10];
    printf("Enter the number of rows and columns of first matrix\n");
    scanf("%d%d", &m, &n);
    printf("Enter the elements of first matrix\n");
    for ( c = 0 ; c < m ; c++ )
        for ( d = 0 ; d < n ; d++ )
            scanf("%d", &first[c][d]);
            printf("Enter the number of rows and columns of second matrix\n");
            scanf("%d%d", &p, &q);
if ( n != p )
        printf("Matrices rows are not equal.\n");
else
{
        printf("Enter the elements of second matrix\n");
    for ( c = 0 ; c < p ; c++ )
        for ( d = 0 ; d < q ; d++ )
            scanf("%d", &second[c][d]);
    for ( c = 0 ; c < m ; c++ )
    {
    for ( d = 0 ; d < q ; d++ )
    {
    for ( k = 0 ; k < p ; k++ )
    {
            sum = sum + first[c][k]*second[k][d];
    }
            multiply[c][d] = sum;
            sum = 0;
    }
    }
    printf("Product of entered matrices:-\n");
    for ( c = 0 ; c < m ; c++ )
    {
    for ( d = 0 ; d < q ; d++ )
            printf("%d\t", multiply[c][d]);
            printf("\n");
    }
}
  return 0;
}
```

Output:
Enter the size of A Mtrix (Row and Col):
2 2
Enter the size of B Mtrix (Row and Col):
2 2
Enter Matrix Value Row by Row
2 2
2 2
Enter Matrix Value Row by Row
2 2
2 2
A Matrix is :
  2 2
  2 2

B Matrix is :
  2 2
  2 2

C Matrix is :
  8 8
  8 8

4.6. Passing Arrays as Function Arguments in C

An array can be passed as argument to the function in the following ways:

Way-1

Passing all the array elements as formal parameters:

```
void main( )
{
myFunction(arrayname);
}
void myFunction(int param[10])
{
}
```

Way-2
Passing individual array element as formal parameters:
```
void main( )
{
for(i = 0;i < n; i++)
myFunction(arrayname[i]);
}
void myFunction(int param)
{
}
```

Example

```
#include <stdio.h>
double getAverage(int arr[], int size);
int main ()
{
    int balance[5] = {1000, 2, 3, 17, 50};
    double avg;
    avg = getAverage( balance, 5 ) ;
    printf( "Average value is: %f ", avg );
  return 0;
}
```

```
double getAverage(int arr[], int size)
{
    int i;
    double avg;
    double sum;
    for (i = 0; i < size; ++i)
    {
        sum += arr[i];
    }
    avg = sum / size;
    return avg;
}
```

Output:
Average value is: 214.400000

Sample Program

```
/* Matrix Multiplication using function */
#include<stdio.h >
#include<conio.h>
int i,j,k;
void main()
{
    int a[10][10],b[10][10],c[10][10],m,n,p,q;
    void mul(int x[10][10],int y[10][10],int z[10][10],int m,int n,int p,int q);
    void read(int x[10][10],int m,int n);
    void display(int x[10][10], int m,int n);
    printf("Enter the size of A Mtrix (Row and Col): \n");
    scanf("%d%d",&m,&n);
    printf("Enter the size of B Mtrix (Row and Col): \n");
    scanf("%d%d",&p,&q);
    if(n!=p)
    {
        printf("Multiplication Not Possible\n Please re-enter\n");
        printf("correct size and try again .....\n");
    }
    else
    {
```

```c
            read(a,m,n);
            read(b,m,n);
            mul(a,b,c,m,n,p,q);
            printf("A Matrix is :\n");
            display(a,m,n);
            printf("B Matrix is :\n");
            display(b,m,n);
            printf("C Matrix is :\n");
            display(c,m,n);
        }
}
void mul(int x[10][10],int y[10][10],int z[10][10],int m,int n,int p,int q)
{
        for (i=0;i<m;i++)
        for(j=0;j<q;j++)
        {
                z[i][j]=0;
        for(k=0;k<n;k++)
                z[i][j]+= x[i][k]*y[k][j];
        }
}
void read(int x[10][10], int m,int n)
{
        printf("Enter Matrix Value Row by Row\n");
        for (i=0;i<m;i++)
        for(j=0;j<n;j++)
        scanf("%d",&x[i][j]);
}
void display(int x[10][10], int m,int n)
{
        for (i=0;i<m;i++)
        {
        for(j=0;j<n;j++)
                printf("%5d",x[i][j]);
                printf("\n");
        }
        printf("\n");
}
```

Output:
Enter the size of A Mtrix (Row and Col):
2 2
Enter the size of B Mtrix (Row and Col):
2 2
Enter Matrix Value Row by Row
2 2
2 2
Enter Matrix Value Row by Row
2 2
2 2
A Matrix is :
    2   2
    2   2

B Matrix is :
    2   2
    2   2

C Matrix is :
    8   8
    8   8

4.7. Sample Program for Arrays

Program 1 : Elements divisible by 5 in Array	Output
| ```c
#include<stdio.h>
#include<conio.h>
void main()
{
    int a[20],i,n;
    clrscr();
    printf("Enter the number of elements:\t");
    scanf("%d",&n);
    printf("Enter %d numbers\n",n);
    for(i=0;i<n;i++)
        scanf("%d",&a[i]);
    printf("\nElements in array\t\t");
    for(i=0;i<n;i++)
        printf("%d\t",a[i]);
    printf("\nElements divisible by 5\n");
    for(i=0;i<n;i++)
    {
        if(a[i]%5==0)
            printf("\n%d in position %d",a[i],i);
    }
    getch();
}
``` | Enter the number of elements: 5<br>Enter 5 numbers<br>2<br>3<br>5<br>10<br>20<br><br>Elements in array<br>  2  3  5  10  20<br><br>Elements divisible by 5<br><br>5 in position 2<br>10 in position 3<br>20 in position 4 |

Program 2 : Delete duplicate elements in Array	Output
| ```c
#include<stdio.h>
int main()
{
    int arr[20], i, j, k, size;
    clrscr();
    printf("\nEnter array size : ");
    scanf("%d", &size);
    printf("\nAccept Numbers : ");
    for (i = 0; i < size; i++)
        scanf("%d", &arr[i]);
    printf("\nArray with Unique list  : ");
    for (i = 0; i < size; i++)
    {
        for (j = i + 1; j < size;)
        {
            if (arr[j] == arr[i])
            {
                for (k = j; k < size; k++)
                    arr[k] = arr[k + 1];
                size--;
            }
            else
                j++;
        }
    }
    for (i = 0; i < size; i++)
        printf("%d ", arr[i]);
}
``` | Enter array size : 6<br><br>Accept Numbers : 1 1 2 3 4 4 2<br><br>Array with Unique list  : 1 2 3 4 |

59

Program 3 : Reversing Array elements	Output
| ```c
#include<stdio.h>
#include<conio.h>
void main()
{
    int a[20],i,n;
    clrscr();
    printf("Enter the number of elements:\t");
    scanf("%d",&n);
    printf("Enter %d numbers\n",n);
    for(i=0;i<n;i++)
        scanf("%d",&a[i]);
    printf("\n Elements in order\t\t");
    for(i=0;i<n;i++)
        printf("%d\t",a[i]);
    printf("\nElements in reverse order\t");
    for(i=n-1;i>=0;i--)
        printf("%d\t",a[i]);
    getch();
}
``` | Enter the number of elements: 6<br>Enter 6 numbers<br>10 20 40 30 70 50<br><br>Elements in order<br>10   20   40   30   70   50<br><br>Elements in reverse order<br>50   70   30   40   20   10 |

Program 4 : Max and Min element in Array	Output
| ```c
#include<stdio.h>
int main ()
{
    int i;
    int a[10] = { 10, 55, 9, 4, 24, 20, 30, 40, 22, 100 };
    int max = a[0];
    int min = a[0];
    clrscr();
    for (i = 0; i < 10; i++)
    {
        if (a[i] > max)
        {
            max = a[i];
        }
        else if (a[i] < min)
        {
            min = a[i];
        }
    }
    printf ("Max element in an array : %d\n", max);
    printf ("Min element in an array : %d\n", min);
    getch();
    return 0;
}
``` | Max element in an array :<br><br>100<br><br>Min element in an array :<br><br>4 |

Program 5 : 3 * 3 Matrix to 4 * 4 Matrix	Output
| ```
#include<stdio.h>
#include<conio.h>
void main()
{
    int a[3][3],b[4][4],i,j;
    clrscr();
    printf("Enter A matrix elements\n");
    for(i=0;i<3;i++)
        for(j=0;j<3;j++)
            scanf("%d",&a[i][j]);
    printf("\nA matrix\n");
    for(i=0;i<3;i++)
    {
        printf("\n");
        for(j=0;j<3;j++)
            printf("%d\t",a[i][j]);
    }
    printf("\nResultant 4X4 matrix\n");
    for(i=0;i<4;i++)
        for(j=0;j<4;j++)
            b[i][j]=0;
    for(i=0;i<3;i++)
        for(j=0;j<3;j++)
            b[i][j]=a[i][j];
    for(i=0;i<3;i++)
        for(j=0;j<3;j++)
            b[i][3]+=b[i][j];
    for(i=0;i<3;i++)
        for(j=0;j<3;j++)
            b[3][i]+=b[j][i];
    for(i=0;i<3;i++)
        b[3][3]+=b[i][3];
    for(i=0;i<4;i++)
    {
        printf("\n");
        for(j=0;j<4;j++)
            printf("%d\t",b[i][j]);
    }
    getch();
}
``` | Enter A matrix elements<br><br>1 2 3<br>4 5 6<br>7 8 9<br><br>A matrix<br><br>1　2　3<br>4　5　6<br>7　8　9<br><br>Resultant 4X4 matrix<br><br>1　2　3　6<br>4　5　6　15<br>7　8　9　24<br>12　15　18　45<br><br>( 4th row values is equal to sum of column values ) |
```

Program 6 : Square of matrix Elements	Output
| ```c
#include<stdio.h>
#include<conio.h>
void sq(int b[5][5],int,int);
void main()
{
    int a[5][5],i,j,r1,c1;
    clrscr();
    printf("\nEnter the order of the matrix\t");
    scanf("%d%d",&r1,&c1);
    printf("\nEnter the matrix elements\n");
    for(i=0;i<r1;i++)
        for(j=0;j<c1;j++)
            scanf("%d",&a[i][j]);
    printf("\n*******matrix*******\n");
    for(i=0;i<r1;i++)
    {
        printf("\n");
        for(j=0;j<c1;j++)
            printf("%d\t",a[i][j]);
    }
    sq(a,r1,c1);
    getch();
}
void sq(int b[5][5],int m,int n)
{
    int i,j;
    for(i=0;i<m;i++)
        for(j=0;j<n;j++)
            printf("\nsquare of %d = %d\n",b[i][j],(b[i][j]*b[i][j]));
}
``` | Enter the order of the matrix<br>3 3<br>Enter the matrix elements<br>1 2 3<br>4 5 6<br>7 8 9<br><br>*******matrix*******<br><br>1  2  3<br>4  5  6<br>7  8  9<br><br>square of 1 = 1<br><br>square of 2 = 4<br><br>square of 3 = 9<br><br>square of 4 = 16<br><br>square of 5 = 25<br><br>square of 6 = 36<br><br>square of 7 = 49<br><br>square of 8 = 64<br><br>square of 9 = 81 |
```

Program 7:Matrix addition using Functions and Pointer	Output
| ```c
#include<stdio.h>
#include<conio.h>
int add(int *,int *);
void main()
{
    int a[2][2],b[2][2];
    int i,j;
    int *p,*q;
    clrscr();
    printf("\n Enter A matrix\n");
    for(i=0;i<2;i++)
        for(j=0;j<2;j++)
            scanf("%d",&a[i][j]);

    printf("\n Enter B matrix\n");
    for(i=0;i<2;i++)
        for(j=0;j<2;j++)
            scanf("%d",&b[i][j]);
    p=a;
    q=b;
    printf("\n\nResultant matrix\n\n");
    for(i=0;i<2;i++)
    {
        for(j=0;j<2;j++)
        {
            printf("%d\t",add(p,q));
            p++;
            q++;
        }
    }
    getch();
}
int add(int *r,int *s)
{
    return(*r + *s);
}
``` | Enter A matrix<br><br>1  2<br>3  4<br><br>Enter B matrix<br><br>5  6<br>7  8<br><br>Resultant matrix<br><br>6   8<br>10  12 |
```

Program 8 : Matrix multiplication	Output
| ```c
#include<stdio.h>
#include<conio.h>
void main()
{
    int a[5][5],b[5][5],c[5][5],i,j,k;
    clrscr();
    printf("\nEnter the A matrix ( 3 X 3 ):\n");
    for(i=0;i<3;i++)
        for(j=0;j<3;j++)
            scanf("%d",&a[i][j]);
    printf("\n A matrix ( 3 X 3 )\n");
    for(i=0;i<3;i++)
    {
        printf("\n");
        for(j=0;j<3;j++)
            printf("%d\t",a[i][j]);
    }
    printf("\nEnter the B matrix ( 3 X 3 ):\n");
    for(i=0;i<3;i++)
        for(j=0;j<3;j++)
            scanf("%d",&b[i][j]);
    printf("\n B matrix ( 3 X 3 )\n");
    for(i=0;i<3;i++)
    {
        printf("\n");
        for(j=0;j<3;j++)
            printf("%d\t",b[i][j]);
    }
    printf("\nProduct matrix\n");
    for(i=0;i<3;i++)
    {
        for(j=0;j<3;j++)
        {
            c[i][j]=0;
            for(k=0;k<3;k++)
                c[i][j]+=a[i][k]*b[k][j];
        }
    }
    for(i=0;i<3;i++)
    {
        printf("\n");
        for(j=0;j<3;j++)
            printf("%d\t",c[i][j]);
    }
    getch();
}
``` | Enter the A matrix ( 3 X 3 ):<br><br>1 2 3<br>4 5 6<br>7 8 9<br><br>A matrix ( 3 X 3 )<br><br>1   2   3<br>4   5   6<br>7   8   9<br><br>Enter the B matrix ( 3 X 3 ):<br><br>1 2 3<br>4 5 6<br>7 8 9<br><br>B matrix ( 3 X 3 )<br><br>1   2   3<br>4   5   6<br>7   8   9<br><br>Product matrix<br><br>30   36   42<br>66   81   96<br>102  126  150 |
```

Program 9 : Matrix transpose	Output

#include<stdio.h>
#include<conio.h>
void main()
{
    int a[5][5],i,j;
    clrscr();
    printf("\nEnter the A matrix (3 X 3):\n");
    for(i=0;i<3;i++)
        for(j=0;j<3;j++)
            scanf("%d",&a[i][j]);
    printf("\n A matrix (3 X 3)\n");
    for(i=0;i<3;i++)
    {
        printf("\n");
        for(j=0;j<3;j++)
            printf("%d\t",a[i][j]);
    }
    printf("\nA matrix transpose (3 X 3):\n");
    for(i=0;i<3;i++)
    {
        printf("\n");
        for(j=0;j<3;j++)
            printf("%d\t",a[j][i]);
    }
    getch();
}
	Enter the A matrix (3 X 3):
	
	1 2 3
	4 5 6
	7 8 9
	
	A matrix (3 X 3)
	
	1 2 3
	4 5 6
	7 8 9
	
	A matrix transpose (3 X 3):
	
	1 4 7
	2 5 8
	3 6 9

Program 10 : Matrix Addition	Output
| ```
#include<stdio.h>
#include<conio.h>
void main()
{
    int a[3][3],b[3][3],i,j,m,n,o,p;
    clrscr();
    printf("\nEnter the number of rows in A matrix\t");
    scanf("%d",&m);
    printf("\nEnter the number of columns in A matrix\t");
    scanf("%d",&n);
    printf("\nEnter the A matrix\n");
    for(i=0;i<m;i++)
        for(j=0;j<n;j++)
            scanf("%d",&a[i][j]);
    printf("\n A matrix\n");
    for(i=0;i<m;i++)
    {
        printf("\n");
        for(j=0;j<n;j++)
            printf("%d\t",a[i][j]);
    }
    printf("\nEnter the number of rows in B matrix\t");
    scanf("%d",&o);
    printf("\nEnter the number of columns in B matrix\t");
    scanf("%d",&p);
    printf("\nEnter the B matrix\n");
    for(i=0;i<o;i++)
        for(j=0;j<p;j++)
            scanf("%d",&b[i][j]);
    printf("\n B matrix\n");
    for(i=0;i<o;i++)
    {
        printf("\n");
        for(j=0;j<p;j++)
            printf("%d\t",b[i][j]);
    }
    if(m==o && n==p)
    {
        printf("\nMatrix addition possible\n");
        printf("\n Sum of two matrix \n");
        for(i=0;i<m;i++)
        {
            printf("\n");
            for(j=0;j<n;j++)
                printf("%d\t",a[i][j]+b[i][j]);
        }
    }
    else
        printf("\n Matrix Addition not possible!\n");
    getch();
}
``` | Enter the number of rows in A matrix<br>3<br><br>Enter the number of columns in A matrix<br>3<br><br>Enter the A matrix<br>1 2 3<br>4 5 6<br>7 8 9<br><br>A matrix<br><br>1   2   3<br>4   5   6<br>7   8   9<br><br>Enter the number of rows in B matrix<br>3<br><br>Enter the number of columns in B matrix<br>3<br><br>Enter the B matrix<br>1 2 3<br>4 5 6<br>7 8 9<br><br>B matrix<br><br>1   2   3<br>4   5   6<br>7   8   9<br><br>Matrix addition possible<br>Sum of two matrix<br><br>2   4   6<br>8   10  12<br>14  16  18 |
```

Program 11 : Sum of the diagonal elements	Output
| ```
#include<stdio.h>
#include<conio.h>
void main()
{
    int a[3][3],i,j,sum=0;
    printf("\nEnter the 3 X 3 matrix\n");
    for(i=0;i<3;i++)
        for(j=0;j<3;j++)
            scanf("%d",&a[i][j]);
    printf("\nEntered matrix");
    for(i=0;i<3;i++)
    {
        printf("\n");
        for(j=0;j<3;j++)
            printf("%d\t",a[i][j]);
    }
    for(i=0;i<3;i++)
        sum+=a[i][i];
    printf("\n\nSum of the diagonal elements = %d\n",sum);
}
``` | Enter the 3 X 3 matrix<br><br>1 2 3<br>4 5 6<br>7 8 9<br><br>Entered matrix<br><br>1 2 3<br>4 5 6<br>7 8 9<br><br>Sum of the diagonal elements = 15 |

67
```

CHAPTER 5

STRING

5.1. Introduction

A group of character enclosed within double quotes is called as **string**. By default a string is terminated by null character "/0". It is also termed as character array.

For Example

"Data Structure"

D	a	t	a		S	t	r	u	c	t	u	r	e	\0

Here "Data Structure " is a string. When compiler encounters strings, it appends null character at the end of string.

5.2. Declaration of Strings

Strings are declared in C in similar manner as arrays. Only difference is that, strings are of char type.

char s[5];

s[0]	s[1]	s[2]	s[3]	s[4]

Strings can also be declared using pointer.

char *p;

5.3. Initialization of String

In C, string can be initialized in different number of ways.

1. char c[]="abcd";
2. char c[5]="abcd";
3. char c[]={'a','b','c','d','\0'};
4. char c[5]={'a','b','c','d','\0'};

c[0]	c[1]	c[2]	c[3]	c[4]
a	b	c	d	\0

String can also be initialized using pointers

char *c="abcd";

5.4. Reading String

char c[20];

scanf("%s",c);

(or)

gets(c);

String variable *C* can only take a word. It is because when white space is encountered, the scanf() function terminates. It is always better to use gets( ) function to read a string.

Program : C program to illustrate how to read string from terminal.
```
#include <stdio.h>
int main()
{
    char name[20];
    printf("Enter name: ");
    scanf("%s",name);
    printf("Your name is %s.",name);
    return 0;
}
```

Output
Enter name: Dennis Ritchie
Your name is Dennis.

Program : C program to illustrate how to read string from terminal using gets( ).
```
#include <stdio.h>
int main()
{
    char name[30];
    printf("Enter name:");
    gets(name);
    printf("Name:");
    puts(name);
    return 0;
}
```

Output
Enter name: Tom Hanks
Name: Tom Hanks

5.5. Passing Strings to Functions

String can be passed to function in similar manner as arrays as, string is also a character array.

Program: Passing Strings to Functions
```
#include <stdio.h>
void Display(char ch[]);
int main()
{
    char c[50];
    printf("Enter string: ");
```

Output:
Enter string: data structure
String Output: data structure

```
            gets(c);
            Display(c);
            return 0;
}
void Display(char ch[])
{
            printf("String Output: ");
            puts(ch);
}
```

5.6. String Manipulations Using Library Functions

Strings are often needed to be manipulated by programmer according to the need of a problem. All string manipulation can be done manually by the programmer but, this makes programming complex and large. To solve this, the C supports a large number of string handling functions.

There are numerous functions defined in "string.h" header file. Few commonly used string handling functions are discussed below:

Function	Work of Function
strlen()	Calculates the length of string
strcpy()	Copies a string to another string
strcat()	Concatenates(joins) two strings
strcmp()	Compares two string
strlwr()	Converts string to lowercase
strupr()	Converts string to uppercase

Strings handling functions are defined under "string.h" header file, i.e, you have to include the code below to run string handling functions.

#include <string.h>
Sample program using gets() and puts()
#include<stdio.h>
int main()
{
            char name[30];
            printf("Enter name: ");
            gets(name);
            printf("Name: ");
            puts(name);
            return 0;
}

Output:
Enter name: data structure
Name: data structure

Sample program to find the frequency of particular character in the given string

```
#include<stdio.h>
int main()
{
    char c[1000],ch;
    int i,count=0;
    printf("Enter a string: ");
    gets(c);
    printf("Enter a character to find frequency: ");
    scanf("%c",&ch);
    for(i=0;c[i]!='\0';++i)
    {
        if(ch= =c[i])
        ++count;
    }
    printf("Frequency of %c = %d", ch, count);
    return0;
}
```

Output:
Enter a string:
This website is awesome.
Enter a character to find frequency: e
Frequency of e = 4

5.7. Sample Programs for String Manipulations

Program 1 : Vowels count in the given string	Output

`#include<stdio.h>`
`#include<conio.h>`
`#include<string.h>`
`void main()`
`{`
`    char str[50];`
`    int i,vowel=0;`
`    puts("\n Enter a Line\n\n");`
`    gets(str);`
`    for(i=0;i<strlen(str);i++)`
`    {`
`        if(str[i]=='a'  ||  str[i]=='e'  ||str[i]=='i'`
`        ||str[i]=='o'   ||str[i]=='u'   ||str[i]=='A'`
`        ||str[i]=='E'   ||str[i]=='i'   ||str[i]=='O'`
`        ||str[i]=='U')`
`            vowel++;`
`    }`
`    printf("\n vowels = %d",vowel);`
`    getch();`
`}`
	Enter a Line
	
	programming and data structures
	
	vowels = 9

Program 2 : String operations	Output

#include<stdio.h>
#include<conio.h>
#include<string.h>
void main()
{
    char str1[30],str2[30];
    clrscr();
    puts("\n Enter a string\n");
    gets(str1);
    printf("\n Entered string is:\t%s",str1);
    strcpy(str2,str1);
    strrev(str1);
    printf("\n reversed string is:\t%s",str1);
    if(strcmp(str1,str2)==0)
    printf("\n Given string %s is palindrome\n",str2);
    else
    printf("\n Given string %s is not palindrome\n",str2);
    getch();
}
	Output 1:
	
	Enter a string
	
	data structure
	
	Entered string is:
	    data structure
	reversed string is:
	    erutcurts atad
	Given string data structure is not palindrome
	
	Output 2:
	
	Enter a string
	
	RADAR
	
	Entered string is RADAR
	reversed string is RADAR
	Given string RADAR is palindrome

Program 3 : Sorting characters in a given string	Output

#include<stdio.h>
#include<conio.h>
#include<string.h>
void main()
{
    char *a;
    int i,j,temp,len=0;
    printf("Enter a string\n");
    gets(a);
    len=strlen(a);
    for(i=0;i<len;i++)
    {
        for(j=i+1;j<len;j++)
        {
            if(a[i]>a[j])
            {
                temp=a[i];
                a[i]=a[j];
                a[j]=temp;
            }
        }
    }
    puts(a);
    getch();
}
	Enter a string
	
	Hai
	
	aiH

Program 4 : Convert character case (Upper & Lower)	Output

#include<stdio.h>
#include<conio.h>
void main()
{
    char a[30];
    int i;
    clrscr();
    printf("Enter a string\n");
    gets(a);
    printf("\nEntered string is %s",a);
    for(i=0;a[i]!='\0';i++)
    {
        if(a[i]>=65 && a[i]<=90)
            a[i]+=32;
        else if(a[i]>=97 && a[i]<=122)
            a[i]-=32;
    }
    printf("\nconverted string is %s",a);
}
	Enter a string
	
	hai
	
	Entered string is hai
	
	converted string is HAI

Program 5 : String Concatenate	**Output**

#include<string.h>
#include<stdio.h>
#include<conio.h>
void main()
{
    char a[20],b[20];
    int i,j;
    clrscr();
    puts("enter a string\n");
    gets(a);
    puts("enter b string\n");
    gets(b);
    for(i=0;a[i]!='\0';i++)
        ;
        for(j=0;b[j]!='\0';j++,i++)
            a[i]=b[j];
    a[i]='\0';
    printf("\n\n Concatenated String\n\n");
    puts(a);
    getch();
}
	enter a string
	
	data
	enter b string
	
	structure
	
	Concatenated String
	
	datastructure

Program 6: String Concatenate using library function	Output

#include<stdio.h>
#include<conio.h>
#include<string.h>
void main()
{
    char a[30]="SQL ";
    char b[30]="SERVER";
    clrscr();
    printf("\n1st string: \t%s",a);
    printf("\n2nd string: \t%s",b);
    printf("\n\nConcatenated string: \t%s",strcat(a,b));
    getch();
}
	1st string: SQL
	2nd string: SERVER
	
	Concatenated string:
	
	SQL SERVER

Program 7 : String comparison	Output

#include<string.h>
#include<stdio.h>
#include<conio.h>
void main()
{
    char *a,*b;
    int i;
    clrscr();
    puts("Enter a string\n");
    gets(a);
    puts("Enter b string\n");
    gets(b);
    for(i=0;a[i]!='\0'&& b[i]!='\0';i++)
    {
        if(a[i] = = b[i])
            continue;
        else
            break;
    }
    if(a[i]==b[i])
    printf("\nThe entered strings are equal\n");
    else
    printf("\nThe entered strings are not equal\n");
    getch();
}
	Enter a string
	
	Hay
	
	Enter b string
	
	Hay
	
	The entered strings are equal

Program 8 : String copy	Output

#include<string.h>
#include<stdio.h>
#include<conio.h>
void main()
{
    char *a,*b;
    int i,j;
    clrscr();
    puts("Enter a string\n");
    gets(a);
 	
    for(i=0;a[i]!='\0';i++)
        b[i]=a[i];
 	
    b[i]='\0';
    printf("\n Copied string is\n");
    puts(b);
    getch();
}
	Enter a string
	
	Hai
	
	Copied string is
	
	Hai

Program 9 : Length of given string	Output

#include<string.h>
#include<stdio.h>
#include<conio.h>
void main()
{
    char *a;
    int i;
    clrscr();
    puts("Enter a string\n");
    gets(a);
    for(i=0;a[i]!='\0';i++)
        ;
    printf("length of '%s' is %d",a,i);
    getch();
}
	Enter a string
	
	Data Structure
	
	length of 'Data Structure ' is 14

Program 10 : Length and Reverse of given string	Output

#include<stdio.h>
#include<conio.h>
void main()
{
    char a[30];
    char t;
    int len=0,i,j;
    clrscr();
    printf("\n Enter a string\n");
    scanf("%s",a);
    while(a[len] != '\0')
        len++;
    printf("\n Length of the string %s is %d\n",a,len);
 	
    for(i=0,j=len-1;i<len/2;i++,j--)
    {
        t=a[i];
        a[i]=a[j];
        a[j]=t;
    }
    printf("Reversed string is %s",a);
    getch();
}
	Enter a string
	
	Data
	
	Length of the string Data is 4
	
	Reversed string is
	
	ataD

CHAPTER 6

PREPROCESSOR

6.1. Introduction

The C Preprocessor is not part of the compiler, but is a separate step in the compilation process. In simplistic terms, a C Preprocessor is just a text substitution tool and they instruct compiler to do required pre-processing before actual compilation.

All preprocessor commands begin with a pound symbol (#). It must be the first nonblank character, and for readability, a preprocessor directive should begin in first column.

6.2. Preprocessor Directives in C

Directive	Description
#define	Substitutes a preprocessor macro
#include	Inserts a particular header from another file
#undef	Undefines a preprocessor macro
#ifdef	Returns true if this macro is defined
#ifndef	Returns true if this macro is not defined
#if	Tests if a compile time condition is true
#else	The alternative for #if
#elif	#else an #if in one statement
#endif	Ends preprocessor conditional
#error	Prints error message on stderr
#pragma	Issues special commands to the compiler, using a standardized method

6.3. Preprocessors Examples

Analyze the following examples to understand various directives.

#define MAX 20

This directive tells the Compiler to replace instances of MAX with 20.

Use *#define* for constants to increase readability.

#include <stdio.h>

#include "myheader.h"

The first line tells the compiler to get stdio.h from **System Libraries** and add the text to the current source file. The next line tells the compiler to get **myheader.h** from the local directory and add the content to the current source file.

```
#undef FILESIZE
#define FILESIZE 42
```
This tells the compiler to undefine existing FILE_SIZE and define it as 42.
```
#ifndef MESSAGE
#define MESSAGE "You wish!"
#endif
```
This tells the compiler to define MESSAGE only if MESSAGE isn't already defined.
```
#ifdef DEBUG
   /* statements */
#endif
```
This tells the compiler to process the statements enclosed if DEBUG is defined.

6.4. Predefined Macros

ANSI C defines a number of macros. Although each one is available for your use in programming, the predefined macros should not be directly modified.

Macro	Description
__DATE__	The current date as a character literal in "MMM DD YYYY" format
__TIME__	The current time as a character literal in "HH:MM:SS" format
__FILE__	This contains the current filename as a string literal.
__LINE__	This contains the current line number as a decimal constant.
__STDC__	Defined as 1 when the compiler complies with the ANSI standard.

Example
```
#include <stdio.h>
void main()
{
            printf("File :%s\n", __FILE__ );
            printf("Date :%s\n", __DATE__ );
            printf("Time :%s\n", __TIME__ );
            printf("Line :%d\n", __LINE__ );
            printf("ANSI :%d\n", __STDC__ );
}
```

Output:
```
File :test.c
Date :Jun 2 2012
Time :03:36:24
Line :8
ANSI :1
```

6.5. Preprocessor Operators

The C preprocessor offers following operators to help in creating macros:

6.5.1 Macro Continuation (\)

A macro usually must be contained on a single line. The macro continuation operator is used to continue a macro that is too long for a single line. For example:

```
#define message_for (a, b) \
printf (#a " and " #b ": We are here!\n")
```

6.5.2 Stringize (#)

The stringize or number-sign operator ('#'), when used within a macro definition, converts a macro parameter into a string constant. This operator may be used only in a macro that has a specified argument or parameter list. For example:

```
#include <stdio.h>
#define  message_for(a, b) \
         printf(#a " and " #b ": We are here!\n")
int main(void)
{
         message_for(Carole, Debra);
   return 0;
}
```

When the above code is compiled and executed, it produces the following result:

Carole and Debra: We are here!

6.5.3 Token Pasting (##)

The token-pasting operator (##) within a macro definition combines two arguments. It permits two separate tokens in the macro definition to be joined into a single token.

For example:

```
#include <stdio.h>
#define tokenpaster(n) printf ("token" #n " = %d", token##n)
int main(void)
{
         int token34 = 40;
         tokenpaster(34);
   return 0;
}
```

When the above code is compiled and executed, it produces the following result:

token34 = 40

How it happened, because this example results in the following actual output from the preprocessor:

printf ("token34 = %d", token34);

This example shows the concatenation of token##n into token34.

6.5.4 The defined() Operator

The preprocessor **defined** operator is used in constant expressions to determine if an identifier is defined using #define. If the specified identifier is defined, the value is true (non-zero). If the symbol is not defined, the value is false (zero). The defined operator is specified as follows:

```
#include <stdio.h>
#if !defined (MESSAGE)
    #define MESSAGE "You wish!"
#endif
int main(void)
{
    printf("Here is the message: %s\n", MESSAGE);
    return 0;
}
```

When the above code is compiled and executed, it produces the following result:

Here is the message: You wish!

6.5.5 Parameterized Macros

One of the powerful functions of the compiler is the ability to simulate functions using parameterized macros. For example,

```
int square(int x)
{
  return x * x;
}
```

The above code can be rewritten using a macro as follows:

#define square(x) ((x) * (x))

Macros with arguments must be defined using the **#define** directive before they can be used. The argument list is enclosed in parentheses and must immediately follow the macro name. Spaces are not allowed between and macro name and open parenthesis. For example:

```
#include <stdio.h>
#define MAX(x,y) ((x) > (y) ? (x) : (y))
int main(void)
{
    printf("Max between 20 and 10 is %d\n", MAX(10, 20));
    return 0;
}
```

When the above code is compiled and executed, it produces the following result:

Max between 20 and 10 is 20

CHAPTER 7

POINTERS

7.1. Introduction

Pointer is a variable that holds the memory address of another variable.every variable is a memory location and every memory location has its address defined which can be accessed using ampersand (&) operator.

7.2. Reference Operator(&)

If *var* is a variable then, &var refers to the address of the variable(var).

```
#include <stdio.h>
int main()
{
    int var=5;
    printf("Value: %d\n",var);
    printf("Address: %u",&var);
    return 0;
}
```

Output
Value: 5
Address: 2686778

The general form of a pointer variable declaration is:

Syntax

type *varname;

7.3. Working of Pointers in C

```
#include <stdio.h>
int main()
{
    int *pc,c;
    c=22;
    printf("Address of c:%d\n",&c);
    printf("Value of c:%d\n\n",c);
    pc=&c;
    printf("Address of pointer pc:%d\n",pc);
```

Output
Address of c: 2686784
Value of c: 22
Address of pointer pc: 2686784
Content of pointer pc: 22
Address of pointer pc: 2686784
Content of pointer pc: 11
Address of c: 2686784
Value of c: 2

```
printf("Content of pointer pc:%d\n\n",*pc);
c=11;
printf("Address of pointer pc:%d\n",pc);
printf("Content of pointer pc:%d\n\n",*pc);
*pc=2;
printf("Address of c:%d\n",&c);
printf("Value of c:%d\n\n",c);
return 0;
}
```

7.4. Variation in Pointer Declarations

Following are the valid pointer declaration:

```
int    *ip;    /* pointer to an integer */
double *dp;    /* pointer to a double */
float  *fp;    /* pointer to a float */
char   *ch;    /* pointer to a character */
```

7.4.1. NULL Pointers in C

It is always a good practice to assign a NULL value to a pointer variable in case the exact address to be assigned is not known. This is done at the time of variable declaration.

A pointer that is assigned NULL is called a **null** pointer.

Example

```
#include <stdio.h>
int main ()
{
int *ptr = NULL;
printf("The value of ptr is : %x\n", ptr );
return 0;
}
```

Output:
The value of ptr is 0

7.4.2. Void Pointers in C

A void pointer is a pointer variable declared using the reserved word **'void'**.

Ex: void *ptr;

Address of any variable of any data type (char, int, float etc.) can be assigned to a void pointer variable.

7.4.3. Dereferencing Operator (*)

Dereferencing Operation is performed to access or manipulate data contained in memory location pointed to by a pointer. Any Operation performed on the de-referenced pointer directly affects the value of variable it pointes to.

Example

#include

void main()

{

    int a=10;

    float b=35.75;

    void *ptr;

    ptr=&a;

    printf("The value of integer variable is= %d",*((int*) ptr));

    ptr=&b;

    printf("The value of float variable is= %f",*((float*) ptr));

}

Output:
The value of integer variable is= 10
The value of float variable is= 37.75

7.5. Function Pointers

Unlike normal pointers, a function pointer points to code, not data. Typically a function pointer stores the start of executable code.

A function pointer can be declared as :

    <returntype of function> (*<name of pointer>) (type of function arguments)

Example

int (*fptr)(int, int)

The above line declares a function pointer 'fptr' that can point to a function whose return type is 'int' and takes two integers as arguments.

Example

```
#include<stdio.h>
void func (int a, int b)
{
        printf("\n a = %d\n",a);
        printf("\n b = %d\n",b);
}
void main(void)
{
   int(*fptr)(int,int);
   fptr = func;
   func(2,3);
   fptr(2,3);
}
```

Output:
a = 2
b = 3
a = 2
b = 3

7.5.1. Function Pointer Without Argument

```
#include <stdio.h>
void fun()
{
        printf( "%d\n", 6*6 );
}
void main()
{
        void (*fp)();
        clrscr();
        fp =fun;
        fp();
        getch();
}
```

Output:
36

7.5.2. Function Pointer with Argument

```
#include <stdio.h>
void fun(int x)
{
    printf( "%d\n", x );
}
void main()
{
    void (*fp)();
    clrscr();
    fp =fun;
    fp(10);
}
```

Output:
10

7.5.3. C - Pointer to Pointer

Pointer is a vaiable that contains the address of a another variable.

Pointer to pointer is a variable, that contains the address of another pointer variable.

int a=65;

int *p1;

int **p2;

```
5000        6000        7000
 65         5000        6000
  a          p1          p2
```

Pointer to pointer variable is declared using double astrics symbol, here p1 is a pointer variable and p2 is a pointer to pointer variable.

Program

```
#include <stdio.h>
int main ()
{
    int  var;
    int *ptr;
    int **pptr;
    var = 3000;
    ptr = &var;
    pptr = &ptr;
    printf("Value of var = %d\n", var );
    printf("Value available at *ptr = %d\n", *ptr );
    printf("Value available at **pptr = %d\n", **pptr);
    return 0;
}
```

Output:

Value of var = 3000

Value available at *ptr = 3000

Value available at **pptr = 3000

7.5.4. Pointer Arithmetic

A pointer in c is an address, which is a numeric value. Therefore arithmetic operations can be performed on a pointer. There are four arithmetic operators that can be used in pointers: ++, --, +, and -

> result = initial address ± constant value (size of pointer type)

ptr++;

Consider the intitial address of pointer variable ptr = 1000. After the above operation, the **ptr** will point to the location 1004 (ptr ++ = ptr + 1).

$$ptr ++ = 1000+1(4)$$
$$= 1004$$

Program

```
#include <stdio.h>
int main()
{
    int *ptr, q,**p;
    q = 50;
    ptr = &q;
    p=&ptr;
    printf("%u\n",*ptr);
    printf("%u\n", p);
    printf("%u\n", **p);
    printf("%u\n", ptr);
    printf("%u\n", ptr+2);
    printf("%u\n", ptr++);
    printf("%u\n", ++ptr);
    printf("%u\n", ptr-2);
    printf("%u\n", --ptr);
    printf("%u\n", ptr--);
    return 0;
}
```

Output:
50
37814052
50
37814048
37814056
37814048
37814056
37814048
37814052
37814052

7.5.5. Pointer and Array

The relationship between Pointer and Array is:

Array name gives address of first element of array.

Array members are accessed using pointer arithmetic.

Program

```
#include <stdio.h>
void fun(int ptr[])
{
    int x = 10;
    printf("sizeof(ptr) = %d\n", sizeof(ptr));
    ptr = &x;
    printf("*ptr = %d ", *ptr);
}
void main()
{
    int arr[] = {10, 20, 30, 40, 50, 60};
    fun(arr);
}
```

Output:

sizeof(ptr) = 4
*ptr = 10

Major Advantages of Pointers are

1. It is used to allocate memory dynamically.
2. It allows passing of arrays and strings to functions more efficiently.
3. It makes possible to pass address of structure instead of entire structure to the functions.
4. They can be used to return multiple values from a function via function arguments.
5. pointers allow C to support dynamic memory management.
6. Pointers provide an efficient tool for manipulating dynamic data structures such as structures, linked lists, queues, stacks and trees.
7. Pointers reduce length and complexity of programs. They increases the execution speed and thus reduce the program execution time.

CHAPTER 8

FUNCTION WITH VARIABLE NUMBER OF ARGUMENTS

8.1. Introduction

Sometimes, there is a need to have a function, which can take variable number of arguments, i.e., parameters, instead of predefined number of parameters.

The C programming language provides a solution for this situation and allow to define a function which can accept variable number of parameters based on the requirement.

The following example shows the definition of such a function.

```
int func(int, ... )
{
---
}
int main()
{
        func(1, 2, 3);
        func(1, 2, 3, 4);
}
```

It should be noted that function **func()** has last argument as ellipses i.e. three dotes (...) and the one just before the ellipses is always an **int** which will represent total number of variable arguments passed.

stdarg.h header file provides functions and macros to implement the functionality of variable arguments with the following steps:

- Define a function with last parameter as ellipses and the one just before the ellipses is always an **int** which will represent number of arguments.
- Create a **va_list** type variable in the function definition. This type is defined in stdarg.h header file.
- Use **int** parameter and **va_start** macro to initialize the **va_list** variable to an argument list. The macro va_start is defined in stdarg.h header file.
- Use **va_arg** macro and **va_list** variable to access each item in argument list.
- Use a macro **va_end** to clean up the memory assigned to **va_list** variable.

8.2. Sample Program

Program which takes variable number of parameters and returns their average.

```c
#include <stdio.h>
#include <stdarg.h>
double average(int num,...)
{
    va_list valist;
    double sum = 0.0;
    int i;
    va_start(valist, num);
    for (i = 0; i < num; i++)
    {
        sum += va_arg(valist, int);
    }
    va_end(valist);
    return sum/num;
}
int main()
{
    printf("Average of 2, 3, 4, 5 = %f\n", average(4, 2,3,4,5));
    printf("Average of 5, 10, 15 = %f\n", average(3, 5,10,15));
}
```

Output:

Average of 2, 3, 4, 5 = 3.500000

Average of 5, 10, 15 = 10.000000

Review Questions

1. Write the rules for naming an identifier?
   - The first character in an identifier must be alphabet.
   - It should not begin with a digit.
   - Keywords cannot be used as an identifier.
   - Identifiers are case sensitive.

2. Write a C program for the following expression
   i) a=5<=8&&6!=5
   ii) a=b++ + ++b where b=50

   Ans : i) #include<stdio.h>

   #include<conio.h>

   void main( )

   {

   int a;

   a=5<=8&&6!=5;

   printf("%d",a);

   }

   output: 1

   iii) #include<stdio.h>
   #include<conio.h>

   void main( )

   {

   int a,b=50;

   a=b++ + ++b where b=50;

   printf("%d",a);

   }

   output:102

3. Write a C program to determine whether a number is 'odd' or 'even' and print the message.

Ans : #include<stdio.h>

#include<conio.h>

void main( )

{

int a,

printf("Enter the number\n")

scanf("%d",&a);

if(a%2==0)

printf("The given no %d is even",a);

else

printf("The given no %d is odd",a);

}

4. Compare while and do-while loop?

While loop	Do..While loop
Condition is tested first and then statements are executed	Statements are executed atleast once and then the conditions are tested
While loop is entry control loop	Do..while is exit control loop

5. Compare break and continue statement?

Break	Continue
Break statement is used to transfer the control of the program to outside loop or switch case statement.	Continue is used to skip some statement of the loop and moves to the next iteration in the loop.
It is used in loop as well as switch case. Syntax : break;	It is used only within loop. Syntax : continue;

6. Write a c program to print the number 10 ten times, the number 9 nine times and so on.
Ans : #include<stdio.h>
#include<conio.h>
void main()
{
    int a=10,i;
    clrscr();
    while(a)
    {
    for(i=a;i>=1;i--)
    {
        printf("%d\t",a);
    }
        a--;
    }
    getch();
}

7. Write a 'C' Program to find factorial of given number using iteration.
#include<stdio.h>
#include<conio.h>
int fact(int);
int main()
{
    int num,f;
    clrscr();
    printf("\nEnter a number :");
    scanf("%d",&num);
    f=fact(num);
    printf("\nFactorial of %d is : %d",num,f);
    getch();
    return();
}
int fact(int n)
{
if(n==1)
return 1;
else
return(n*fact(n-1));
}

8. Define an Array. Give an example? (Nov/Dec 2014)

An array is a collection of similar data item that are stored under a common name, the value in an array is identified by index, subscript enclosed by square brackets with array name.

int a[10];

int b[10]={1,2,3,4,5};

9. Write any four features of arrays
   1. Array is a derived data type.
   2. String array always terminates with null character ('\0').
   3. Array elements are countered from 0 to n-1.
   4. Array elements can be accessed with base address (index) and subscripts define the position of the element.

10. How will you declare and initialize one-dimensional array? Give example?

Syntax: data-type array-variable [size] = {list of values};

E.g. int a[10] = {1,2,4,6,7,9,5,8,3,12};

Where

    int is the data type of the array.

    a is the array name.

    10 is the size of the array.

11. How will you declare and initialize two-dimensional array? Give example?

Syntax: data-type array-variable [row-size][column-size]={list of values};

int n[2][3] = {{1,6,4},{2,8,9}};

12. Differentiate between Array and Structure?

S.No	ARRAY	STRUCTURE
1.	An array is a collection of similar data items.	A structure is a collection of dissimilar data items.
2.	It is a derived data type.	It is a user-defined data type.
3.	It behaves like a built in data type.	It must be declared and defined.
4.	It can be increased or decreased.	A structure element can be added if necessary.
5.	Array elements are accessed with the help of index or subscript.	The structure members can be accessed using structure variable.

13. Define string? Give example?

The group of character, digits, and symbols enclosed within double quotation marks are called as string. The string can be initialized as follows.

    char name[]= "Welcome";

String terminates with NULL character ('\0').

14. How will you declare and initialize string array?

Syntax:

data-type array-variable[size]={list of values};

The string can be initialized as follows.

    char name[]= "Welcome";

15. List some string functions?

    strlen( ) strcpy( )

    strcat( ) strcmp( )

    strlwr( ) strrev( )

16. Define a float array of size 5 and assign 5 values to it?

```
Void main()
{
float a[5] ={1.1,2.2,3.3,4.4,5.5);
int i;
for ( i = 0 ; i < 5 ; i ++ )
printf(" %f " , a [ i ] );
}
```

17. What is recursion?

The Process of calling the function by itself again and again until some condition is satisfied.

```
Syntax :
void recursion()
{
     recursion(); /*function calls itself*/
}
int main()
{
     recursion();
}
```

18. What is Pointer? How is pointer initialized?

Pointer is a variable whose value is the address of another variable .i.e., direct address of the memory location. General syntax of pointer declaration is,

    data-type *pointer_name;

    Pointer Initialization:

It is the process of assigning address of a variable to pointer variable. Pointer variable contains address of variable of same data type. In C language address operator & is used to determine the address of a variable. The & (immediately preceding a variable name) returns the address of the variable associated with it.

Eg1:	Eg2:
int a = 10 ;	#include<stdio.h>
int *ptr ; //pointer declaration	int main()
ptr = &a ; //pointer initialization	{
(or)	int a = 10;
//initialization and declaration together	int *ptr;
int *ptr = &a ;	ptr = &a;
	printf("\nValue of ptr : %u",ptr);
	return(0);
	}
	OUTPUT
	Value of ptr : 65524

19. Write notes on Call by value & Call by reference.

Call by Value:

This is the usual method to call a function in which only the value of the variable is passed as an argument.

Call by reference:

In this method, the address of the variable is passed as an argument.

20. Give example on call by reference.(Nov/Dec2014)

```
#include <stdio.h>
#include <conio.h>
void main()
{
void swap(int *,int *);
int a,b;
printf("\n Enter any 2 numbers");
scanf("%d%d",&a,&b0;
printf("\n Before swapping a=%d,b=%d",a,b);
swap(&a,&b);//call by value
printf("\n after swapping a=%d,b=%d",a,b);
getch();
}
void swap(int *x, int *y)
{
int z;
```

```
z=*x;
*x=*y;
*y=z;
}
```
Output
Enter any 2 numbers : 20 30

Before swapping a=20,b=30

After swapping a=30,b=20

21. Write a C function to check whether the given year is leap or not.

```
void main()
{
int a;
clrscr();
printf("Enter the Year: ");
scanf("%d",&a);
if(a%4==0)
printf("%d leap year",a);
else
printf("%d It is not leap year" ,a);
getch();
}
```

Output:

Enter the year : 2008

2008 leap year

22. Determine the output for the following printf statements

```
main()
{
char *ptr="string";
printf("%c",*ptr++);
printf("%c",*(++ptr);
printf("%c",(*ptr)++);
printf("%c",++*ptr);
}
```

Output: srrt

23. What is function prototyping? Why is it necessary?

   A function prototype is a function declaration before the main program.

   This is done to inform the compiler that there is a user defined function in the program.

24. What is the need for functions?
    - It provides modularity to the program.
    - Easy code Reusability. You just have to call the function by its name to use it.
    - In case of large programs with thousands of code lines, debugging and editing becomes easier if you use functions.

25. What are the uses of pointers?
    - Pointers are used to return more than one value to the function.
    - Pointers are more efficient in handling the data in arrays.
    - Pointers reduce the length and complexity of the program.
    - They increase the execution speed.
    - The pointers saves data storage space in memory.

26. What is a function?
    - A function is a self-contained block or a sub-program of one or more statements that performs a special task when performed.
    - A function is a set of instructions that are used to perform specified tasks which repeatedly occurs in the main program.

27. What are the operators exclusively used with pointers? What is an address operator and indirection operator?

    * (asterisk) and & (ampersand) are the operators exclusively used with pointers.

    *operator : deference or indirection operator.

    &operator : address operator.

    → indirection operator used to point the value of pointer variable

28. Give two examples of C preprocessor with syntax.(Apr/May2015)

   Pre-processor directives are....

   File Inclusion - #include "file name" or #include<file name>

   ex: #include<stdio.h>

   Macro substitution - # define identifier string/ integer

   ex: # define PI 3.14

29. What is meant by storage classes? List the different storage classes in C?

In 'C' language, through declaration statements, memory is allocated temporarily for the entire variable defined. The size of the allocated memory varies with respect to the type of the variable. 'C' supports 4 types of storage classes and these are used to specify the scope of different variables defined with in function blocks and programs. the different storage classes in c are.....

a) auto

b) static

c) extern

d) register

30. Define macro with an example?(May/Jun2014)

It used to define symbolic constants in the source program.

Syntax: #define identifier string / integer

#define PI 3.14

31. With the help of the printf function show how C handles functions with variable number of arguments.(May/Jun2014)

Functions with variable number of arguments is handled using the header file "stdarg.h".

va_start,

va_arg,

va_list,

va_end

All these Macros are supported in stdarg.h header file to handle functions with variable number of arguments.

32. What are function pointers in C ? Explain with example(Apr/may2015)

Function pointer stores the address of the executable code.

#include <stdio.h>

void fun(int a)

{

printf("Value of a is %d\n", a); }

void main()

{

void (*fun_ptr)(int) = fun;

fun_ptr(10); }

Output: Value of a is 10

PART II

- Structure and Union
- File Operations
- Sample Programs
- Review Questions with Solution

CHAPTER 9

STRUCTURE AND UNION

9.1. Introduction

Structure is a user defined data type. It isa collection of dissimilar data items.Unlike array, the structure members occupy different memory location.

9.2. Defining a Structure

To define a structure, the keyword **struct** should be used. The structure tag is optional.

Syntax

```
struct [structure tag]
{
    Datatype member 1;
    .....
    Datatypemember n;
} [one or more structure variables];
```

Example : Book structure
```
struct Books
{
    char title[50];
    char author[50];
    char subject[100];
    int  book_id;
} book;
```

9.3. Accessing Structure Members

To access the structure members, the **member access operator (.)**should be used.

Example

```
#include <stdio.h>
#include <string.h>
struct Books
{
    char title[50];
    char author[50];
    char subject[100];
    int  book_id;
};
```

Output:
Enter the Book title
Programming and Data Structure
Enter the Author Name
Hema Priya
Enter the Subject Name
Data structure
Enter the Book ID
101
Book title : Programming and Data Structure
Book author : Hema Priya
Book subject : Data structure
Book book_id : 101

101

```
int main( )
{
    struct Books B;
    printf("Enter the Book title \n");
    gets(B.title);
    printf("Enter the Author Name\n");
    gets(B.author);
    printf("Enter the Subject Name \n");
    gets(B.subject);
    printf("Enter the Book ID \n");
    scanf("%d",&B.book_id);
    printf( "Book  title : %s\n", B.title);
    printf( "Book  author : %s\n", B.author);
    printf( "Book  subject : %s\n", B.subject);
    printf( "Book  book_id : %d\n", B.book_id);
    return 0;
}
```

9.4. Structure as Function Argument

Structure can be passed as an argument to a function by passing the structure variable to the function.

Example

```
#include <stdio.h>
#include <string.h>
struct Books
{
    char title[50];
    char author[50];
    char subject[100];
    int book_id;
};
void printBook( struct Books book );
int main( )
{
    struct Books B1;
    printf("Enter book title");
    gets(B1.title);
    printf("Enter author Name");
    gets(B1.author);
    printf("Enter subject name");
    gets(B1.subject);
```

Output:
Enter book title Programming and data structure
Enter author Name Jeffrey
Enter subject nameData structure
Enter book id101
Book title : Programming and data structure
Book author : Jeffrey
Book subject : Data structure
Book book_id : 101

```
            printf("Enter book id");
            scanf("%d",&B1.book_id);
            printBook( B1 );
   return 0;
}
void printBook( struct Books book )
{
            printf( "Book title : %s\n", book.title);
            printf( "Book author : %s\n", book.author);
            printf( "Book subject : %s\n", book.subject);
            printf( "Book book_id : %d\n", book.book_id);
}
```

9.5. Structure and Pointer

Pointer to structurecan be defined as follows:

struct Books *structpointer;

To access the members of a structure using a pointer the operator ->should be used as follows:

structpointer ->title;

Let us re-write above example using structure pointer, hope this will be easy for you to understand the concept:

```
#include <stdio.h>
#include <string.h>
struct Books
{
            char  title[50];
            char  author[50];
            char  subject[100];
            int   book_id;
};
void printBook( struct Books *book );
int main( )
{
            struct Books Book1;
            strcpy( Book1.title, "Programming and Data Structure");
            strcpy( Book1.author, "Vinston Raja");
            Book1.book_id = 6495407;
            printBook( &Book1 );
}
```

Output:
Book title : Programming and Data Structure
Book author : Vinston Raja
Book book_id : 6495407

```
void printBook( struct Books *book )
{
            printf( "Book title : %s\n", book->title);
            printf( "Book author : %s\n", book->author);
            printf( "Book book_id : %d\n", book->book_id);
}
```

9.6. Array of Structure

Structure is collection of different datatypes (variables) which are grouped together. Whereas, array of structures is a collection of structures.

Example: To Store Information of 10 students Using Structure

```
#include <stdio.h>
struct student
{
            char name[50];
            int roll;
            float marks;
};
int main()
{
            struct student s[10];
            int i,n;
            printf("Enter the number of students:\n");
            scanf("%d",&n);
            printf("Enter information of students:\n");
            for(i=0;i<n;++i)
            {
                        s[i].roll=i+1;
                        printf("\nFor roll number %d\n",s[i].roll);
                        printf("Enter name: ");
                        scanf("%s",s[i].name);
                        printf("Enter marks: ");
                        scanf("%f",&s[i].marks);
                        printf("\n");
            }
            printf("Displaying information of students:\n\n");
            for(i=0;i<n;++i)
            {
                        printf("\nInformation for roll number %d:\n",i+1);
                        printf("Name: ");
                        puts(s[i].name);
                        printf("Marks: %.1f",s[i].marks);
            }
            return 0; }
```

Output:

Enter the number of students: 2

Enter information of students:
For roll number 1
Enter name: Vinston
Enter marks: 100

For roll number 2
Enter name: Hemapriya
Enter marks: 100

Displaying information of students:

Information for roll number 1:
Name: Vinston
Marks: 100.0

Information for roll number 2:
Name: Hemapriya
Marks: 100.0

9.7. Self-Referential Structure

A self-referential structure is essentially a structure definition which includes atleast one member that is a pointer to the structure of its own kind. A chain of such structures can thus be expressed as follows.

```
struct name
{
    member 1;
    member 2;
    ...
    struct name *pointer;
};
```

9.8. Union

A union is a user defined data type. Union is also like structure, i.e. collection of different data types which are grouped together. Each element in a union is called member. Union and structure in C are same in concepts, except allocating memory for their members. Structure allocates storage space for all its members separately. Whereas, Union allocates one common storage space for all its members.

Defining a Union

To define a union, the keyword **union** should be used. The **union tag** is optional.

Syntax

```
union [union tag]
{
    Datatype member1;
    Datatype member2;
} [one or more union variables];
```

The memory occupied by a union will be large enough to hold the largest member of the union.

In below example, union abcd will occupy 20 bytes of memory space because this is the maximum space amoung all the union members.

Example

```
#include <stdio.h>
#include <string.h>
union abcd
{
        int i;
        float f;
        char  str[20];
};
int main( )
{
        union abcda;
        printf( "Memory size occupied by abcd : %d\n", sizeof(a));
        return 0;
}
```

Output:
Memory size occupied by abcd : 20

9.9.   Accessing Union Members

To access the union members, the **member access operator (.)** should be used.

Example 1

```
#include <stdio.h>
#include <string.h>
union Data
{
        int i;
        float f;
        char  str[20];
};
int main( )
{
        union Data data;
        data.i = 10;
        data.f = 220.5;
        strcpy( data.str, "Data structure");
        printf( "data.i : %d\n", data.i);
        printf( "data.f : %f\n", data.f);
        printf( "data.str : %s\n", data.str);
        return 0;
}
```

Output:
data.i : 1917853763
data.f 4122360580327794900000000000000.000000
data.str : Data structure

Example 2

```
#include <stdio.h>
#include <string.h>
union Data
{
    int i;
    float f;
    char str[20];
};
int main( )
{
    union Data data;
    data.i = 10;
    printf( "data.i : %d\n", data.i);
    data.f = 220.5;
    printf( "data.f : %f\n", data.f);
    strcpy( data.str, "Data structure");
    printf( "data.str : %s\n", data.str);
    return 0;
}
```

Output:
data.i : 10
data.f : 220.500000
data.str : Data structure

9.10. Difference between Structure and Union

Sl.NO	STRUCTURE	UNION
1.	Keyword **struct** should be used.	Keyword **union** should be used.
2.	Collection of dissimilar data items.	Collection of dissimilar data items.
3.	User – Defined data type	User – Defined data type
4.	Memory occupied = Sum of the bytes occupied by individual structure members.	Memory occupied = size of the largest union member.
5.	All the structure members occupy different memory location.	All the union members occupy same memory location.
6.	All the structure members can be accessed simultaneously	Only one union member can be accessed at a time.

9.11. Type Def in C

The C programming language provides a keyword called **typedef**, which can be used to define a new datatype.

Example

typedef int mark;

After this type declaration, the identifier mark can be used as datatype

mark m1,m2;

Example

```
#include <stdio.h>
#include <string.h>
typedef struct Books
{
    char title[50];
    char author[50];
    int book_id;
} Book;
int main( )
{
    Book book;
    strcpy( book.title, "Data Structure");
    strcpy( book.author, "Hemapriya");
    book.book_id = 6495407;
    printf( "Book title : %s\n", book.title);
    printf( "Book author : %s\n", book.author);
    printf( "Book book_id : %d\n", book.book_id);
    return 0;
}
```

Output:
Book title : Data Structure
Book author : Hemapriya
Book book_id : 6495407

9.12. Sample Programs using Structure and Union

Program:1 Structure program for Bank operations.	Ouput

#include<stdio.h>
#include<conio.h>
void create();
void display();
void deposit();
void withdraw();
struct bank
{
int accno;
char name[25];
long balance;
};
struct bank b;
 	
void main()
{
int ch;
clrscr();
do
{
printf("\n\t\t*********Menu********\n");
printf("\n1.create");
printf("\n2.deposit");
printf("\n3.withdraw");
printf("\n4.display");
printf("\n5.exit");
printf("\nenter your choice: ");
scanf("%d",&ch);
switch(ch)
{
case 1:
	*********Menu********
	1.create
	2.deposit
	3.withdraw
	4.display
	5.exit
	enter your choice: 1
	Enter your a/c.no: 123456
	Enter your name: xxxx
	Enter the initial deposit:10000
	
	enter your choice: 2
	Enter the amount to be deposited: 2000
	Available balance in the account is 12000

108

```
                create();
                break;
    case 2:
                deposit();
                break;
    case 3:
                withdraw();
                break;
    case 4:
                display();
                break;
    case 5:
                exit(0);
    default:
                printf("\nWrong choice");
                printf("\n Thank you for using the system");
    }
    }
    while(ch<6);
    getch();
    }
    void create()
    {
    printf("\nEnter your a/c.no: ");
    scanf("%d",&b.accno);
    printf("\nEnter your name: ");
    scanf("%s",b.name);
    printf("\n Enter the initial deposit: ");
    scanf("%ld",&b.balance);
    }
    void withdraw()
    {
    long wd,amount;
    printf("\nEnter amount to withdraw: ");
    scanf("%ld",&wd);
    amount=b.balance-wd;
    if(amount<500)
    {
    printf("\nMinimum balance 500 should be maintained.!!!!! withdrawl not possible\n");
    }
    else
    {
    printf("\nWithdrawl amount is %ld",wd);
    printf("\nAvailable balance in the acct is %ld\n",amount);
    b.balance=amount;
    }
    }
    void deposit()
    {
    long dep;
    printf("Enter the amount to be deposited: ");
    scanf("%ld",&dep);
    b.balance+=dep;
    printf("\nAvailable balance in the account is %ld",b.balance);
    }
    void display()
    {
    printf("\n*********Account Details*********\n");
    printf("\nAccount Number: %d",b.accno);
    printf("\nA/C Holder Name: %s",b.name);
    printf("\nBalance: %ld",b.balance);
    }
```

Program 2:print the students mark and total	output
| ```c
#include<stdio.h>
#define SIZE 50

struct student
{
  char name[30];
  int rollno;
  int sub[3];
};
void main()
{
  int i, j, max, count, total, n, a[SIZE], ni;
  struct student st[SIZE];
  printf("Enter how many students: ");
  scanf("%d", &n);
  /* for loop to read the names and roll numbers*/
  for (i = 0; i < n; i++)
  {
    printf("\nEnter name and roll number for student %d : ", i+1);
    scanf("%s", &st[i].name);
    scanf("%d", &st[i].rollno);
  }

  /* for loop to read ith student's jth subject*/
  for (i = 0; i < n; i++) {
    for (j = 0; j <= 2; j++) {
      printf("\nEnter marks of student %d for subject %d : ", i+1, j+1);
      scanf("%d", &st[i].sub[j]);
    }
  }

  /* for loop to calculate total marks of each student*/
  for (i = 0; i < n; i++) {
    total = 0;
    for (j = 0; j < 3; j++) {
      total = total + st[i].sub[j];
    }
    printf("\nTotal marks obtained by student %s are %d", st[i].name,total);
  }
}
``` | Enter how many students: 2<br>Enter name and roll number for student 1:<br>aaa    1<br>Enter name and roll number for student 2:<br>bbb    2<br>Enter marks of student 1 for subject 1 :<br>100<br>Enter marks of student 1 for subject 2 :<br>90<br>Enter marks of student 1 for subject 3:<br>90<br>Enter marks of student 2 for subject 1 :<br>70<br>Enter marks of student 2 for subject 2 :<br>60<br>Enter marks of student 2 for subject 3 :<br>80<br>Total marks obtained by student aaa are 280<br>Total marks obtained by student bbb are 210 |
```

Program 3: Structure to add two complex numbers	Output

#include <stdio.h>
#include<conio.h>
struct complex
{
  int real, img;
};
void main()
{
  struct complex a, b, c;
  clrscr();
  printf("Enter a and b where a + ib is the first
                complex number.\n");
  printf("a = ");
  scanf("%d", &a.real);
  printf("b = ");
  scanf("%d", &a.img);
  printf("Enter c and d where c + id is the second
                complex number.\n");
  printf("c = ");
  scanf("%d", &b.real);
  printf("d = ");
  scanf("%d", &b.img);
 	
  c.real = a.real + b.real;
  c.img = a.img + b.img;
 	
  if (c.img >= 0)
    printf("Sum of two complex numbers = %d +
              %di\n", c.real, c.img);
  else
    printf("Sum of two complex numbers = %d
              %di\n", c.real, c.img);
}
	Enter a and b where a + ib is the first complex number
	
	a = 3
	b = 5
	
	Enter c and d where c + id is the second complex number.
	
	c = 4
	d = 8
	
	Sum of two complex numbers = 7 + 13i

CHAPTER 10

FILE HANDLING CONCEPTS

10.1. Introduction

A file represents a set of records containing numbers, symbols and text that can be accessed through various file functions.

10.2. Need for a File

To store the records permanently, files are required.

To transfer the data from one computer to other, files are required.

10.3. File Operations

Following operations can be performed on a file.

- Opening an existing File.
- Reading from the File.
- Writing into the File.
- Appending to a File.
- Closing a File.

10.4. Types of File

There are two types of File

- Text File.
- Binary File.

Let us discuss each one in detail.

10.4.1. Text File

It is a computer file that only contains text and has no special features such as multimedia contents.

10.4.1.1. File Open

Any file has to be opened to perform operations. **fopen( )** is used to create a new file or to open an existing file.

Syntax

FILE *fp;

fp = fopen(const char * filename, const char * mode);

Example

fp = fopen("Test.txt", "w");

fopen function is used to open a file. Where, fp is file pointer to the data type "FILE". Test.txt is the filename,which is opened in writemode "w".

Text File Modes

File Mode	Meaning of Mode	During Inexistence of file
r	Open for reading.	If the file does not exist, fopen() returns NULL.
w	Open for writing.	If the file exists, its contents are overwritten. If the file does not exist, it will be created.
a	Open for append. i.e, Data is added to end of file.	If the file does not exists, it will be created.
r+	Open for both reading and writing.	If the file does not exist, fopen() returns NULL.
w+	Open for both reading and writing.	If the file exists, its contents are overwritten. If the file does not exist, it will be created.
a+	Open for both reading and appending.	If the file does not exists, it will be created.

10.4.1.2. File Close

To close a file, use the fclose( ).

Syntax

fclose(FILE *fp);

The **fclose( )** returns zero on success, or **EOF** if there is an error in closing the file. This function actually, flushes any data still pending in the buffer, closes the file, and releases memory used for the file. The EOF is a constant defined in the header file **stdio.h** which marks the End Of the File.

10.4.1.3. Writing a File

Following functions are used to write a file

File handling functions	Description
putw ()	putw () functions writes an integer to file.
putc (), fputc ()	putc () and fputc () functions write a character to file.
puts ()	puts () function writes line to o/p screen.
fprintf ()	fprintf () function writes formatted data to a file.
printf ()	printf () function writes formatted data to screen.

Syntax

fputc(char c, FILE *fp);

fputc() writes the character value to the output stream referenced by fp.

Syntax

fputs(const char *s, FILE *fp);

fputs() writes the string **s** to the output stream referenced by fp.

Syntax

fprintf(FILE *fp,control string, variable);

fprintf( ) writes the contents to the output stream referenced by fp.

Example

```
#include <stdio.h>
    int main()
    {
    int num;
    FILE *fptr;
    fptr = fopen("C:\\program.txt","w");
    if(fptr == NULL)
    {
    printf("Error!");
    exit(1);
    }
    printf("Enter num: ");
    scanf("%d",&num);
    fprintf(fptr,"%d",num);
    fputs("\nFile write successful",fptr);
    fclose(fptr);
    return 0;
    }
```

Output:

Enter num: 200

```
200
File write successful
```

10.4.1.4. Reading a File

Following Functions are Used to Read Contents from the File

File handling functions	Description
getw ()	getw () function reads an integer from file.
getc (), fgetc ()	getc () and fgetc () functions read a character from file.
gets ()	gets () function reads line from keyboard.
fgets ()	fgets () function reads string from a file, one line at a time.
feof ()	feof () function finds end of file.
fgetc ()	fgetc () function reads a character from file.
fscanf ()	fscanf () function reads formatted data from a file.
scanf ()	scanf () function reads formatted data from keyboard.

Syntax to read a single character from a file:

char c = fgetc(FILE * fp);

Syntax to read a string from a file:

char *fgets(char *buf, int n, FILE *fp);

The **fgets()** reads up to n-1 characters from the input stream referenced by fp. It copies the read string into the buffer **buf**, appending a **null** character to terminate the string.

Syntax to read thecontent from a file:

fscanf(FILE *fp, const char *format, ...)

This function reads string from a file till first space character encounters.

#include <stdio.h>

int main()

{

int num;

FILE *fptr;

if ((fptr = fopen("C:\\program.txt","r")) == NULL)

    {

    printf("Error! opening file");

    exit(1);

}

Output:
Value of n=200

fscanf(fptr,"%d",&num);

printf("Value of n=%d",num);

fclose(fptr);

return 0;

}

10.4.2. Binary File

It contains formatted text, non text characters or other data not interpreted as text.

Example: Program files and Image files.

It is useful to store the block of data into the file rather than individual elements. Each block has some fixed size; it may be of structure or of an array.

Hence it is easy to read the entire block from file or write the entire block to the file.

10.4.2.1. Binary File Modes

These are following modes used in binary file.

File Mode	Meaning of Mode	During Inexistence of file
rb	Open for reading in binary mode.	If the file does not exist, fopen() returns NULL.
wb	Open for writing in binary mode.	If the file exists, its contents are overwritten. If the file does not exist, it will be created.
ab	Open for append in binary mode. i.e, Data is added to end of file.	If the file does not exists, it will be created.
rb+	Open for both reading and writing in binary mode.	If the file does not exist, fopen() returns NULL.
wb+	Open for both reading and writing in binary mode.	If the file exists, its contents are overwritten. If the file does not exist, it will be created.
ab+	Open for both reading and appending in binary mode.	If the file does not exists, it will be created.

10.4.2.2. Binary I/O Functions

File handling functions	Description
fwrite()	Writes an entire block to a given file
fread()	Reads an entire block from a given file

1. fwrite()

This function is used for writing an entire block to a given file.

Syntax

fwrite(ptr, size, nst, fptr);

- Size is the size of the structure.
- nst is the number of the structure.
- fptr is a file pointer.

Example

```
#include<stdio.h>
#include<conio.h>
void main()
{
    struct emp
    {
        int eno;
        char ename[20];
        float sal;
```

Output:
Enter employee num: 10
Enter employee name : Jeffrey
Enter employee salary : 10000
One record stored successfully.

```
}e;
FILE *fp;
fp=fopen("emp.dat", "wb");
clrscr();
printf("Enter employee number");
scanf("&d",&e.eno);
printf("Enter employee name");
fflush(stdin);
scanf("%s",e.ename);
printf("Enter employee salary");
scanf("%f",&e.sal);
fwrite(&e,sizeof(e),1,fp);
printf("One record stored successfully");
getch();
}
```

2. fread( )

This function is used to read an entire block from a given file.

Syntax

fread (ptr , size , nst , fptr);

- Size is the size of the structure
- nst is the number of the structure
- fptr is a filepointer.

Example

```
#include<stdio.h>
#include<conio.h>
void main()
{
struct emp
{
         int eno;
         char ename[20];
         float sal;
```

OUTPUT:
Employee number is 10
Employee name is Joshua
Employee salary is 10000.
One record read successfully.

```
}e;
FILE *fp;
fp=fopen("emp.dat", "rb");
clrscr();
if(fp==NULL)
printf("File cannot be opened");
else
fread(&e,sizeof(e),1,fp);
printf("\nEmployee number is %d",e.eno);
printf("\nEmployee name is %s",e.ename);
printf("\nEmployee salary is %f",e.sal);
printf("One record read successfully");
getch();
}
```

Random Access to File

There is no need to read each record sequentially, if a particular record needs to be accessed. Theseare the functions used for random access file processing.

File handling functions	Description
fseek ()	fseek () function moves file pointer position to given location.
SEEK_SET	SEEK_SET moves file pointer position to the beginning of the file.
SEEK_CUR	SEEK_CUR moves file pointer position to given location.
SEEK_END	SEEK_END moves file pointer position to the end of file.
ftell ()	ftell () function gives current position of file pointer.
rewind ()	rewind () function moves file pointer position to the beginning of the file.
fflush ()	fflush () function flushes a file.

1. fseek( )

This function is used for seeking the pointer position in the file at the specified byte.

Syntax

fseek (file pointer, displacement, pointer position);

Where,

File pointer- It is the pointer which points to the file.

Displacement - It is positive or negative. This is the number of bytes which are skipped backward (if negative) or forward (if positive) from the current position.

Pointer position- This sets the pointer position in the file.

Value	Pointer position
0	Beginning of file.
1	Current position
2	End of file

Example

fseek(p,10,0)

0 means pointer position is on beginning of the file; from this statement pointer position is skipped 10 bytes from the beginning of the file.

fseek(p,5,1)

1 means current position of the pointer position. From this statement pointer position is skipped 5 bytes forward from the current position.

fseek(p,-5,1)

From this statement pointer position is skipped 5 bytes backward from the current position.

2. ftell()

This function returns the value of the current pointer position in the file. The value is count from the beginning of the file.

Syntax

ftell(fptr);

Where fptr is a file pointer.

3. rewind()

This function is used to move the file pointer to the beginning of the given file.

Syntax

rewind(fptr);

Where fptr is a file pointer.

Example

Program to read last 'n' characters of the file

```
#include<stdio.h>
    #include<conio.h>
    void main()
    {
       FILE *fp;
       char ch;
       clrscr();
       fp=fopen("file1.c", "r");
       if(fp==NULL)
        printf("file cannot be opened");
       else
       {
           printf("Enter value of n  to read last 'n' characters");
           scanf("%d",&n);
           fseek(fp,-n,2);
           while((ch=fgetc(fp))!=EOF)
           {
              printf("%c\t",ch);
           }
       }
       fclose(fp);
       getch();
    }
```

program - Notepad
Random access file program

Output:
Enter value of n to read last 'n' characters
12
file program

Sample Programs

Program 1 : File Program for Data, even and odd elements	Output
#include<stdio.h>	How many numbers?
#include<conio.h>	
#include<process.h>	5
void main()	
{	Enter contents of DATA file:
int a,n,i;	
FILE *fp1,*fp2,*fp3;	1 2 3 4 5
clrscr();	Contents of ODD file:
fp1=fopen("DATA","w");	
if(fp1==NULL)	1 3 5
{	
printf("File could not open!!");	Contents of EVEN file:
exit(0);	
}	2 4

```c
    printf("How many numbers?");
    scanf("%d",&n);
    printf("Enter contents of DATA file:\n");
    for(i=0;i<n;++i)
    {
        scanf("%d",&a);
        putw(a,fp1);
    }
    fclose(fp1);
    fp1=fopen("DATA","r");
    fp2=fopen("ODD","w");
    fp3=fopen("EVEN","w");
    if(fp1==NULL||fp2==NULL||fp3==NULL)
    {
        printf("File could not open!!");
        exit(0);
    }
    while((a=getw(fp1))!=EOF)
    {
            if(a%2!=0)
                    putw(a,fp2);
            else
                    putw(a,fp3);
    }
    fclose(fp1);
    fclose(fp2);
    fclose(fp3);
    fp2=fopen("ODD","r");
    fp3=fopen("EVEN","r");
    if(fp2==NULL||fp3==NULL)
    {
            printf("File could not open!!");
            exit(0);
    }
    printf("\nContents of ODD file:\n");
    while((a=getw(fp2))!=EOF)
            printf("%d ",a);
    printf("\n\nContents of EVEN file:\n");
    while((a=getw(fp3))!=EOF)
            printf("%d ",a);
    fclose(fp2);
    fclose(fp3);
    getch();
}
```

Program 2 : C program to read a file from last to first and write in another file	Output
| ```c
#include<stdio.h>
#include<conio.h>
void main()
{
FILE *f1,*f2;
char *a,ch;
int i,n;
clrscr();
f1=fopen("c:\\a.txt","w");
if(f1!=NULL)
{
printf("\nEnter a string to be written in the file\n");
gets(a);
fputs(a,f1);
}
fclose(f1);
f1=fopen("c:\\a.txt","r");
f2=fopen("c:\\b.txt","w");
if(f1!=NULL && f2!=NULL)
{
fseek(f1,0,2);
n=ftell(f1);
for(i=1;i<=n;i++)
{
fseek(f1,-i,2);
ch=fgetc(f1);
fputc(ch,f2);
}
}
fclose(f1);
fclose(f2);
getch();
}
``` | Enter a string to be written in the file<br>welcome to PDS LAB<br>file: a.txt<br>welcome to PDS LAB<br>file: b.txt<br>BAL SDP ot emoclew |

Program 3: Program to Find the Number of Lines in a Text File	Output
| ```c
#include <stdio.h>
int main()
{
FILE *fileptr;
int count_lines = 0;
char filechar[40], chr;
fileptr = fopen("c:\\sample.txt", "r");
chr = fgetc(fileptr);
while (chr != EOF)
{
if (chr == '\n')
{
count_lines = count_lines + 1;
}
chr = fgetc(fileptr);
}
fclose(fileptr); //close file.
printf("There are %d lines in a file\n", count_lines+1);
return 0;
}
``` | sample - Notepad<br>File Edit Format View Help<br>Programming<br>Data<br>Structure<br>Part1<br><br>There are 4 lines in a file |

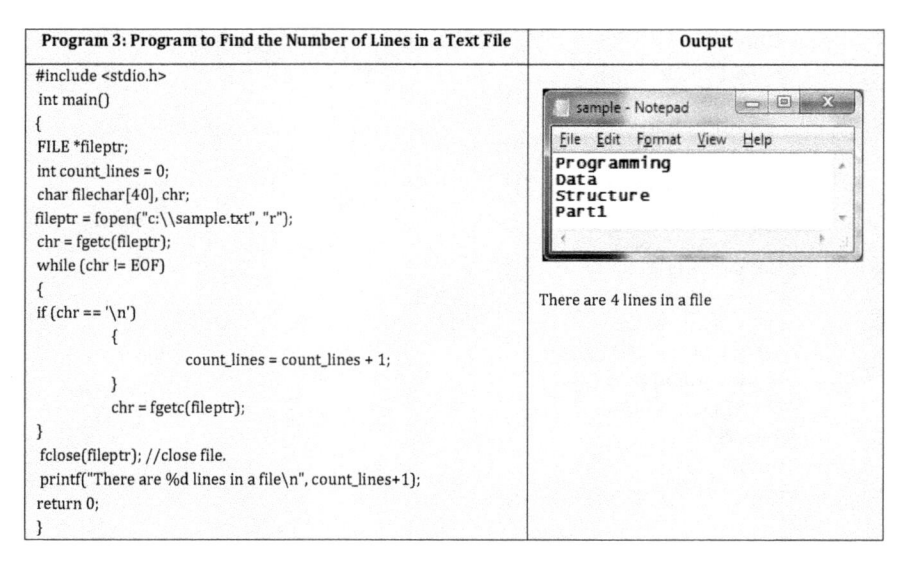

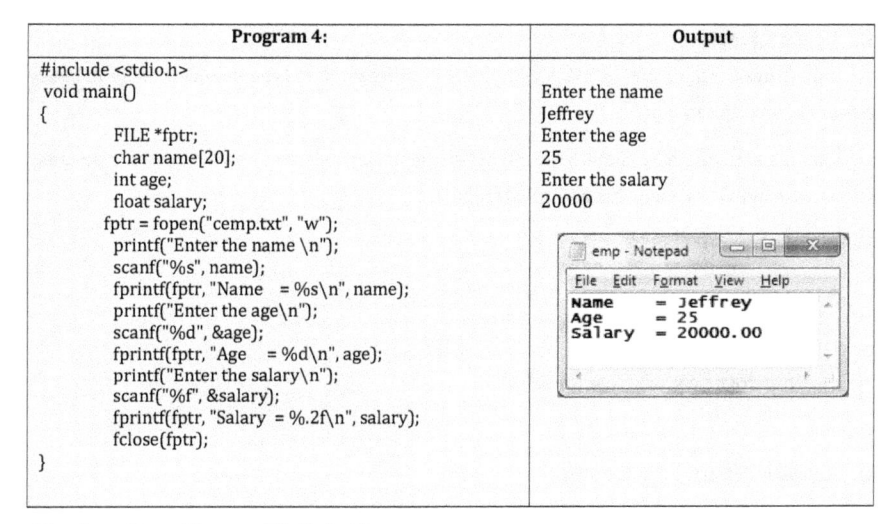

Program 4:	Output

#include <stdio.h>
void main()
{
    FILE *fptr;
    char name[20];
    int age;
    float salary;
    fptr = fopen("cemp.txt", "w");
    printf("Enter the name \n");
    scanf("%s", name);
    fprintf(fptr, "Name = %s\n", name);
    printf("Enter the age\n");
    scanf("%d", &age);
    fprintf(fptr, "Age = %d\n", age);
    printf("Enter the salary\n");
    scanf("%f", &salary);
    fprintf(fptr, "Salary = %.2f\n", salary);
    fclose(fptr);
}
	Enter the name
	Jeffrey
	Enter the age
	25
	Enter the salary
	20000
	
	emp - Notepad
	File Edit Format View Help
	Name = Jeffrey
	Age = 25
	Salary = 20000.00

Review Questions with Solution

1. Compare array and structure.

Array	Structure
An array is a collection of data items of same data type.	A structure is a collection of data item of different data types.
There is no keyword for array.	The keyword for structure is struct
Array elements are stored in continuous memory location	Structure memebrs are stored in different memory locations
Array elements are accessed with index	Structure members are accessed with dot operator.
An array cannot have bitfields.	A structure may contain bitfields.

2. Compare structure and union.

Structure	Union
Everymember has its own memory	All members use the same memory.
The keyword used is struct	The keyword used is union.
All members occupy separate memory location, hence different interpretations of the same memory location are not possible.	Different interpretations forthe same memory location arepossible.
Individual member can be accessed at a time	Only one member can be accessed at a time.

struct stu
{
    char c;
    int l;
    float p;
};
Total memory = 1+2+4 = 7 Bytes
	union stu
	{
	    char c;
	    int l;
	    float p;
	};
	Total memory = 4 Bytes (Largest Union member)

3. Define Structure in C.

A structure contains one or more data items of different data type in which the individual elements can differ in type.

A simple structure may contain the integer elements, float elements and character elements etc. and the individual elements are called members.

Example

   struct result

   {

       intmarks; float avg; char grade;

   }std;

4. Rules for declaring a structure?
   - A structuremustend with a semicolon.
   - Usually a structure appears at the top of the source program.
   - Each structure element must be terminated.
   - The structure must be accessed with structure variable with dot (.)operator.

5. Define structure pointers

   Pointer is a avariable, it contain address of another variable and the structure pointers are declared by placing * in front of a structure variable name.

Example

   struct result

   {

      intmarks;

      float avg;

      char grade;

   };

   structresult*sam;

6. Define union?

   A union is a collection of variables of different types, just like structure. Union is aderived data type and the difference between union and structureis in terms of storage. In structure each member has its own storage location, where as all the members of union use the same memory location.

Example

union result

{

    intmarks; float avg; char grade;

}std;

7. Define file?(nov/dec2014)

A file represents a set of records containing numbers, symbols and text that can be accessed through various file functions.

Example: FILE *infile; FILE *outfile;

8. Define binary files?

Binary file contains formatted text, non text characters or other data not interpreted as text. Example: Program files and Image files. It is useful to store the block of data into the file rather than individual elements. Each block has some fixed size; it may be of structure or of an array. Hence it is easy to read the entire block from file or write the entire block to the file.

9. Define opening a file?

A file requires to be opened first with the file pointer positioned on the first character. No input-output functions on astream can be performed unless itis opened. When astream is opened, it is connected to named DOS device or file.

Syntax

FILE *fopen(char *filename, char *mode);

10. Definefseek()?

This function is used for seeking the pointer position in the file at the specified byte.

Syntax

          fseek (file pointer, displacement, pointer position);

Where,

File pointer - It is the pointer which points to the file.

Displacement - It is positive or negative. This is the number of bytes which are skipped backward (if negative) or forward (if positive) from the current position.

Pointer position - This sets the pointer position in the file.

Value	Pointer position
0	Beginning of file.
1	Current position
2	End of file

11. Functions of bit fields?

- Bitfields do not have address.
- It is not an array.
- It cannot be accessed using pointer.
- It cannot be store values beyond their limits. If larger values are assigned, the output is undefined.

12. What are the ways to detect End of File?

In Text File

- Special character EOF denotes the end of file.
- As soon as character is read, end of the file can be detected
- EOF is defined in stdio.h.
- Equivalent value of EOF is -1.

In Binary File

- feof( ) is used to detect the end of file.
- It can be used in text file.
- feof( ) returns TRUE if end of the file is reached.

Syntax: feof(FILE *fp);

13. What are key functions required to process a file?

- fopen( )
- fclose( )
- fseek( )
- fread( )
- fwrite( )

14. List out the file handling functions

fopen()-create a new file or open an existing file.

fclose( ) –close a file.

getc()-reads a character from a file.

putc()-writes a characterto file.

fscanf()–reads a set of data from a file.

15. Give application in which union rather than structure can be used.(may/jun2014)

Union is used in the CPU registers.

Union is used in embedded programming or in situation where direct access to the hardware/memory is needed.

16. Will the following declaration work. Justify your answer(may/jun2014)

```
struct student
{
    int rollno=12;
    float mark[ ]={ 55,60,56 };
    char gender;
};
```

No, the following declaration will not work, because initialization of structure member is not possible when the structure members are declared.

17. Need for union.(nov/dec2014)

Proper use of union saves memory.

Union is used in the CPU registers.

Union is used in embedded programming or in situation where direct access to the hardware/memory is needed.

18. What are the statements used for reading a file ? (Nov/dec2014)
    1. fscanf ( )
    2. fread ( )
    3. fgets ( )
    4. fgetc ( )

19. What is the difference between getc() and getchar() ? Explain. (apr/may2015)

The difference between getc() and getchar() is getc() can read from any input stream, but getchar() reads from standard input.

So getchar() is equivalent to getc(stdin).

Syntax:

int getchar(void);

int getc(FILE *stream);

20. Explain the syntax as given below. (apr/may2015)

fread(&my_record,sizeof(struct rec),1,ptr_myfile);

fread( ) function is mainly used to read contents from binary file. Here it is used to read one record from the file pointed by the file pointer ptr_myfile and store the read record in the address of &my_record.

PART III

- Overview of Linear Data Structure
- List ADT
- Singly Linked list
- Doubly Linked List
- Circular Linked List
- Polynomial ADT
- Review Questions with Solutions

CHAPTER 11

OVERVIEW OF LINEAR DATA STRUCTURE-LIST

11.1. Introduction to Data Structures

A data structure is a specialized format for organizing and storing data.

General data structure types include the array, the file, the record, the table, the tree, and so on.

Any data structure is designed to organize data to suit a specific purpose so that it can be accessed and worked with in appropriate ways.

> A data structure is a way of organizing, storing, retrieving data and their relationship with each other.

Terms to be known

(i) Data

A collection of facts, concepts, figures, observations, occurrences or instructions in a formalized manner.

(ii) Information

Processed data is called as information.

(iii)   Record

Collection of related fields.

(iv) Data Type

Set of elements that share common set of properties used to solve a program.

11.2.   Application of Data Structures

- Operating systems.
- Compiler design.
- Statistical and numerical analysis.
- Database management systems.
- Expert systems.
- Network analysis.

11.3. Classification of Data Structure

There are two main types of Data Structure classification.

1. Primitive Data Structure.
2. Non-primitive Data Structure

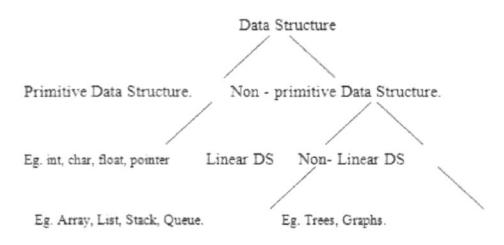

```
                        Data Structure
                       /             \
          Primitive Data Structure.   Non - primitive Data Structure.
                /                      /            \
   Eg. int, char, float, pointer   Linear DS    Non- Linear DS
                                      /              \
                        Eg. Array, List, Stack, Queue.   Eg. Trees, Graphs.
```

(i) **Primitive Data Structure:** It is a basic Data structure which can be directly operated by the machine instruction.

(ii) **Non-Primitive Data Structure:** It is a Data structure which emphasize on structuring of a group of homogeneous or heterogeneous data items. It is further classified into two types. They are:

- Linear Data Structures.
- Non- Linear Data Structures.

(iii) **Linear Data Structures:** It is a data structure which contains a linear arrangement of elements in the memory.

(iv) **Non-Linear Data Structure:** It is a data structure which represents a hierarchical arrangement of elements.

11.4. Abstract Data Type(ADT)

Abstract data types are mathematical models of a set of data values or information that share similar behavior or qualities and that can be specified and identified independent of specific implementations. Abstract data types, or ADTs, are typically used in algorithms. An abstract data type is defined in term of its data items or its associated operations rather than by its implementation.

ADT is a set of operations that are written once in the program and can be used any time from any part of the program.

Benefits of Using ADTs

Modularity: Each data type can be considered independently.

Testing: Data type implementations can be tested separately to check that they meet the specifications.

Division of labour: Separate implementation of data types according to agreed specifications.

Reusability: Implemented data types can be reused.

Change of implementation: The implementation can be changed with no effect to users.

11.5. List ADT

A list is a linear data structure. It is a collection of elements. In general the List is in the form of elements $A_1, A_2, ..., A_N$, where N is the size of the list associated with a set of operations listed below.

- Insert( ): Add an element e.g. Insert(X,5)-Insert the element X after the position 5.
- Delete( ): Remove an element e.g. Delete(X)-The element X is deleted.
- Find( ): Find the position of an element (search) e.g. Find(X,L)-Returns the position of X in List L.
- PrintList( ): Display all the elements from the list.
- MakeEmpty( ): Make the list as empty list.

11.5.1. Methods to Implement a List

There are two ways to implement List.

1. Array implementation of list.
2. Linked list implementation of list.

11.5.2. Array Implementation of List

A set of data elements of same data type is called array. Array is a static data structure i.e., the memory should be allocated in advance and the size is fixed.

This will waste the memory space when used space is less than the allocated space.

The basic operations performed on a list of elements are:

a. Creation of List.
b. Insertion of data element in the List.

c. Deletion of data elementfrom the List.
d. Display all dataelementsin the List.
e. Searching for a dataelement in the list.

Global Declaration

#define maxsize 10

int list[maxsize], n ;

a) Create Operation

Initially the array is fixed with maximum size of 10 elements in our example. In the above global declaration section, list[maxsize] represents the array name as ' list ', and ' n ' denotes the number of elements present in the list.

Create( ) is used to initialize the list with ' n ' number of elements read from the user. The array elements are stored in the consecutive array locations (i.e.) list [0], list [1] and so on.

```
void Create()
{
int i;
printf("\nEnter the number of elements to be added in the list:\t");
scanf("%d",&n);
printf("\nEnter the array elements:\t");
for(i=0;i<n;i++)
scanf("%d",&list[i]);
Display();
}
```

b) Insert Operation

Insert operation is used to insert an element at particular position in the list. Inserting the element in the last position of an array is easy.

But inserting the element at a particular position in an array is quite difficult since it involves all the datas from the specified position to be moved one position right in the array.

Consider an array with 5 elements [max elements = 10]

	10	20	30	40	50					
Index	0	1	2	3	4	5	6	7	8	9

If data 15 is to be inserted in the 1st index then data 50 has to be moved to index 5, 40 has to be moved to index 4, 30 has to be moved to index 3 and 20 has to be moved to index 2.

	10	20	30	40	50				
Index	0	1	2	3	4	5	6	7	8	9

	10		20	30	40	50			
Index	0	1	2	3	4	5	6	7	8	9

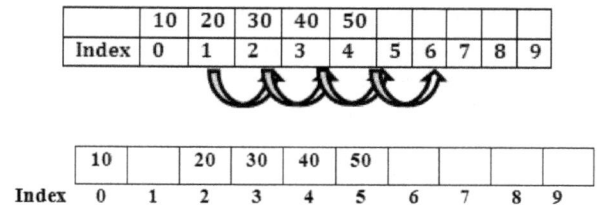

After four data movement, 15 is inserted in the index 1 of the array.

	10	15	20	30	40	50			
Index	0	1	2	3	4	5	6	7	8	9

```
void Insert( )
{
    int i,data,pos;
    printf("\nEnter the data to be inserted:\t");
    scanf("%d",&data);
    printf("\nEnter the position at which element to be inserted:\t");
    scanf("%d",&pos);
    for(i = n-1 ; i >= pos-1 ; i--)
        list[i+1] = list[i];
    list[pos-1] = data;
    n+=1;
    Display();
}
```

Here the elements are inserted one at a time. Once the element is inserted, the number of elements in the array 'n' is incremented by 1. Hence inserting an element at particular position in the array is costly and time consuming since it involves many data movements.

c) Deletion Operation

Delete operation is used to delete one element from the array. An element can be deleted from any position in the array.

Deleting the element from the last position of an array is easy. But deleting the element at a particular position in an array is quite difficult since it involves all the datas from the specified position to be moved one position left in the array.

Consider an array with 5 elements [max elements = 10]

	10	15	20	30	40	50			
Index	0	1	2	3	4	5	6	7	8	9

If data 15 is to be delete from the 1st index then data 20 has to be moved to index 1, 30 has to be moved to index 2, 40 has to be moved to index 3 and 50 has to be moved to index 4.

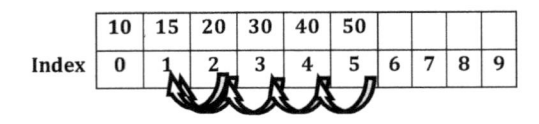

	10	15	20	30	40	50				
Index	0	1	2	3	4	5	6	7	8	9

After four data movement, 15 is deleted from the index 1 of the array.

	10	20	30	40	50				
Index	0	1	2	3	4	5	6	7	8	9

```
void Delete()
{
int i,pos;
printf("\nEnter the position of the data to be deleted:\t");
scanf("%d",&pos);
printf("\nThe data deleted is:\t %d", list[pos-1]);
for(i=pos-1;i<n-1;i++)
list[i]=list[i+1];
n=n-1;
Display();
}
```

d) Display Operation

Display( ) is used to display all the elements stored in the list. The elements are stored from the index 0 to n-1. Using a for loop, the elements in the list are viewed.

```
void display()
{
int i;
printf("\n*********Elements in the array*********\n");
for(i=0;i<n;i++)
   printf("%d\t",list[i]);
}
```

e) Search Operation

Search( ) is used to determine whether a particular element is present in the list or not. Input the search element to be checked in the list. There are two types of searching algorithm. They are Linear Search and Binary Search.

Here Linear search technique is applied to search an element in the array.

```
void Search()
{
int search,i,count = 0;
printf("\nEnter the element to be searched:\t");
scanf("%d",&search);
for(i=0;i<n;i++)
{
if(search == list[i])
count++;
}
if(count==0)
printf("\nElement not present in the list");
else
printf("\nElement present in the list");
}
```

Program for Array Implementation of List

```
#include<stdio.h>
#include<conio.h>
#define maxsize 10
int list[maxsize],n;
void Create();
void Insert();
void Delete();
void Display();
void Search();
void main()
{
	int choice;
	clrscr();
	do
	{
	printf("\n Array Implementation of List\n");
	printf("\t1.create\n");
	printf("\t2.Insert\n");
	printf("\t3.Delete\n");
	printf("\t4.Display\n");
	printf("\t5.Search\n");
	printf("\t6.Exit\n");
	printf("\nEnter your choice:\t");
	scanf("%d",&choice);
	switch(choice)
	{
```

```c
            case 1: Create();
                        break;
            case 2: Insert();
                        break;
            case 3: Delete();
                        break;
            case 4: Display();
                        break;
            case 5: Search();
                        break;
            case 6: exit(1);
            default: printf("\nEnter option between 1 - 6\n");
                        break;
            }
            }while(choice<7);
}
void Create()
{
            int i;
            printf("\nEnter the number of elements to be added in the list:\t");
            scanf("%d",&n);
            printf("\nEnter the array elements:\t");
            for(i=0;i<n;i++)
            scanf("%d",&list[i]);
            Display();
}
void Insert()
{
            int i,data,pos;
            printf("\nEnter the data to be inserted:\t");
            scanf("%d",&data);
            printf("\nEnter the position at which element to be inserted:\t");
            scanf("%d",&pos);
            for(i = n-1 ; i >= pos-1 ; i--)
            list[i+1] = list[i];
            list[pos-1] = data;
            n+=1;
            Display();
}
void Delete( )
{
            int i,pos;
            printf("\nEnter the position of the data to be deleted:\t");
            scanf("%d",&pos);
            printf("\nThe data deleted is:\t %d", list[pos-1]);
            for(i=pos-1;i<n-1;i++)
```

```
            list[i]=list[i+1];
            n=n-1;
            Display();
}
void Display()
{
            int i;
            printf("\n**********Elements in the array**********\n");
            for(i=0;i<n;i++)
            printf("%d\t",list[i]);
}
void Search()
{
            int search,i,count = 0;
            printf("\nEnter the element to be searched:\t");
            scanf("%d",&search);
            for(i=0;i<n;i++)
            {
            if(search == list[i])
            {
            count++;
            }
            }
            if(count==0)
            printf("\nElement not present in the list");
            else
            printf("\nElement present in the list");
}
```

Output

```
Array Implementation of List
        1.create
        2.Insert
        3.Delete
        4.Display
        5.Search
        6.Exit
Enter your choice:    1
Enter the number of elements to be added in the list:  3
Enter the array elements:    10 20 30
**********Elements in the array**********
0       20      30
Array Implementation of List
        1.create
        2.Insert
        3.Delete
        4.Display
        5.Search
        6.Exit
Enter your choice:
```

Limitation of Array Implementation

- An array size is fixed at the start of execution and can store only the limited number of elements.
- Insertion and deletion operation in array are expensive. Since insertion is performed by pushing the entire array one position down and deletion is performed by shifting the entire array one position up.

A better approach is to use a *Linked List* implementation of List.

11.5.3. Linked List Implementation of List

Linked Lists

A linked list is a collection of nodes(Structure). Every node has a data field and an address field. The Address field contains the address of its successor.

Types of Linked List

1. Singly Linked List or One Way List.
2. Doubly Linked List or Two-Way Linked List.
3. Circular Linked List.

11.5.4. Singly Linked List (SLL)

In this type of linked list two successive nodes are linked together in linear fashion. Each node contain address of the next node to be followed. In singly linked list only linear or forward sequential movement is possible. Elements are accessed sequentially, no direct access is allowed.

DATA	LINK (or)NEXT

SLL NODE

First node does not have predecessor while last node does not have any successor. last node have successor reference as "NULL". Each SLL has a header node L to avoid confusion during Insertion and Deletion operation.

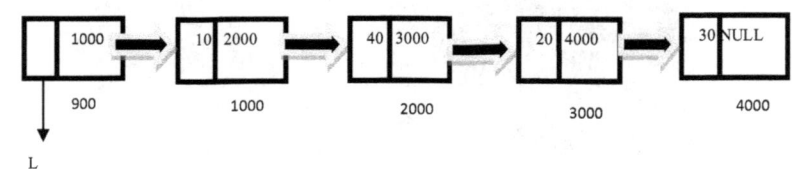

```
L → 1000 → 10|2000 → 40|3000 → 20|4000 → 30|NULL
    900    1000      2000      3000      4000
```

Basic operations on a singly-linked list are:

1. Insert( ) – Inserts a new node in the list.
2. Delete( ) – Deletes any node from the list.
3. Find( )–Finds the position(address) of any node in the list.
4. FindPrevious( ) –Finds the position(address) of the previous node in the list.

Declaration of Linked List

void insert(int X,List L,position P);

void find(List L,int X);

void delete(int x , List L);

typedef struct node *position;

position L,p,newnode,temp;

Node Structure for Singly Linked List

```
struct node
{
        int data;
        position next;
};
```

Routine to Insert an Element in List

```
void Insert(int X,List L,position p)
{
        position newnode;
        newnode=malloc(sizeof(struct node));
        if(newnode==NULL)
                Fatal error("Out of Space");
        else
        {
                Newnode->data=x;
                Newnode->next=p->next;
                P ->next=newnode;
        }
}
```

Routine to Insert an Element in the List

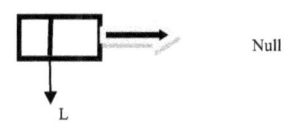

Insert(L,10) - A new node with data 10 is inserted and the next field is updated to NULL. The next field of previous node is updated to store the address of new node.

```
    [ 1000 ]  →  [ 10 | NULL ]
       900              1000
       ↓
       L
```

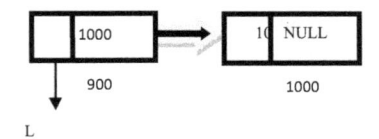

Insert(L,20) - A new node with data 20 is inserted and the next field is updated to NULL. The next field of previous node is updated to store the address of new node.

```
    [ ] → [ 10 | ] → [ 20 | ] → Null
     ↓
     L
```

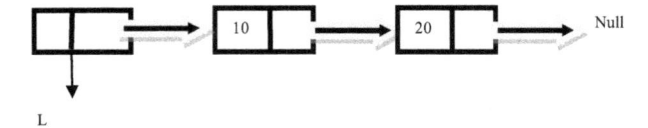

Insert(L,30) - A new node with data 30 is inserted and the next field is updated to NULL. Thenext field of previous node is updated to store the address of new node.

```
    [ ] → [ 10 | ] → [ 20 | ] → [ 30 | ] → Null
     ↓              ↑
     L              P
```

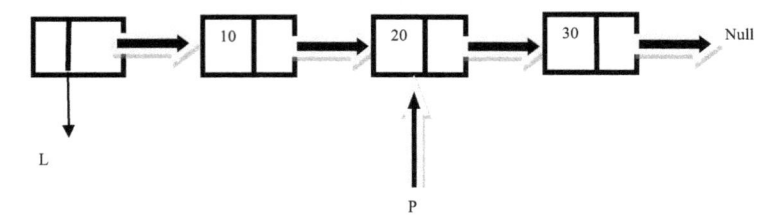

Routine to Check Whether a List is Empty

```
int IsEmpty(List L)
{
if (L->next==NULL)
                return(1);
}
```

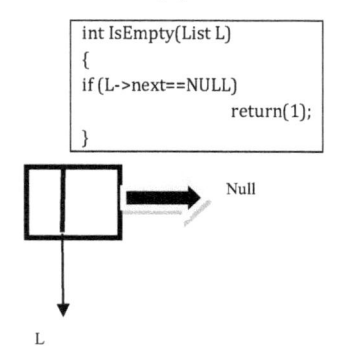

```
    [ | ] → Null
     ↓
     L
```

141

Routine to Check Whether the Current Position is Last in the List

```
int IsLast(List L , position p)
{
    if(p->next==NULL)
        return(1);
}
```

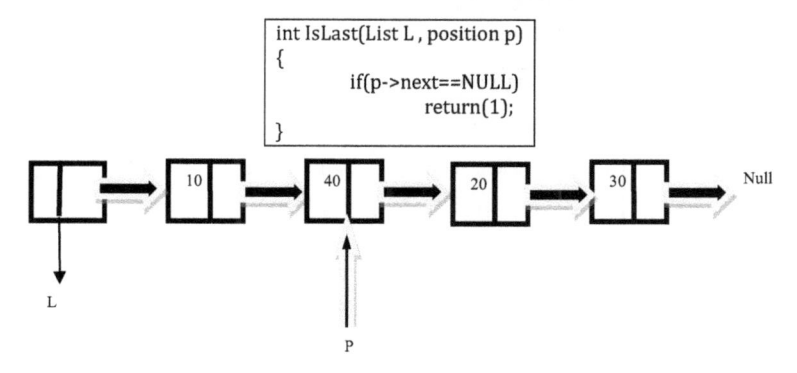

Routine to Find the Element in the List

```
position find(List L,int X)
{
    position p;
    p=L->next;
    while(p!=NULL && p->data!=X)
        p=p->next;
    return(p);
}
```

Find(L,20) - To find an element in the list, start from the first node of the list and traverse the list till the element is found.

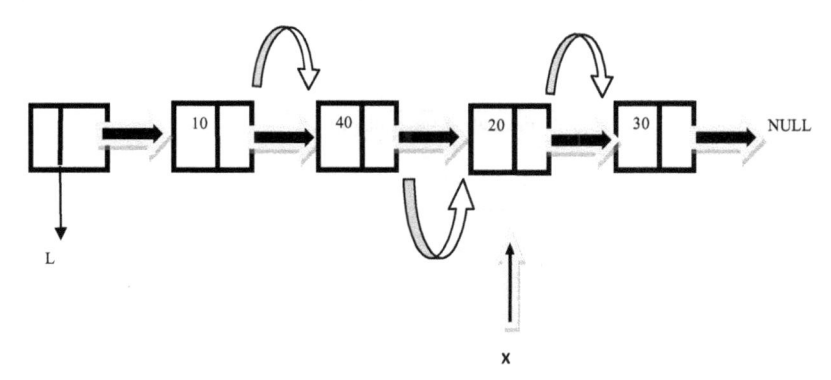

Routine to Find Previous Node

It returns the position of its predecessor.

```
position FindPrevious (int X, List L)
{
        position p;
        p=L;
        while(p->next!=NULL && p->next->data!=X)
                p=p->next;
        return P;
}
```

Routine to Count the Element in the List

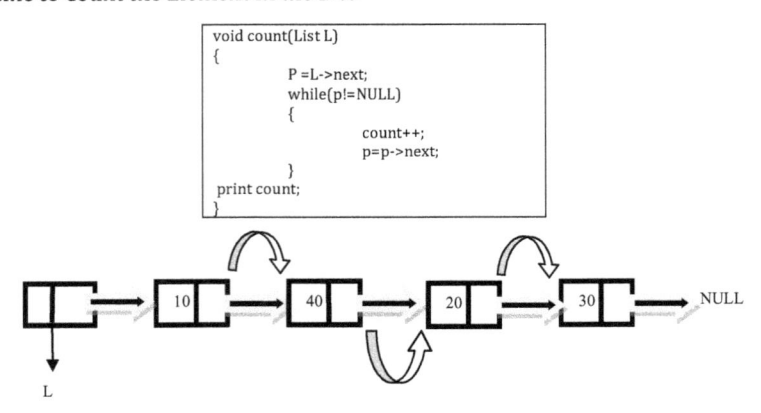

```
void count(List L)
{
        P =L->next;
        while(p!=NULL)
        {
                count++;
                p=p->next;
        }
        print count;
}
```

[Diagram: Linked list L → 10 → 40 → 20 → 30 → NULL]

Routine to Delete an Element from the List

Delete(20,L) - A node with data 20 is found. Mark the node to be deleted as **temp**. Update the address part of the previous node from the temp node. Using free( ) release the memory of temp node.

```
void Delete(int x , List L)
{
position p,Temp;
p=FindPrevious(X,L);
if(!IsLast(p,L))
{
        temp=p->next;
        P ->next=temp->next;
        free(temp);
}
}
```

143

Before Deletion

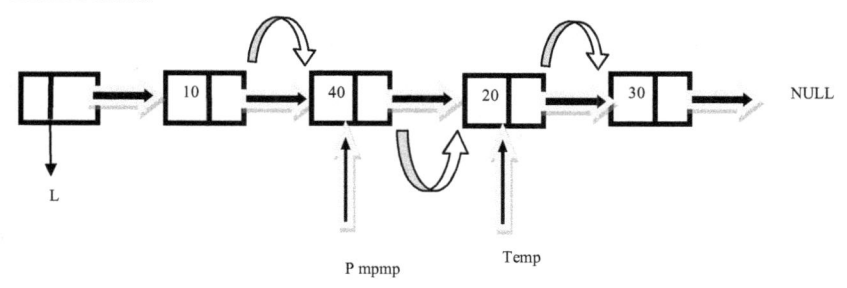

```
L → □ → 10 → 40 → 20 → 30 → NULL
              ↑P mpmp   ↑Temp
```

After Deletion

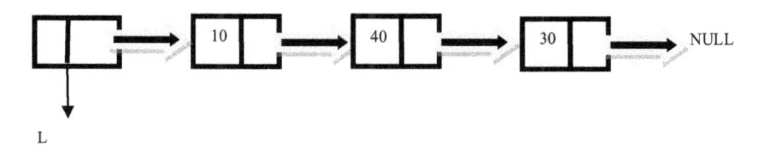

```
L → □ → 10 → 40 → 30 → NULL
```

Routine to Delete the List

```
void Delete_list(List L)
{
position P,temp;
P=L->next;
L->next=NULL;
while(P!=NULL)
{
        temp=P->next;
        free(P);
        P=temp;
}
}
```

Routine to Find Next Element in the List

```
void FindNext(int X, List L)
{
position P;
P=L->next;
while(P!=NULL && P->data!=X)
        P = P->next;
return P->next;
}
```

11.5.5. Doubly Linked List (DLL)

It is a more sophisticated form of linked list. It is a collection of nodes where each node has three fields.

PREV	DATA	NEXT
	DLL NODE	

PREV – Stores the address of the previous node.

DATA – Stores the actual data.

NEXT- Stores the address of the next node.

In comparison to singly-linked list, doubly-linked list requires handling of more pointers but less information is required as one can use the previous links to observe the preceding element. It has a dynamic size, which can be determined only at run time.

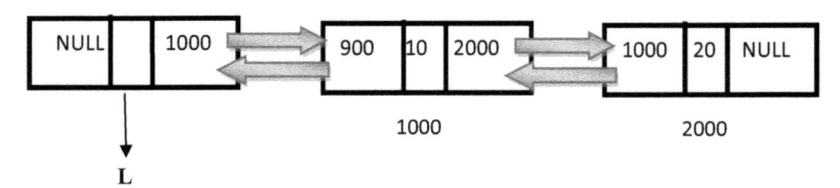

| NULL | 1000 | ⇄ | 900 | 10 | 2000 | ⇄ | 1000 | 20 | NULL |

```
        ↓                    1000                    2000
        L
```

Doubly linked list operations:

1. Insert( ) – Inserts a new element at the end of the list.
2. Delete( ) – Deletes any node from the list.
3. Find( ) – Finds any node in the list.
4. Print( ) – Prints the list.

Declaration of Doubly Linked List

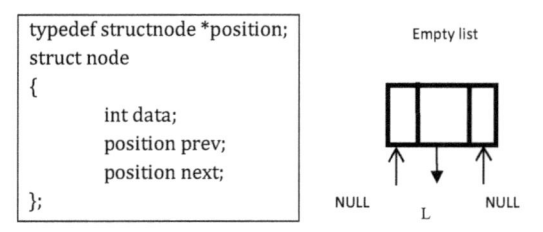

```
typedef structnode *position;
struct node
{
        int data;
        position prev;
        position next;
};
```

Empty list

```
     ↑   ↓   ↑
    NULL  L  NULL
```

Routine to Insert an Element

```
void Insert (int x,List L,position p)
{
    position newnode;
    newnode = malloc(sizeof(struct node));
    if(newnode==NULL)
    Fatal error ("out of space");
    else
    {
        newnode ->data = x;
        newnode ->next =p->next;
        p->next ->prev = newnode;
        p->next= newnode;
        newnode ->prev =p;
    }
}
```

i) Insert(L,10) - A newnode with data 10 is inserted, the next field is updated to NULL and the previous field is updated to store the address of the previous node. The next field of previous node is updated to store the address of new node.

```
NULL | 1000        900 | 10 | NULL
        |              1000
        L            (Newnode)
```

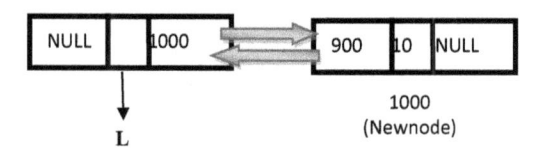

ii) Insert(L,20) - A newnode with data 20 is inserted, the next field is updated to NULL and the previous field is updated to store the address of the previous node. The next field of previous node is updated to store the address of new node.

```
NULL | 1000       900 | 10 | 2000       1000 | 20 | NULL
        |               1000                  2000
        L
```

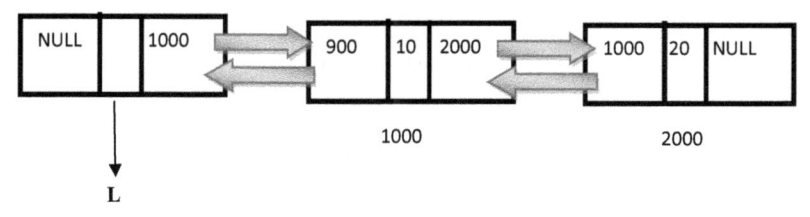

iii) Insert(L,30) - A new node with data 30 is inserted, the next field is updated to NULL and the previous field is updated to store the address of the previous node. The next field of previous node is updated to store the address of new node.

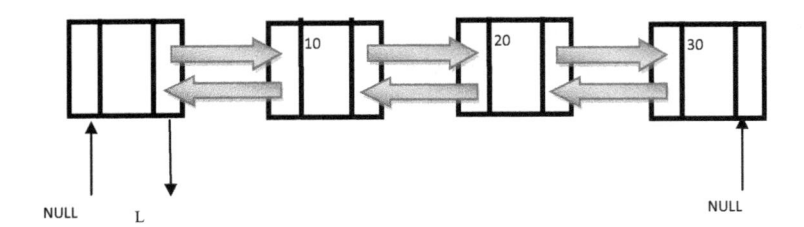

iv) Insert(L,40,P) - A new node with data 40 is inserted, the next field is updated to NULL and the previous field is updated to store the address of the previous node. The next field of previous node is updated to store the address of new node.

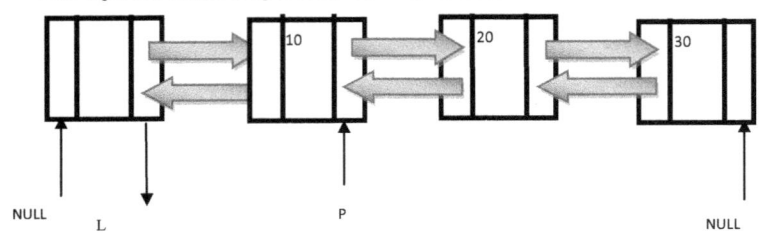

Inserting element 40 at the particular position in the list

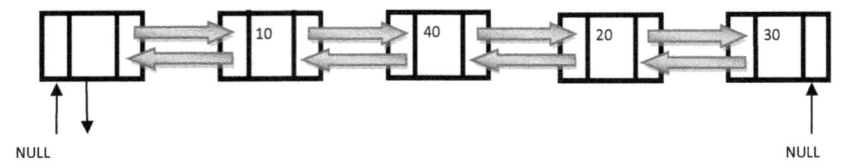

Routine to Display List Element

```
void Display(List L)
{
P =L->next;
while (p!=NULL)
{
   print p->data;
   p=p->next;
}
print NULL
}
```

```
┌───┬───┬───┐   ┌───┬────┬───┐   ┌───┬────┬───┐   ┌───┬────┬───┐
│   │ 10│   │⇄│   │ 40 │   │⇄│   │ 20 │   │⇄│   │ 30 │   │
└───┴───┴───┘   └───┴────┴───┘   └───┴────┴───┘   └───┴────┴───┘
   ↓                                                      ↓
   L                                                    NULL
```

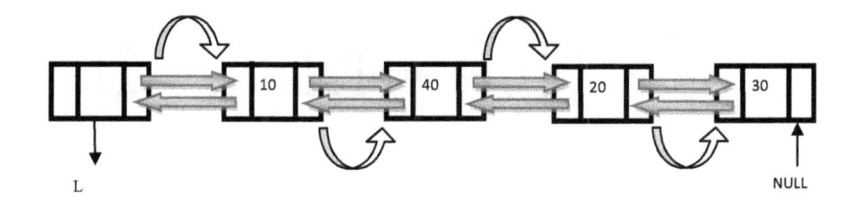

Routine to Delete Anelement

```
void Delete (int x ,List L)
{
Position p , temp;
P = Find(x,L);
if(isLast(p,L))
{
temp =p;
   p->prev->next=NULL;
   free(temp);
}
else
{
 temp = p;
 p->prev->next=p->next;
 p->next->prev = p->prev;
 free(temp);
}
```

Delete(L,10) - A node with data 10 is found, the next and previous fields are updated to store the NULL value. The next field of previous node is updated to store the address of node next to the deleted node. The previous field of the node next to the deleted one is updated to store the address of the node that is before the deleted node.

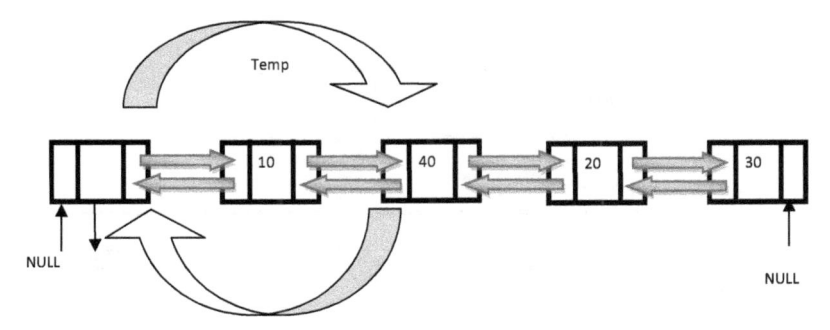

```
         Temp
      ⌒⟶⟶⟶⌒
┌───┬───┬───┐   ┌───┬────┬───┐   ┌───┬────┬───┐   ┌───┬────┬───┐
│   │ 10│   │⇄│   │ 40 │   │⇄│   │ 20 │   │⇄│   │ 30 │   │
└───┴───┴───┘   └───┴────┴───┘   └───┴────┴───┘   └───┴────┴───┘
   ↑                                                      ↓
 NULL    ⌢⟵⟵⟵⌢                                         NULL
```

148

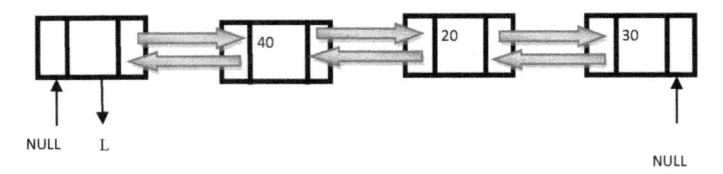

Find(start,10) 'Element Not Found'

To print start from the first node of the list and move to the next with the help of the address stored in the next field.

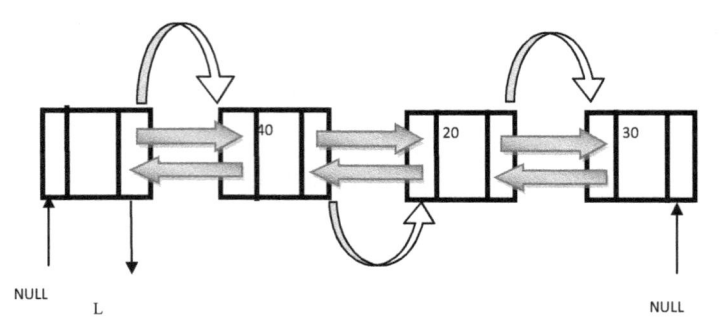

11.5.6. Circular Linked List

Circular linked list is a more complicated linked list. All nodes are linked in a continuous circle without using NULL. The next node after the last node is the first node.

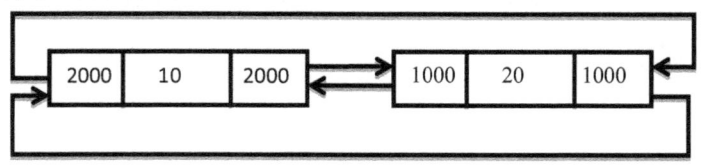

Types of Circular Linked List

1. Singly circular linked list

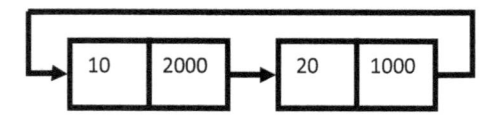

2. Doubly circular linked list

Basic operations of a singly circular linked list are same as SLL:
1. Insert ( )– Inserts a new element at the end of the list.
2. Delete( ) – Deletes any node from the list.
3. Find( ) – Finds any node in the list.
4. Print( ) – Prints the list.

Declaration of Linked List

void insert(int X,List L,position P);

void find(List L,int X);

void delete(int x , List L);

typedef struct node *position;

position L,p,newnode;

struct node

{

    int data;

    position next;

};

Routine to Insert an Element in List

```
void Insert(int X, List L, position p)
{
        position newnode;
        newnode = malloc( sizeof( struct node ));
        if( newnode = = NULL )
                Fatal error( " Out of Space " );
        else
        {
                Newnode -> data = x ;
                Newnode -> next = p ->next ;
                P -> next = newnode ;
        }
}
```

singly circular with 1 node

| 10 | 1000 |

Insert(Start,20) - A new node with data 20 is inserted and the next field is updated to store the address of start node.

The next field of previous node is updated to store the address of new node.

| 10 | 2000 | → | 20 | 1000 |

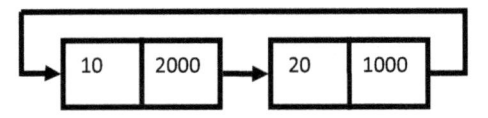

Insert(Start,30) - A new node with data 30 is inserted and the next field is updated to store the address of start node.

The next field of previous node is updated to store the address of new node.

| 10 | 2000 | → | 20 | 3000 | → | 30 | 1000 |

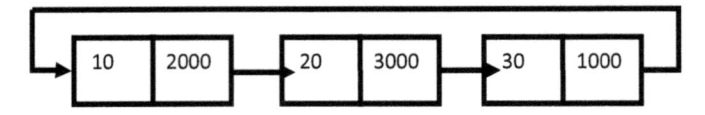

Find Previous

It returns the position of its predecessor.

```
position FindPrevious (int X, List L)
{
        position p;
        p = L;
        while( p -> next ! = NULL && p -> next -> data! = X )
                p = p -> next;
        return P;
}
```

Routine to Delete an Element from the List

```
void Delete( int x , List L)
{
        position p, Temp;
        p = FindPrevious( X, L);
        if( ! IsLast (p, L))
        {
                temp = p -> next;
                P -> next = temp -> next;
                free ( temp );
        }
}
```

151

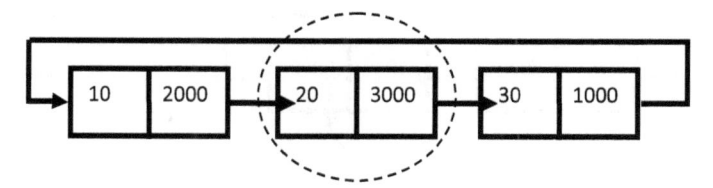

```
┌─────────────────────────────────────────────────┐
│  ┌────┬──────┐   ┌────┬──────┐   ┌────┬──────┐  │
└─▶│ 10 │ 2000 │──▶│ 20 │ 3000 │──▶│ 30 │ 1000 │──┘
   └────┴──────┘   └────┴──────┘   └────┴──────┘
                   ( dashed circle around 20|3000 )
```

Routine to Delete the List

```
void Delete_list(List L)
{
        position P,temp;
        P=L->next;
        L->next=NULL;
        while(P!=NULL)
        {
                temp=P->next;
                free(P);
                P=temp;
        }
}
```

Routine to Find Next Element in the List

```
void FindNext(int X, List L)
{
        position P;
        P=L->next;
        while(P!=NULL && P->data!=X)
                P = P->next;
        return P->next;
}
```

Routine to Find the Element in the List

```
position find(List L, int X)
{
        position p;
        p=L->next;
        while(p!=NULL && p->data!=X)
                p=p->next;
        return(p);
}
```

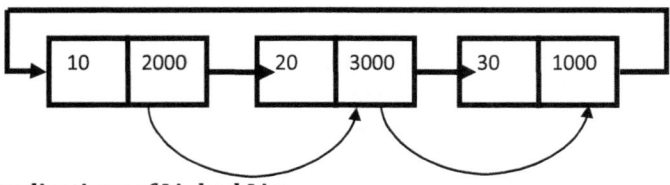

11.6. Applications of Linked List

Linked list is applicable in the following areas

1. Polynomial Manipulation
2. Multi list
3. Set operations
4. Radix sort
5. Dynamic memory management

Polynomial Manipulation

Polynomial manipulations such as addition, subtraction & differentiation etc.. can be performed using linked list.

Declaration for Linked List Implementation of Polynomial ADT

```
struct poly
{
int coeff;
int power;
struct poly * Next;
}*list1,*list2,*list3;
```

Creation of the Polynomial

```
poly create(poly*head1,poly*newnode1)
{
        poly *ptr;
        if(head1==NULL)
        {
                head1=newnode1;
                return (head1);
        }
        else
        {
                ptr=head1;
                while(ptr->next!=NULL)
                ptr=ptr->next;
                ptr->next=newnode1;
        }
        return(head1);
}
```

Addition of Two Polynomials

```
void add()
{
        Poly*ptr1,*ptr2,*newnode;
        ptr1=list1;
        ptr2=list2;
        while(ptr1!=NULL&&ptr2!=NULL)
        {
                Newnode=malloc(sizeof(struct poly));
                if(ptr1->power==ptr2->power)
                {
                        Newnode->coeff=ptr1->coeff+ptr2->coeff;
                        Newnode->power=ptr1->power;
                        Newnode->next=NULL;
                        list3=create(list3,newnode);
                        ptr1=ptr1->next;
                        ptr2=ptr2->next;
                }
                else if(ptr1->power>ptr2->power)
                {
                        Newnode->coeff=ptr1->coeff;
                        Newnode->power=ptr1->power;
                        Newnode->next=NULL;
                        list3=create(list3,newnode);
                        ptr1=ptr1->next;
                }
                else
                {
                        Newnode->coeff=ptr2->coeff;
                        Newnode->power=ptr2->power;
                        Newnode->next=NULL;
                        list3=create(list3,newnode);
                        ptr2=ptr2->next;
                }}
}
```

Subtraction of Two Polynomial

```
void sub()
{
    Poly *ptr1, *ptr2, *newnode;
    ptr1 = list1;
    ptr2 = list2;
    while( ptr1 != NULL && ptr2 != NULL )
    {
        Newnode = malloc(sizeof(struct poly));
        if(ptr1->power==ptr2->power)
        {
            newnode->coeff=(ptr1-coeff)-(ptr2->coeff);
            newnode->power=ptr1->power;
            newnode->next=NULL;
            list3=create(list3,newnode);
            ptr1=ptr1->next;
            ptr2=ptr2->next;
        }
        else
        {
            if(ptr1-power>ptr2-power)
            {
                newnode->coeff=ptr1->coeff;
                newnode->power=ptr1->power;
                newnode->next=NULL;
                list3=create(list3,newnode);
                ptr1=ptr1->next;
            }
            else
            {
                newnode->coeff=-(ptr2->coeff);
                newnode->power=ptr2->power;
                newnode->next=NULL;
                list3=create(list3,newnode);
                ptr2=ptr2->next;
            }
        }
    }
}
```

11.7. Sample Programs

Program 1: Implementation of Singly linked List	Output
#include<stdio.h>	1.create
#include<conio.h>	2.display
#include<stdlib.h>	3.insert
void create();	4.find
void display();	5.delete
void insert();	
void find();	
void delete();	Enter your choice
typedef struct node *position;	
position L,p,newnode;	1
struct node	
{	Enter the number of nodes to be inserted
int data;	5
position next;	
};	Enter the data
void main()	1
{	2
int choice;	3
clrscr();	4
do	5
{	1.create
printf("1.create\n2.display\n3.insert\n4.find\n5.delete\n\n\n");	2.display
printf("Enter your choice\n\n");	3.insert
scanf("%d",&choice);	4.find
switch(choice)	5.delete
{	
case 1:	
create();	Enter your choice
break;	
case 2:	2
display();	1 -> 2 -> 3 -> 4 -> 5 -> Null
break;	1.create
case 3:	2.display
insert();	3.insert
break;	4.find
case 4:	5.delete
find();	
break;	
case 5:	Enter your choice
delete();	
break;	3
case 6:	
exit(0);	Enter ur choice
}	
}	1.first

```
while(choice<7);
getch();
}
void create()
{
int i,n;
L=NULL;
newnode=(struct node*)malloc(sizeof(struct node));
printf("\n Enter the number of nodes to be inserted\n");
scanf("%d",&n);
printf("\n Enter the data\n");
scanf("%d",&newnode->data);
newnode->next=NULL;
L=newnode;
p=L;
for(i=2;i<=n;i++)
{
newnode=(struct node *)malloc(sizeof(struct node));
scanf("%d",&newnode->data);
newnode->next=NULL;
p->next=newnode;
p=newnode;
}
}
void display()
{
p=L;
while(p!=NULL)
{
 printf("%d -> ",p->data);
p=p->next;
}
printf("Null\n");
}
void insert()
{
int ch;
printf("\nEnter ur choice\n");
printf("\n1.first\n2.middle\n3.end\n");
scanf("%d",&ch);
switch(ch)
{
case 2:
        {
        int pos,i=1;
        p=L;
        newnode=(struct node*)malloc(sizeof(struct node));
        printf("\nEnter the data to be inserted\n");
```

2.middle
3.end
1

Enter the data to be inserted
7
7 -> 1 -> 2 -> 3 -> 4 -> 5 -> Null
1.create
2.display
3.insert
4.find
5.delete

Enter your choice

```
                scanf("%d",&newnode->data);
                printf("\nEnter the position to be inserted\n");
                scanf("%d",&pos);
                newnode->next=NULL;
                 while(i<pos-1)
                {
                 p=p->next;
                 i++;
                }
                newnode->next=p->next;
                p->next=newnode;
                p=newnode;
                display();
                break;
                }
      case 1:
                {
                p=L;
                newnode=(struct node*)malloc(sizeof(struct node));
                printf("\nEnter the data to be inserted\n");
                scanf("%d",&newnode->data);
                newnode->next=L;
                L=newnode;
                display();
                break;
                }
      case 3:
                {
                p=L;
                newnode=(struct node*)malloc(sizeof(struct node));
                printf("\nEnter the data to be inserted\n");
                scanf("%d",&newnode->data);
                while(p->next!=NULL)
                p=p->next;
                newnode->next=NULL;
                p->next=newnode;
                p=newnode;
                display();
                break;
                }
}
}
void find()
{
int search,count=0;
printf("\n Enter the element to be found:\n");
scanf("%d",&search);
p=L;
```

```c
while(p!=NULL)
{
if(p->data==search)
{
 count++;
 break;
}
p=p->next;
}
if(count==0)
printf("\n Element Not present\n");
else
printf("\n Element present in the list \n\n");
}
void delete()
{
position p,temp;
int x;
p=L;
if(p==NULL)
{
printf("empty list\n");
}
else
{
printf("\nEnter the data to be deleted\n");
scanf("%d",&x);
if(x==p->data)
{
temp=p;
L=p->next;
free(temp);
display();
}
else
{
while(p->next!=NULL && p->next->data!=x)
{
p=p->next;
}
temp=p->next;
p->next=p->next->next;
free(temp);
display();
}
}
}
```

Program 2 :Implementation of Doubly linked list	Output

#include<stdio.h>
#include<conio.h>
void insert();
void delete();
void display();
void find();
struct list
{
int info;
struct list *next;
struct list *prev;
}*node,*ptr,*head=NULL,*temp;
void main()
{
int choice;
clrscr();
do
{
printf("\n1.INSERT");
printf("\n2.DELETE");
printf("\n3.DISPLAY");
printf("\n4.FIND");
printf("\n5.EXIT");
printf("\nEnter ur option");
scanf("%d",&choice);
switch(choice)
{
case 1:
insert();
break;
case 2:
delete();
break;
case 3:
display();
break;
case 4:
find();
break;
case 5:
exit(1);
}
}while(choice!=5);
getch();
}
void insert()
{
int pos,i;
	1.INSERT
	2.DELETE
	3.DISPLAY
	4.FIND
	5.EXIT
	Enter ur option
	1
	
	Enter the data to be inserted5
	
	1.INSERT
	2.DELETE
	3.DISPLAY
	4.FIND
	5.EXIT
	Enter ur option1
	
	Enter the data to be inserted 7
	
	Enter the position where the data is to be inserted 2
	
	1.INSERT
	2.DELETE
	3.DISPLAY
	4.FIND
	5.EXIT
	Enter ur option3
	
	The elements in the stack are
	57
	1.INSERT
	2.DELETE
	3.DISPLAY
	4.FIND
	5.EXIT
	Enter ur option1
	
	Enter the data to be inserted 8
	
	Enter the position where the data is to be inserted 1

160

```
temp=(struct list*)malloc(sizeof(struct list));
printf("\nEnter the data to be inserted");
scanf("%d",&temp->info);
if(head==NULL)
{
head=temp;
head->next=NULL;
head->prev=NULL;
}
else
{
printf("\nEnter the position where the data is to be inserted");
scanf("%d",&pos);
if(pos==1)
{
temp->next=head;
temp->prev=NULL;
head->prev=temp;
head=temp;
}
else
{
ptr=head;
for(i=1;i<pos-1&&ptr->next!=NULL;i++)
{
ptr=ptr->next;
}
temp->next=ptr->next;
ptr->next=temp;
temp->prev=ptr;
ptr->next->prev=temp;
}
}
}
void delete()
{
int pos,i;
if(head==NULL)
printf("\nThe list is empty");
else
{
printf("\nEnter the position of the data to be deleted");
scanf("%d",&pos);
temp=head;
if(pos==1)
{
printf("\nThe deleted element is %d",temp->info);
head=temp->next;
head->prev=NULL;
```

```
1.INSERT
2.DELETE
3.DISPLAY
4.FIND
5.EXIT
Enter ur option3

The elements in the stack
are
857
1.INSERT
2.DELETE
3.DISPLAY
4.FIND
5.EXIT
Enter ur option
```

```c
}
else
{
ptr=head;
for(i=1;i<pos-1;i++)
ptr=ptr->next;
node=ptr->next;
printf("\nThe deletedelement is %d",node->info);
ptr->next=node->next;
node->next->prev=ptr;
}
}
}
void display()
{
if(head==NULL)
printf("\nNo of elements in the list");
else
{
printf("\nThe elements in the stack are\n");
for(ptr=head;ptr!=NULL;ptr=ptr->next)
printf("%d",ptr->info);
}
}
void find()
{
int a,flag=0,count=0;
if(head==NULL)
printf("\nThe list is empty");
else
{
printf("\nEnter the elements to be searched");
scanf("%d",&a);
for(ptr=head;ptr!=NULL;ptr=ptr->next)
{
count++;
if(ptr->info==a)
{
flag=1;
printf("\nThe element is found");
printf("\nThe position is %d",count);
break;
}
}
if(flag==0)
printf("\nThe element is not found");
}
}
```

Program 3: Implementation of Polynomial Addition	Output

#include<stdio.h>
 #include<malloc.h>
 #include<conio.h>
 struct link
 {
 int coeff;
 int pow;
 struct link *next;
 };
 struct link *poly1=NULL,*poly2=NULL,*poly=NULL;
 void create(struct link *node)
 {
 char ch;
 do
 {
 printf("\nEnter coeff:");
 scanf("%d",&node->coeff);
 printf("\nEnter power:");
 scanf("%d",&node->pow);
 node->next=(struct link*)malloc(sizeof(struct link));
 node=node->next;
 node->next=NULL;
 printf("\ncontinue(y/n):");
 ch=getch();
 }
 while(ch=='y'||ch=='Y');
 }
 void show(struct link *node)
 {
 while(node->next!=NULL)
 {
 printf("%dx^%d",node->coeff,node->pow);
 node=node->next;
 if(node->next!=NULL)
 printf("+");
 }
	Enter the 1st number:
	 Enter coeff:4
	
	 Enter power:2
	
	 continue(y/n):
	 Enter coeff:
	 5
	
	 Enter power:2
	
	 continue(y/n):
	 Enter coeff:
	 6
	
	 Enter power:1
	
	 continue(y/n):
	 Enter the 2nd number:
	 Enter coeff:6
	
	 Enter power:4
	
	 continue(y/n):
	 1st number:4x^2+5x^2+6x^1
	 2nd number:6x^4 Press any key to continue...

163

```
}
void polyadd(struct link *poly1,struct link *poly2,struct link *poly)
{
while(poly1->next&&poly2->next)
{
if(poly1->pow>poly2->pow)
{
poly->pow=poly1->pow;
poly->coeff=poly1->coeff;
poly1=poly1->next;
}
else if(poly1->pow<poly2->pow)
{
poly->pow=poly2->pow;
poly->coeff=poly2->coeff;
poly2=poly->next;
}
else
{
poly->pow=poly1->pow;
poly->coeff=poly1->coeff+poly2->coeff;
poly1=poly1->next;
poly2=poly2->next;
}
poly->next=(struct link *)malloc(sizeof(struct link));
poly=poly->next;
poly->next=NULL;
}
while(poly1->next||poly2->next)
{
if(poly1->next)
{
poly->pow=poly1->pow;
poly->coeff=poly1->coeff;
poly1=poly1->next;
}
if(poly2->next)
```

```
{
poly->pow=poly2->pow;
poly->coeff=poly2->coeff;
poly2=poly2->next;
}
poly->next=(struct link *)malloc(sizeof(struct link));
poly=poly->next;
poly->next=NULL;
}
}
main()
{
char ch;
clrscr();
do{
poly1=(struct link *)malloc(sizeof(struct link));
poly2=(struct link *)malloc(sizeof(struct link));
poly=(struct link *)malloc(sizeof(struct link));
printf("\nEnter the 1st number:");
create(poly1);
printf("\nEnter the 2nd number:");
create(poly2);
printf("\n1st number:");
show(poly1);
printf("\n2nd number:");
show(poly2);
polyadd(poly1,poly2,poly);
printf("\nAdded Polynomial:");
show(poly);
printf("\nAdd two more numbers:");
ch=getch();
}
while(ch=='y'||ch=='Y');
}
```

Review Questions with Solutions

1) Define data structures.

A data structure is a mathematical or logical way of organizing data in the memory that consider not only the items stored but also the relationship to each other and also it is characterized by accessing functions. Ex. List, Stack, Queue etc.

2) What are the types of data structures? Give examples.

The types of data structures are linear data structures and non-linear data structures.

Linear Data Structures: It is a data structure which contains a linear arrangement of elements in the memory. Ex: Stack, Queue, Linked List, Array etc.

Non-Linear Data Structure: It is a data structure which represents a hierarchical arrangement of elements. Ex: Graphs, Trees etc.

3) List down any four applications of data structures?
- Compiler design.
- Operating System.
- Database Management system.
- Network analysis.

4) Define ADT?(Apr\May2015)

ADT refers to the basic mathematical concept that defines the data type. It is a set of operations.

Implementation of the operations are written once in the program and any other part of the program that needs to perform an operation on the ADT can do so by calling the appropriate function.

Eg. Objects such as list, set and graph along with their operations can be viewed as ADT.

5) What are abstract data type?(Nov\Dec2014)

ADT refers to the basic mathematical concept that defines the data type. It is a set of operations. Implementation of the operations are written once in the program and any other part of the program that needs to perform an operation on the ADT can do so by calling the appropriate function.

Eg. Stack, List, Queue, Tree

6) What are the operations of ADT?

Union, Intersection, size, complement and find are the various operations of ADT

7) What is list? Mention its types.

A list can be defined as a collection of elements. Data processing involves storing and processing data organized as a list. The list is maintained in two ways, through arrays and linked list.

The general form of the list is $A_1, A_2, A_3 \ldots\ldots\ldots A_N$

Where, A_1- First element of the list

A_N- Last Element of the list.

N-Size of the list

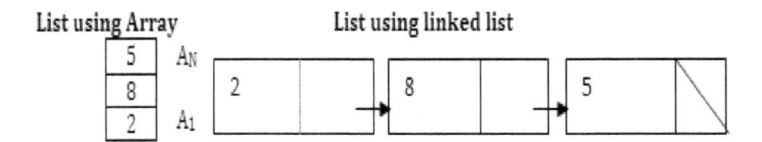

List using Array

5	A_N
8	
2	A_1

List using linked list

| 2 | → | 8 | → | 5 | \ |

8) Mention the methods of implementing the list.

There are three methods of implementing the list. They are

1. Array implementation.
2. Linked List implementation.

9) Define linked list

A linked list is a chain of structures or collection of nodes which contain a pointer to the next element. It is dynamic in nature. Items may be added to it or deleted..

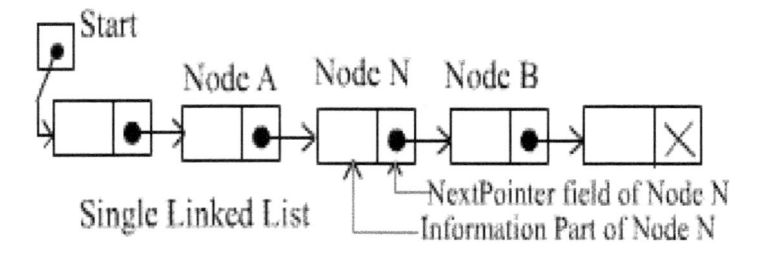

Single Linked List — Start, Node A, Node N, Node B — NextPointer field of Node N — Information Part of Node N

Each Node of the List has Two Elements

- The item being stored in the list and
- A pointer to the next item in the list

10) Write the difference between array and linked list.

Arrays	Linked Lists
Size of an array is fixed	Size of list is variable
It is necessary to specify number of elements during declaration	It is not necessary to specify number of elements during declaration
Insertions and deletions are difficult and costly.	Insertions and deletions are done in less time
It occupies less memory than a linked list	It occupies more memory
Coding is easy	Careful coding is needed to avoid memory errors.

11) Mention the types of linked list.

There are three types of Linked List. They are:

1. Singly Linked List
2. Doubly Linked List
3. Circular Linked List.

Circular Linked List can be again classified as two types. They are:

- Singly Circular linked list.
- Doubly Circular linked list.

12) Define doubly linkedlist.

A doubly linked list is a collection of nodes. Each node has three parts. They are:

- Data part which contains the data element.
- Address part which points to the previous node.
- Address part which points to the next node.

Pictorial Representation

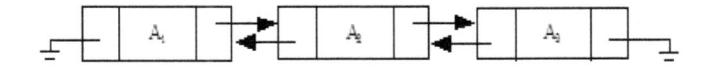

13) Name the three fields in doubly linked list.

- Data field contain data element.
- Left Address field points to previous node.
- Right Address field points to next node.

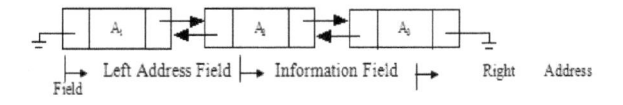

Left Address Field   Information Field   Right Address Field

14) List out basic operations carried out in linked list.
- Insert
- Delete
- Find
- Findk^{th} node in the list
- FindPrevious of a node in the list
- PrintList

15) Define head pointer and NULL pointer.

Each node of the list contains a pointer to its successive node. The last node does not have a successive node. Hence its address part contains NULL. This is called NULL Pointer. A pointer which always points to the first node of the list is labeled as **head pointer**. This node is never used to hold data.

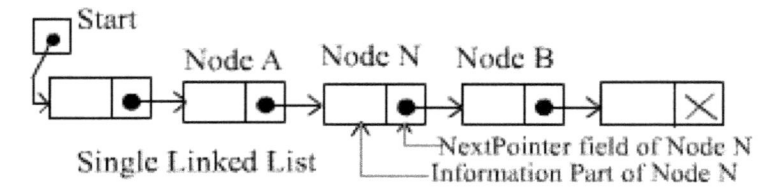

Here, Start is the Header or head pointer. The last node contains the NULL Pointer, which is denoted by

16) What is the need for the header?

The principal advantage of using a header which is also called as sentinel is that it simplifies the programming of certain operations. In order to access a linked list, a pointer variable often called head is used to store a pointer to the first node of list. It makes the operations like insertion, deletion at the front of the list easier.

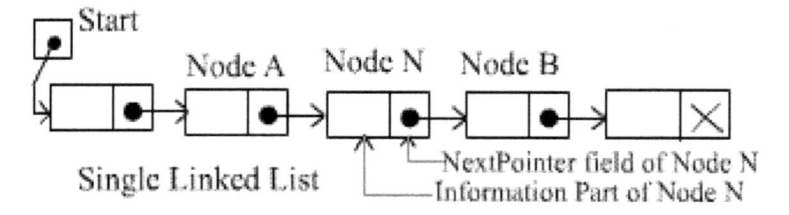

Here, Start is the head node which is called as Header.

17) State the advantages and disadvantages of doubly linked list.

Advantages
1. Traversing the list is easier, since each node contains the address of the next and previous node.
2. Searching time is less.
3. Forward and backward traversing is possible in the doubly linked list.
4. Deletion is made simple.

Disadvantages
1. Insertion and deletion takes long time since the linkages have to be done for both next and previous nodes properly.
2. Memory space requirement is more because of the extra link (previous link) for each node.

18) Give any three applications of linked list.
- The Polynomial ADT.
- Tree
- Graph
- Stack
- Queue
- LRU/MRU
- Symbol table management in compiler design
- Hash table
- Radix Sort.
- Multilists.

19) Why is linked list used for polynomial arithmetic
- Each term in polynomial is contained in one cell, and the cells are sorted in decreasing order of exponents. The operations would then be straight forward to implement.
- When more number of degrees are zero in a polynomial, it is easy to represent in linked list and also utilizes less space.

20) Should arrays or linked list be used for the following types of applications? Justify your answer.(May/Jun2014)
 a) Many search operations in sorted list.
 b) Many search operations in unsorted list.

Array can be used in the search operations in sorted list. Linked List can be used in the search operations in unsorted list.

21) What is the advantage of an ADT?(May/Jun2014)

ADT refers to the basic mathematical concept that defines the data type. It is a set of operations. Implementation of the operations are written once in the program and any other part of the program that needs to perform an operation on the ADT can do so by calling the appropriate function.

22) What is Circular Linked List?(Nov\Dec2014)

In a circularly linked list, all nodes are linked in a continuous circle, without using null. For lists with a front and a back (such as a queue), one stores a reference to the last node in the list. The next node after the last node is the first node.

23) What is static linked list? State any two application of it.(Apr\May2015)

Static linked listuses an array of a specific maximum length, and all storage is allocated beforerun-time. Used in Stack, Queue etc.

PART IV

- Stack ADT
- Application of Stack
- Queue ADT
- Circular Queue
- Double Ended Queue
- Review Questions with Solutions

CHAPTER 12

LINEAR DATA STRUCTURES-STACK

12.1. Introduction

Stack is a Linear Data Structure that follows Last In First Out(LIFO) principle.Insertion and deletion can be done at only one end of the stack called TOP of the stack.

Example: Pile of coins.

TOP Pointer

It will always point to the last element inserted in the stack. For empty stack, top will be pointing to -1. (TOP = -1)

12.2. Stack Model

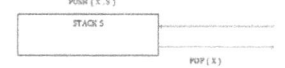

```
            PUSH ( X .S )
           ┌─────────┐
           │ STACK S │───────────────
           └─────────┘
                      POP ( X )
```

12.3. Operations on Stack(Stack ADT)

Two fundamental operations performed on the stack are PUSH and POP.

(a) PUSH:It is the process of inserting a new element at the Top of the stack.

For every push operation:

1. Check for Full stack (overflow).
2. Increment Top by 1. (Top = Top + 1)
3. Insert the element X in the Top of the stack.

(b) POP: It is the process of deleting the Top element of the stack.

For every pop operation:

1. Check for Empty stack (underflow).
2. Delete (pop) the Top element X from the stack
3. Decrement the Top by 1. (Top = Top - 1)

Exceptional Conditions of Stack

1. Stack Overflow

- An Attempt to insert an element X when the stack is Full, is said to be stack overflow.
- For every Push operation, check this condition.

2. **Stack Underflow**
   - An Attempt to delete an element when the stack is empty, is said to be stack underflow.
   - For every Pop operation, we need to check this condition.

12.4. Implementation of Stack

Stack can be implemented in 2 ways.
1. Static Implementation (Array implementation of Stack).
2. Dynamic Implementation (Linked List Implementation of Stack).

12.4.1. Array Implementation of Stack

- Each stack is associated with a Top pointer.
- For Empty stack, Top = -1.
- Stack is declared with its maximum size.

Array Declaration of Stack

#define ArraySize 5
int S [Array Size];
   or
int S [5];

(i) Stack Empty Operation

- Initially Stack is Empty.
- With Empty stack Top pointer points to – 1.
- It is necessary to check for Empty Stack before deleting(pop) an element from the stack.

Routine to Check Whether Stack is Empty

```
int IsEmpty ( Stack S )
{
   if( Top = = - 1 )
   return(1);
}
```

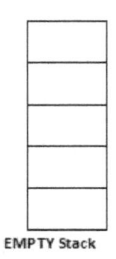

EMPTY Stack
TOP = -1

(ii) Stack Full Operation

- As we keep inserting the elements, the Stack gets filled with the elements.
- Hence it is necessary to check whether the stack is full or not before inserting a new element into the stack.

Routine to Check Whether a Stack is Full

```
int IsFull ( Stack S )
{   if( Top = = Arraysize – 1 )
       return(1);
}
```

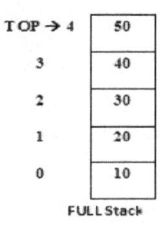

TOP → 4

3	50
2	40
1	30
0	20
	10

FULL Stack

(iii) Push Operation

- It is the process of inserting a new element at the Top of the stack.
- It takes two parameters. Push(X, S) the element X to be inserted at the Top of the Stack S.
- Before inserting an Element into the stack, check for Full Stack.
- If the Stack is already Full, Insertion is not possible.
- Otherwise, Increment the Top pointer by 1 and then insert the element X at the Top of the Stack.

Routine to Push an Element Into the Stack

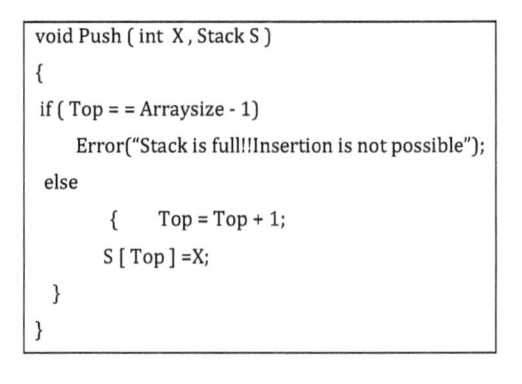

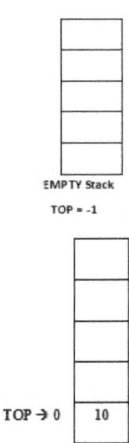

```
void Push ( int X , Stack S )
{
if ( Top = = Arraysize - 1)
    Error("Stack is full!!Insertion is not possible");
else
    {   Top = Top + 1;
        S [ Top ] =X;
    }
}
```

EMPTY Stack
TOP = -1

TOP → 0 | 10

PUSH (10, S)

175

(iv) Pop Operation

- It is the process of deleting the Top element of the stack.
- It takes only one parameter. Pop(X). The element X to be deleted from the Top of the Stack.
- Before deleting the Top element of the stack, check for Empty Stack.
- If the Stack is Empty, deletion is not possible.
- Otherwise, delete the Top element from the Stack and then decrement the Top pointer by 1.

Routine to Pop the Top Element of the Stack

```
void Pop ( Stack S )
{
  if ( Top = = - 1)
  Error ( "Empty stack! Deletion not possible");
  else
  {   X = S [ Top ] ;
      Top = Top – 1 ;
  }
}
```

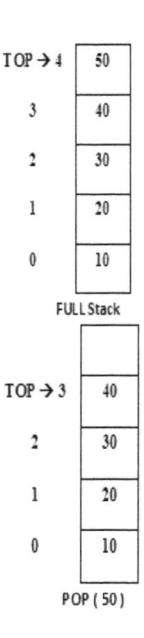

TOP → 4 | 50
3 | 40
2 | 30
1 | 20
0 | 10

FULL Stack

TOP → 3 | 40
2 | 30
1 | 20
0 | 10

POP (50)

(v) Return Top Element

- Pop routine deletes the Top element in the stack.
- If the user needs to know the last element inserted into the stack, then the user can return the Top element of the stack.
- To do this, first check for Empty Stack.
- If the stack is empty, then there is no element in the stack.
- Otherwise, return the element which is pointed by the Top pointer in the Stack.

Routine to Return top Element of the Stack

```
int TopElement(Stack S)
{
  if(Top==-1)
  {
    Error("Empty stack!!No elements");
    return 0;
  }
  else
    return S[Top];
}
```

EMPTY Stack
TOP = -1

TOP → 4	50
3	40
2	30
1	20
0	10

FULL Stack

Implementation of Stack Using Array

```
/* static implementation of stack*/
#include<stdio.h>
#include<conio.h>
#define size 5
int stack [ size ];
int top;
void push( )
{
    int n;
    printf( "\n Enter item in stack" );
    scanf( "%d", &n );
    if( top = =size - 1)
    {
            printf("\nStack is Full");
    }
    else
    {
            top=top+1;
            stack[top]=n;
    }
}
void pop()
{
    int item;
    if(top==-1)
```

177

```c
        {
                printf("\n Stack is empty");
        }
        else
        {
                item=stack[top];
                printf("\n item popped is=%d", item);
                top--;
        }
}
void display()
{
    int i;
    printf("\n item in stack are");
    for(i =top; i >=0; i --)
    printf("\n %d", stack[ i] );
}
void main()
{
    char ch,ch1;
    ch ='y';
    ch1='y';
    top=-1;
    clrscr();
    while(ch!='n')
    {
            push();
            printf("\n Do you want to push any item in stack y/n");
            ch=getch();
    }
    display();
    while(ch1!='n')
    {
            printf("\n Do you want to delete  any item in stack y/n");
            ch1=getch();
            pop();
    }
    display();
    getch();
}
```

```
DOSBox 0.74, Cpu speed: max 100% cycles, Frameskip 0, Program:    TC

Enter item in stack:56

Do you want to push any item in stack y/n
Enter item in stack:4

Do you want to push any item in stack y/n
Enter item in stack:90

Do you want to push any item in stack y/n
Item in stack are
90
4
56
Do you want to delete  any item in stack y/n
item popped is=90
Do you want to delete  any item in stack y/n
item popped is=4
Do you want to delete  any item in stack y/n
item popped is=56
Do you want to delete  any item in stack y/n
Stack is empty
Do you want to delete  any item in stack y/n
Stack is empty
Item in stack are
```

12.4.2. Linked List Implementation of Stack

- Stack elements are implemented using SLL (Singly Linked List) concept.
- Dynamically, memory is allocated to each element of the stack as a node.

Type Declarations for Stack Using SLL

```
struct node;
typedef struct node *stack;
typedef struct node *position;
stack S;
struct node
{
int data;
position next;
};
int IsEmpty(Stack S);
void Push(int x, Stack S);
void Pop(Stack S);
int TopElement(Stack S);
```

(i) Stack Empty Operation

- Initially Stack is Empty.
- With Linked List implementation, Empty stack is represented as S -> next = NULL.
- It is necessary to check for Empty Stack before deleting (pop) an element from the stack.

Routine to Check Whether the Stack is Empty

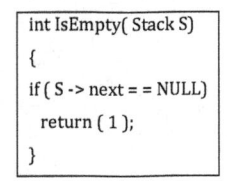

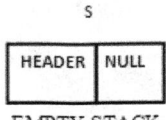

```
int IsEmpty( Stack S)
{
    if ( S -> next = = NULL)
        return ( 1 );
}
```

```
        S
┌────────┬──────┐
│ HEADER │ NULL │
└────────┴──────┘
   EMPTY STACK
```

(ii) Push Operation

- It is the process of inserting a new element at the Top of the stack.
- With Linked List implementation, a new element is always inserted at the Front of the List.(i.e.) S -> next.
- It takes two parameters. Push(X, S) the element X to be inserted at the Top of the Stack S.
- Allocate the memory for the newnode to be inserted.
- Insert the element in the data field of the newnode.
- Update the next field of the newnode with the address of the next node which is stored in the S -> next.

Push Routine /*Inserts Element at Front of the List

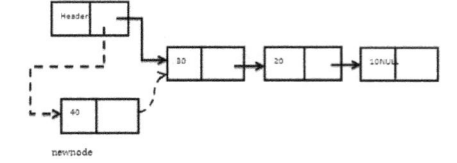

Before Insertion

Push Routine /*Inserts Element at Front of the List

```
void push(int X, Stack S)
{
    Position newnode, Top;
    newnode = malloc (sizeof( struct node ) );
    newnode -> data = X;
    newnode -> next = S -> next;
    S -> next = newnode;
    Top = newnode;
}
```

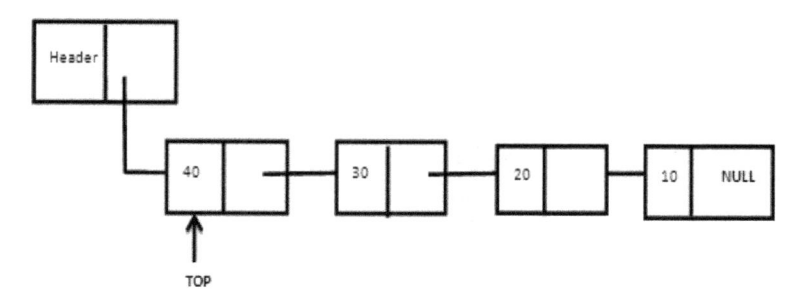

After Insertion

(iii) **Pop Operation**
- It is the process of deleting the Top element of the stack.
- With Linked List implementations, the element at the Front of the List (i.e.) S -> next is always deleted.
- It takes only one parameter. Pop(X).The element X to be deleted from the Front of the List.
- Before deleting the front element in the list, check for Empty Stack.
- If the Stack is Empty, deletion is not possible.
- Otherwise, make the front element in the list as "temp".
- Update the next field of header.
- Using free ( ) function, Deallocate the memory allocated for temp node.

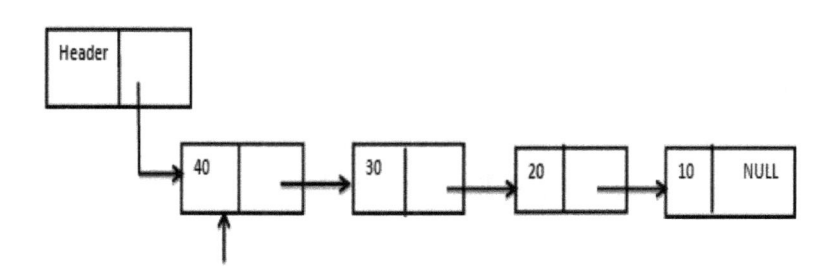

Before Deletion

181

Pop Routine/*Deletes the Element at Front of List

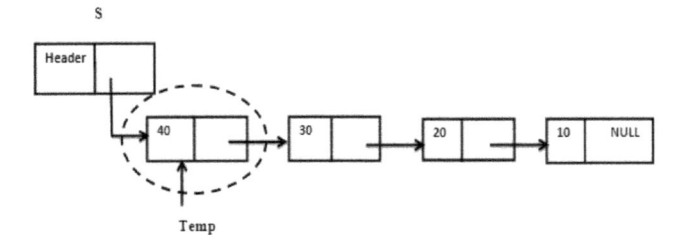

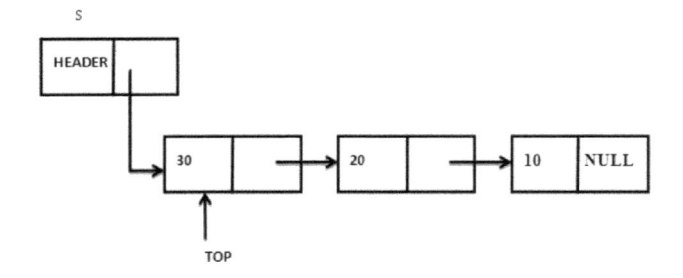

```
void Pop(Stack S)
{
Position temp,Top;
Top=S->next;
  if(S->next==NULL)
        Error("empty stack! Pop not possible");
  else
  {
        Temp = S -> next;
        S -> next = temp -> next;
        free(temp);
        Top = S -> next;
  }
}
```

After Deletion

(iv) Return Top Element

- Pop routine deletes the Front element in the List.
- If the user needs to know the last element inserted into the stack, then the user can return the Top element of the stack.
- To do this, first check for Empty Stack.
- If the stack is empty, then there is no element in the stack.
- Otherwise, return the element present in the S -> next -> data in the List.

Routine to Return Top Element

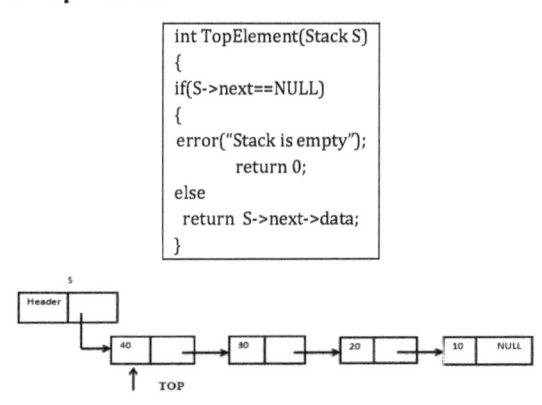

```
int TopElement(Stack S)
{
if(S->next==NULL)
{
error("Stack is empty");
        return 0;
else
  return S->next->data;
}
```

Implementation of Stack Using 'Linked List'

C Program for Linked List Implementation of Stack

```
#include<stdio.h>
#include<conio.h>
#include<stdlib.h>
typedef struct node *position;
struct node
{
        int data;
        position next;
};
void create();
void push();
void pop();
void display();
position s,newnode,temp,top; /* Global Declarations */
void main()
{
        /* Main Program */
        int op;
        clrscr();
        do
        {
                printf("\n ### Linked List Implementation of STACK Cperations ### \n\n");
```

```c
            printf("\n Press 1-create\n 2-Push\n 3-Pop\n 4-Display\n5-Exit\n");
            printf("\n Your option ? ");
            scanf("%d", &op);
            switch (op)
    {
    case 1:
            create();
            break;
        case 2:
            push();
            break;
        case 3:
            pop();
            break;
        case 4:
            display();
            break;
        case 5:
            exit(0);
    }
}while(op<5);
getch();
}
void create()
{
        int n,i;
        s=NULL;
        printf("Enter the no of nodes to be created\n");
        scanf("%d",&n);
        newnode=(struct node*)malloc(sizeof(struct node));
        printf("Enter the data\t");
        scanf("%d",&newnode->data);
        newnode->next=NULL;
        top=newnode;
        s=newnode;
for(i=2;i<=n;i++)
{
        newnode=(struct node*)malloc(sizeof(struct node));
        printf("Enter the data\t");
        scanf("%d",&newnode->data);
```

```
            newnode->next=top;
            s=newnode;
            top=newnode;
}
}
void display()
{
            top=s;
while(top!=NULL)
{
            printf("%d->",top->data);
            top=top->next;
}
            printf("NULL\n");
}
void push()
{
            top=s;
            newnode=(struct node*)malloc(sizeof(struct node));
            printf("Enter the data\t");
            scanf("%d",&newnode->data);
            newnode->next=top;
            top=newnode;
            s=newnode;
            display();
}
void pop()
{
            top=s;
            if(top==NULL)
            printf("Empty stack\n\n");
            else
{
            temp=top;
            printf("Deleted element is \t %d\n\n",top->data);
            s=top->next;
            free(temp);
            display();
}
}
```

```
DOSBox 0.74, Cpu speed: max 100% cycles, Frameskip 0, Program:  TC
### Linked List Implementation of STACK Operations ###

Press 1-create
2-Push
3-Pop
4-Display
5-Exit

Your option ? 1
Enter the no of nodes to be created
2
Enter the data  10
Enter the data  20

### Linked List Implementation of STACK Operations ###

Press 1-create
2-Push
3-Pop
4-Display
5-Exit

Your option ?
```

12.5. Applications of Stack

Application of Stack

1. Evaluating the arithmetic expressions
   - Conversion of Infix to Postfix Expression
   - Evaluating the Postfix Expression
2. Balancing the Symbols
3. Function Call
4. Tower of Hanoi
5. 8 Queen Problem

12.5.1. Evaluating the Arithmetic Expression

There are 3 types of Expressions

- Infix Expression
- Postfix Expression
- Prefix Expression

Infix Expression

Operators appears between operands

Eg. A+B

A/B+C

186

Postfix Expression

Operators appears after the operands

E.g. AB+

AB/C+

Prefix Expression

Operators appears before the operands

E.g. +AB

+/ABC

Evaluating Arithmetic Expressions

1. Convert the given infix expression to Postfix expression
2. Evaluate the postfix expression using stack.

Algorithm to Convert Infix Expression to Postfix Expression

1. Print operands as they arrive.
2. If the stack is empty or contains a left parenthesis on top push the incoming operator onto the Stack.
3. If the character read is a left parenthesis, push it on the stack.
4. If the character readis a right parenthesis, pop the stack and print the operators until you see a left parenthesis. Discard the pair of parentheses.
5. If the character readhas higher precedence than the top of the stack, push it on the stack.
6. If the character readhas equal precedence with the top of the stack, use association. If the association is left to right, pop and print the top of the stack and then push the incoming operator.
If the association is right to left, push the incoming operator.
7. If the character readhas lower precedence than the symbol on the top of the stack, pop the stack and print the top operator. Then test the incoming operator against the new top of stack.
8. At the end of the expression, pop and print all operators on the stack. (No parentheses should remain.)

E.g. Consider the following Infix expression: - A*B+(C-D/E)#

Read char	Stack	Output
A		A
*	*	A
B	+ *	AB
+	+	AB*
(	(+	AB*
C	(+	AB*C

188

-	- (+	AB*C
D	 - (+	AB*CD
/	 / - (+	
E	 / - (+	AB*CDE

|) | /
 -
 (
 + | AB*CDE/- |
| # | | AB*CDE/-+ |

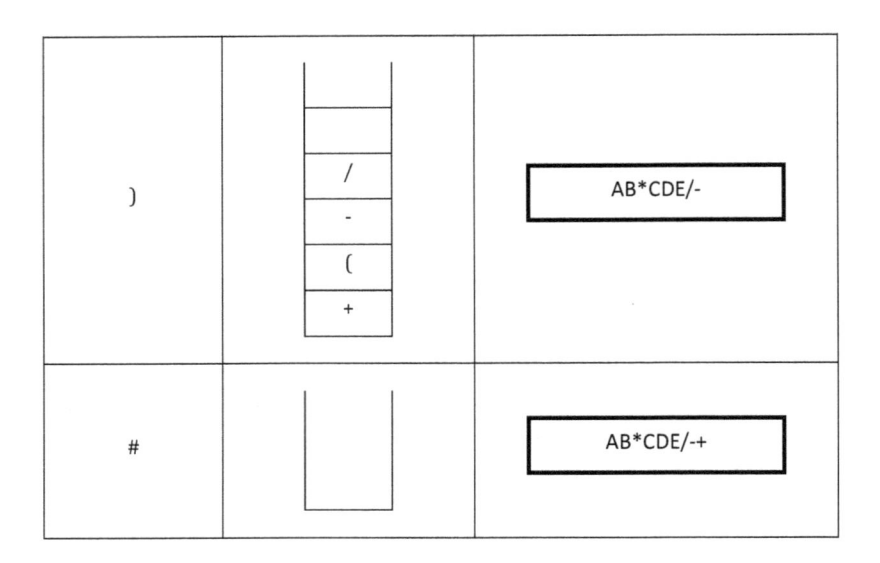

Output: Postfix expression:- AB*CDE/-+

Evaluating the Postfix Expression

Algorithm to Evaluate the Obtained Postfix Expression

1. Create a stack to store operands (or values).
2. Scan the given expression and do following for every scanned element.
   a) If the element is a operand, push its value into the stack.
   b) If the element is an operator, pop 2 values from the stack. Apply the operator and push the Result back to the stack.
3. when the expression is ended, the number in the stack is the final answer

E.g consider the obtained **Postfix expression:- AB*CDE/-+**

Operand	Value
A	2
B	3
C	4
D	4
E	2

Char Read	Stack
A	2
B	3 2
*	6
C	4 6
D	4 4 6
E	2 4 4 6
/	2 4 6
-	2 6
+	8

OUTPUT = 8

Example 2: Infix Expression:- (a+b)*c/d+e/f#

Read char	Stack	Output
(	(	
a	(	a
+	+ (	a
b	+ (	ab
)		ab+
*	*	ab+
c	*	ab+c
/	/	ab+c*
d	/	ab+c*d
+	+	ab+c*d/
e	+	ab+c*d/e
/	/ +	ab+c*d/e
f	/ +	ab+c*d/ef
#		ab+c*d/ef/+

Postfix expression:- ab+c*d/ef/+

Evaluating the Postfix Expression

Operand	Value
a	1
b	2
c	4
d	2
e	6
f	3

Char Read	Stack
a	1
b	2 1
+	3
c	4 3
*	12
d	2 12
/	6
e	6 6
f	3 6 6
/	2 6
+	8

Output = 8

C program for Infix to Postfix Conversion	Output

`#define SIZE 50`   `/* Size of Stack */`
`#include <ctype.h>`
`char s[SIZE];`
`int top=-1;`   `/* Global declarations */`
 	
`void push(char elem)`
`{`
`  s[++top]=elem;`
`}`
 	
`char pop()`
`{`
`  return(s[top--]);`
`}`
 	
`int pr(char elem)`
`{`   `/* Function for precedence */`
`  switch(elem)`
`  {`
`  case '#': return 0;`
`  case '(': return 1;`
`  case '+':`
`  case '-': return 2;`
`  case '*':`
`  case '/': return 3;`
`  }`
`  return 0;`
`}`
 	
`Void main()`
`{`   `/* Main Program */`
`  char infx[50],pofx[50],ch,elem;`
`  int i=0,k=0;`
`  printf("\nRead the Infix Expression ? ");`
`  scanf("%s",infx);`
`  push('#');`
`  while( (ch=infx[i++]) != '\0')`
`  {`
`    if( ch == '(') push(ch);`
`    else`
`      if(isalnum(ch)) pofx[k++]=ch;`
`      else`
`        if( ch == ')')`
`        {`
`           while( s[top] != '(')`
`              pofx[k++]=pop();`
`           elem=pop(); /* Remove */`
`        }`
`        else`
`        {   /* Operator */`
`           while( pr(s[top]) >= pr(ch) )`
`              pofx[k++]=pop();`
`           push(ch);`
`        }`
`  }`
`  while( s[top] != '#')   /* Pop from stack till empty */`
`     pofx[k++]=pop();`
`  pofx[k]='\0';     /* Make pofx as valid string */`
`  printf("\n\nGiven Infix Expn: %s  Postfix Expn:%s\n",infx,pofx);`
`}`
	Read the Infix Expression ?
	(a+b)-(c-d)
	
	Given Infix Expn: (a+b)*(c-d)
	Postfix Expn: ab+cd-*

194

12.5.2. Towers of Hanoi

Towers of Hanoi can be easily implemented using recursion. Objective of the problem is moving a collection of N disks of decreasing size from one pillar to another pillar. The movement of the disk is restricted by the following rules.

Rule 1 : Only one disk could be moved at a time.

Rule 2 : No larger disk could ever reside on a pillar on top of a smaller disk.

Rule 3 : A 3rd pillar could be used as an intermediate to store one or more disks, while moving the disk from source to destination.

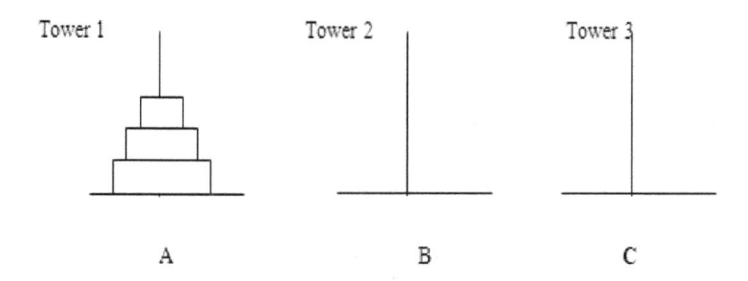

Initial Setup of Tower of Hanoi

Recursive Solution

N - Represents the Number of Disks

Step 1. If N = 1, move the disk from A to C.

Step 2. If N = 2, move the 1st disk from A to B. Then move the 2nd disk from A to C, The move the 1st

disk from B to C.

Step 3. If N = 3, Repeat the step (2) to more the first 2 disks from A to B using C as intermediate. Then the 3rd disk is moved from A to C. Then repeat the step (2) to move 2 disks from B to C using A as intermediate.

In general, to move N disks. Apply the recursive technique to move N - 1 disks from A to B using C as an intermediate. Then move the Nth disk from A to C. Then again apply the recursive technique to move N - 1 disks from B to C using A as an intermediate.

Recursive Routine for Towers of Hanoi

```
void hanoi (int n, char s, char d, char i)
{
/* n    no. of disks, s    source, d    destination i    intermediate */
if (n = = 1)
{
print (s, d);
return;
}
else
{
hanoi (n - 1, s, i, d);
print (s, d)
hanoi (n-1, i, d, s);
return;
}
}
```

Source Pillar Intermediate Pillar Destination Pillar

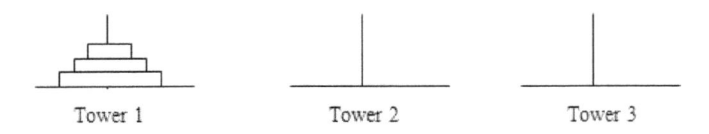

Tower 1   Tower 2   Tower 3

1. Move Tower 1 to Tower 3

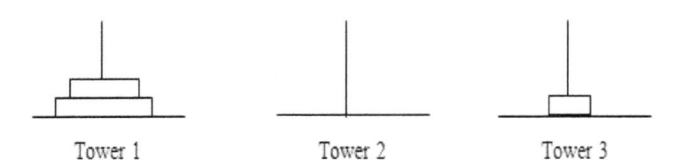

Tower 1   Tower 2   Tower 3

2. Move Tower 1 to Tower 2

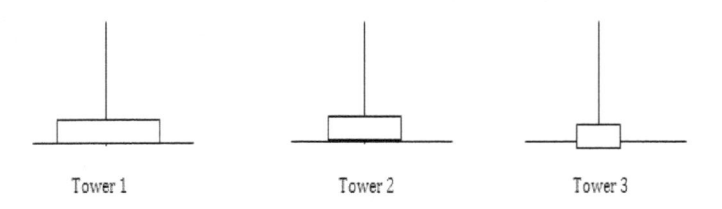

Tower 1   Tower 2   Tower 3

3. Move Tower 3 to Tower 2

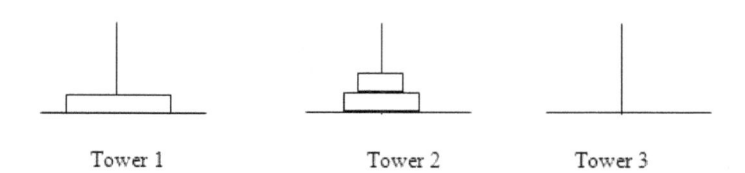

　　　　　Tower 1　　　　　Tower 2　　　　　Tower 3

4. Move Tower 1 to Tower 3

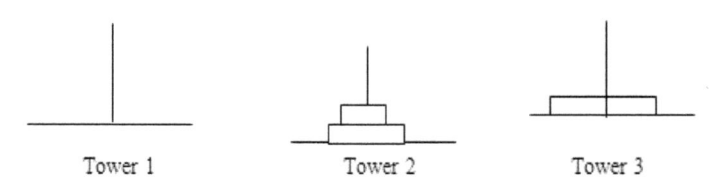

　　　　　Tower 1　　　　　Tower 2　　　　　Tower 3

5. Move Tower 2 to Tower 1

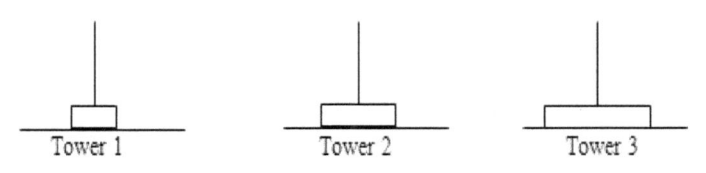

　　　　　Tower 1　　　　　Tower 2　　　　　Tower 3

6. Move Tower 2 to Tower 3

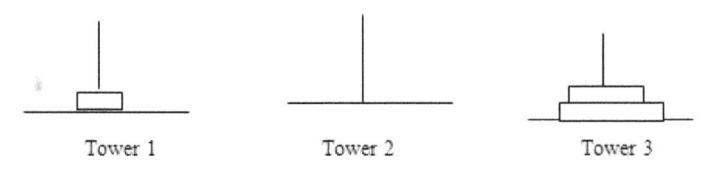

　　　　　Tower 1　　　　　Tower 2　　　　　Tower 3

7. Move Tower 1 to Tower 3

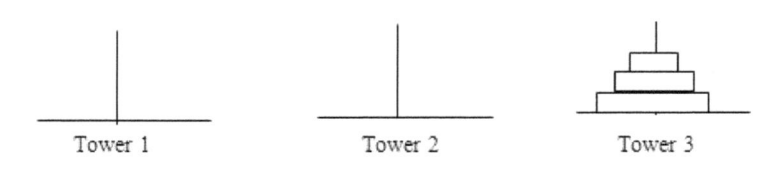

　　　　　Tower 1　　　　　Tower 2　　　　　Tower 3

Since disks are moved from each tower in a LIFO manner, each tower may be considered as a Stack. Least Number of moves required solvingtheproblem according to our algorithm is given by,

$$O(N)=O(N-1)+1+O(N-1) = 2^N-1$$

12.5.3. Function Calls

When a call is made to a new function all the variables local to the calling routine need to be saved, otherwise the new function will overwrite the calling routine variables. Similarly the current location address in the routine must be saved so that the new function knows where to go after it is completed.

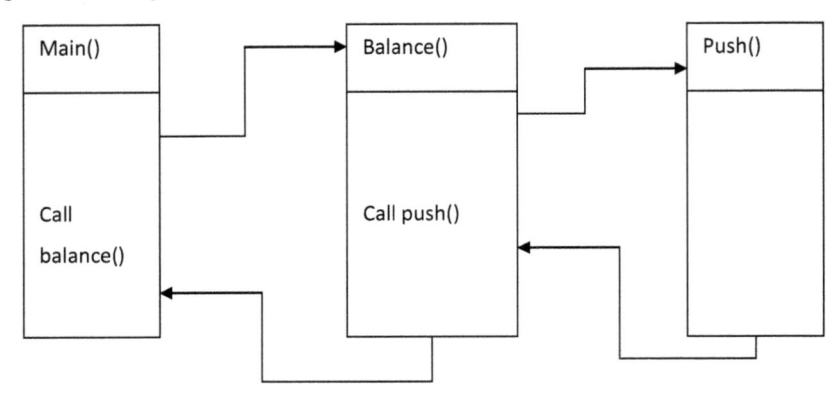

```
Main()                    Balance()                  Push()



Call                      Call push()
balance()
```

Recursive Function to Find Factorial

```
int fact(int n)
{
int S;
if(n==1)
    return(1);
else
        S=n*fact(n - 1);
        return(S)
}
```

12.5.4. Balancing the Symbols

- Compilers check the programs for errors, a lack of one symbol will cause an error.
- A Program that checks whether everything is balanced.
- Every right parenthesis should have its left parenthesis.
- Check for balancing the parenthesis brackets braces and ignore any other character.

Algorithm for Balancing the Symbols

Read one character at a time until it encounters the delimiter `#`.

Step 1 : If the character is an opening symbol, push it onto the stack.

Step 2 : If the character is a closing symbol, and if the stack is empty report an error as missing opening symbol.

Step 3 : If it is a closing symbol and if it has corresponding opening symbol in the stack, POP it from the stack. Otherwise, report an error as mismatched symbols.

Step 4 : At the end of file, if the stack is not empty, report an error as Missing closing symbol. Otherwise, report as balanced symbols.

E.g. Let us consider the expression ((B*B)-{4*A*C}/[2*A]) #

((B*B)-{4*A*C}/[2*A]) #	
Read Character	Stack
(	(
(	((
)	(
{	{ (

199

}	┌─┐ ├─┤ (
[	[
]	┌─┐ ├─┤ (
)	┌─┐ ├─┤ └─┘

Empty stack, hence the symbols the balanced in the given expression.

CHAPTER 13

QUEUE

13.1. Introduction

- It is a Linear Data Structure that follows First in First out(FIFO) principle.
- Insertion of element is done at one end of the Queue called "**Rear** "end of the Queue.
- Deletion of element is done at other end of the Queue called "**Front**"end of the Queue.
- Example: - Waiting line in the ticket counter.

Front Pointer

It always points to the first element inserted in the Queue.

Rear Pointer

It always points to the last element inserted in the Queue.

For Empty Queue

Front (F)= - 1
Rear(R) = - 1

13.2. Queue Model

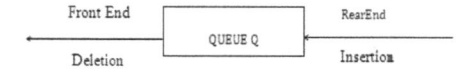

Front End — QUEUE Q — RearEnd
Deletion   Insertion

13.3. Operations on Queue

Fundamental operations performed on the queue are,

1. EnQueue
2. DeQueue

1) EnQueue Operation

- It is the process of inserting a new element at the rear end of the Queue.
- For every EnQueue operation.
  - Check for Full Queue.
  - If the Queue is full, Insertion is not possible.
  - Otherwise, increment the rear end by 1 and then insert the element in the rear end of the Queue.

2) De Queue Operation

- It is the process of deleting the element from the front end of the queue.
- For every DeQueue operation.
    - Check for Empty queue.
    - If the Queue is Empty, Deletion is not possible.
    - Otherwise, delete the first element inserted into the queue and then increment the front by 1.

Exceptional Conditions of Queue

- Queue Overflow.
- Queue Underflow.

1) Queue Overflow

- An Attempt to insert an element X at the Rear end of the Queue when the Queue is full is said to be Queue overflow.
- For every Enqueue operation, we need to check this condition.

2) Queue Underflow

- An Attempt to delete an element from the Front end of the Queue when the Queue is empty is said to be Queue underflow.
- For every DeQueue operation, we need to check this condition.

13.4. Implementation of Queue

Queue can be implemented in two ways.

1. Implementation using Array (**Static Queue**).
2. Implementation using Linked List (**Dynamic Queue**).

13.4.1 Array Implementation of Queue

- Each Queue is associated with Front pointer and rear Pointer.
- For Empty Queue, Front = - 1 and Rear = -1.
- Queue is declared with its maximum size.

Array Declaration of Queue

```
#define ArraySize 5
int Q [ ArraySize];
    or
int Q [ 5 ];
```

Initial Configuration of Queue

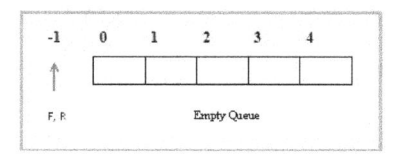

```
     -1    0    1    2    3    4
      ↑  ┌────┬────┬────┬────┬────┐
         │    │    │    │    │    │
         └────┴────┴────┴────┴────┘
     F, R            Empty Queue
```

1. Queue Empty Operation

- Initially Queue is Empty.
- With Empty Queue, Front (F) and Rear (R) points to – 1.
- It is necessary to check for Empty Queue before deleting (DeQueue) an element from the Queue (Q).

Routine to Check for Empty Queue

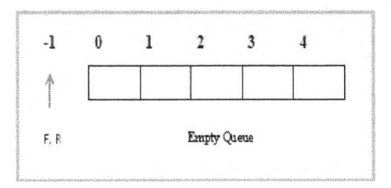

```
int IsEmpty ( Queue Q )
{
    if( ( Front = = - 1) && ( Rear = = - 1 ) )
        return ( 1 );
}
```

```
     -1    0    1    2    3    4
      ↑  ┌────┬────┬────┬────┬────┐
         │    │    │    │    │    │
         └────┴────┴────┴────┴────┘
     F, R            Empty Queue
```

2. Queue Full Operation

- As we keep inserting the new elements at the Rear end of the Queue, the Queue becomes full.
- When the Queue is Full, Rear reaches its maximum Araysize.
- For every Enqueue Operation, we need to check for full Queue condition.

Routine to Check for Full Queue

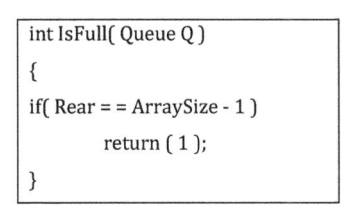

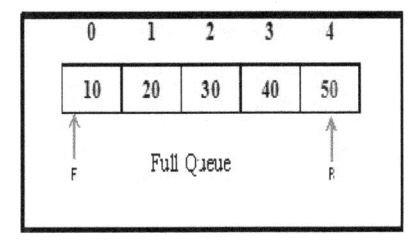

```
int IsFull( Queue Q )
{
    if( Rear = = ArraySize - 1 )
        return ( 1 );
}
```

```
       0    1    2    3    4
     ┌────┬────┬────┬────┬────┐
     │ 10 │ 20 │ 30 │ 40 │ 50 │
     └────┴────┴────┴────┴────┘
       ↑                    ↑
       F     Full Queue     R
```

3. Enqueue Operation

- It is the process of inserting a new element at the Rear end of the Queue.

- It takes two parameters, Enqueue(X, Q). The elements X to be inserted at the Rear end of the Queue Q.
- Before inserting a new Element into the Queue, check for Full Queue.
- If the Queue is already Full, Insertion is not possible.
- Otherwise, Increment the Rear pointer by 1 and then insert the element X at the Rear end of the Queue.
- If the Queue is Empty, Increment both Front and Rear pointer by 1 and then insert the element X at the Rear end of the Queue.

Routine to Insert an Element in a Queue

```
void EnQueue (int X , Queue Q)
{
if ( Rear == Arraysize-1)
print (" Full Queue !!!!. Insertion not possible");
else if (Rear = = - 1)
{
Front = Front + 1;
Rear = Rear + 1;
Q [Rear] = X;
}
else
{
Rear = Rear + 1;
Q [Rear] = X;
}
}
```

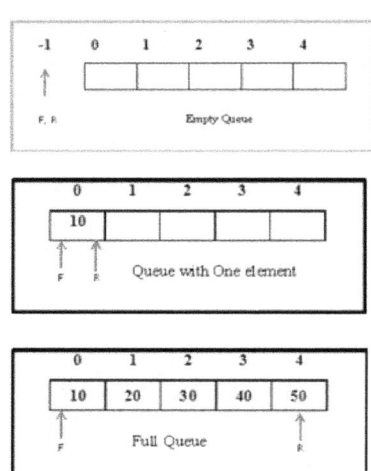

4. De Queue Operation

- It is the process of deleting a element from the Front end of the Queue.
- It takes one parameter, DeQueue (Q). Always front element in the Queue will be deleted.
- Before deleting an Element from the Queue, check for Empty Queue.
- If the Queue is empty, deletion is not possible.
- If the Queue has only one element, then delete the element and represent the empty queue by updating Front = - 1 and Rear = - 1.
- If the Queue has many Elements, then delete the element in the Front and move the Front pointer to next element in the queue by incrementing Front pointer by 1.

Routine for Dequeue

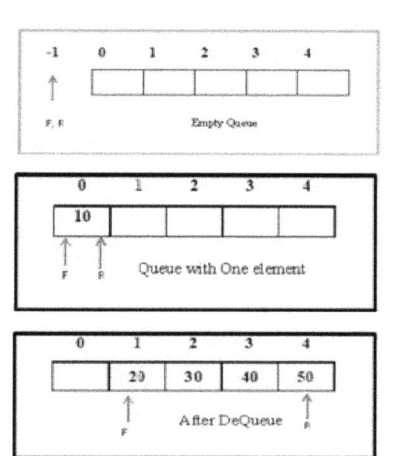

```
void DeQueue ( Queue Q )
{
    if ( Front = = - 1)
        print (" Empty Queue !. Deletion not possible ");
    else if( Front = = Rear )
    {
        X = Q [Front];
            Front = - 1;
            Rear = - 1;
    }
        else
        {
            X = Q [ Front ];
            Front = Front + 1 ;
        }
}
```

Array Implementation of Queue

```
#include<stdio.h>
#include<conio.h>
#define SIZE 5
int front=-1;
int rear=-1;
int q[SIZE];
void insert();
void del();
void display();
void main()
{
    int choice;
    clrscr();
    do
    {
        printf("\t Menu");
        printf("\n 1. Insert");
        printf("\n 2. Delete");
        printf("\n 3. Display ");
        printf("\n 4. Exit");
        printf("\n Enter Your Choice:");
        scanf("%d",&choice);
        switch(choice)
        {
            case 1:
```

205

```
                              insert();
                              display();
                              break;
                  case 2:
                              del();
                              display();
                              break;
                  case 3:
                              display();
                              break;
                  case 4:
                              printf("End of Program....!!!!");
                              exit(0);
            }
      }while(choice!=4);
}
void insert()
   {
         int no;
         printf("\n Enter No.:");
         scanf("%d",&no);
         if(rear < SIZE-1)
         {
                  q[++rear]=no;
                  if(front==-1)
                  front=0;// front=front+1;
         }
         else
         {
                  printf("\n Queue overflow");
         }
   }
   void del()
   {
         if(front==-1)
         {
                  printf("\nQueue Underflow");
                  return;
         }
         else
         {
         printf("\nDeleted Item:-->%d\n",q[front]);
         }
```

```
            if(front==rear)
            {
                        Front=-1;
                        Rear=-1;
            }
            else
            {
                        Front=front+1;
            }
}
void display()
{
            int i;
            if(front==-1)
            {
                        printf("\nQueue is empty....");
                        return;
            }
            for(i =front; i<=rear;i++)
                        printf("\t%d",q[i]);
}
```

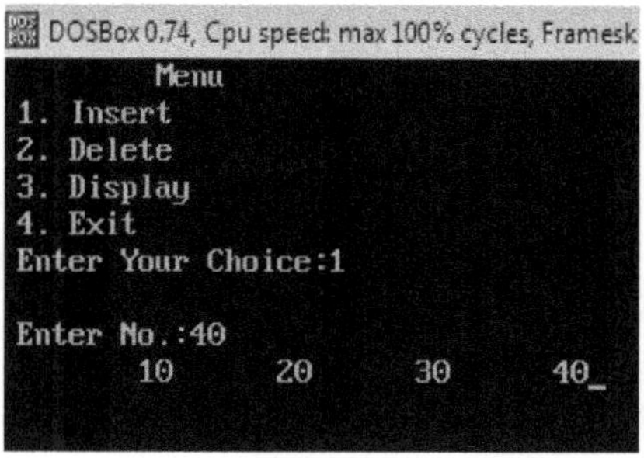

```
DOSBox 0.74, Cpu speed: max 100% cycles, Framesk
                Menu
1. Insert
2. Delete
3. Display
4. Exit
Enter Your Choice:1
Enter No.:40
          10      20      30      40_
```

13.4.2 Linked List Implementation of Queue

- Queue is implemented using SLL (Singly Linked List) node.
- Enqueue operation is performed at the end of the Linked list and DeQueue operation is performed at the front of the Linked list.
- With Linked List implementation, for Empty queue

Front = NULL & Rear = NULL

Linked List representation of Queue with 4 elements

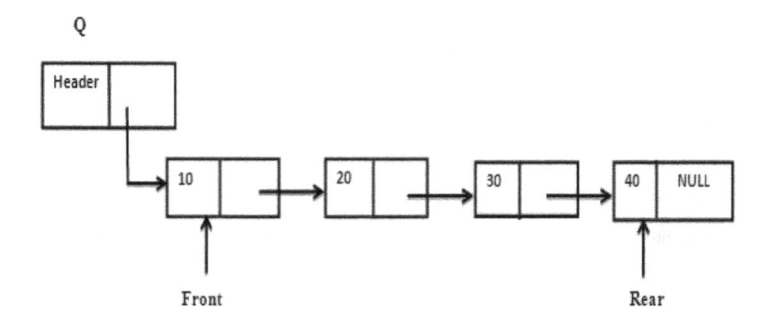

Declaration for Linked List Implementation of Queue ADT

```
struct node;
typedef struct node * Queue;
typedef struct node * position;
int IsEmpty (Queue Q);
Queue CreateQueue (void);
void MakeEmpty (Queue Q);
void Enqueue (int X, Queue Q);
void Dequeue (Queue Q);
struct node
{
int data ;
position next;
}* Front = NULL, *Rear = NULL;
```

1. Queue Empty Operation

- Initially Queue is Empty.
- With Linked List implementation, Empty Queue is represented as S -> next = NULL.
- It is necessary to check for Empty Queue before deleting the front element in the Queue.

Routine to Check Whether the Queue is Empty

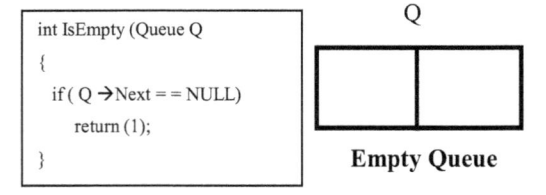

```
int IsEmpty (Queue Q
{
    if ( Q →Next = = NULL)
        return (1);
}
```

Q

Empty Queue

2. EnQueue Operation

- It is the process of inserting a new element at the Rear end of the Queue.
- It takes two parameters, EnQueue (int X , Queue Q). The elements X to be inserted into the Queue Q.
- Using malloc ( ) function allocate memory for the newnode to be inserted into the Queue.

- If the Queue is Empty, the newnode tobe inserted will become first and last node in the list. Hence Front and Rear points to the newnode.
- Otherwise insert the newnode in the Rear -> next and update the Rear pointer.

Routine to EnQueue an Element in Queue

```
void EnQueue (int X, Queue Q )
{
struct node *newnode;
newnode = malloc (sizeof (struct node));
if (Rear = = NULL)
{
newnode →data = X;
newnode→next = NULL;
Q -> next = newnode;
Front = newnode;
Rear = newnode;
}
else
{
newnode →data = X;
newnode →next = NULL;
Rear →next = newnode;
Rear = newnode;
}
}
```

Q

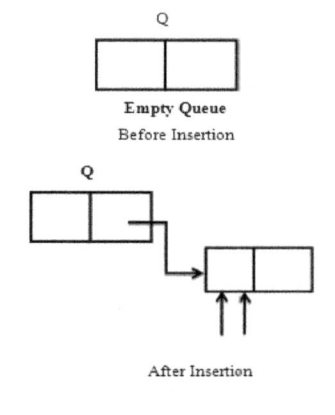

Empty Queue
Before Insertion

Q

After Insertion

3. DeQueue Operation

- It is the process of deleting the front element from the Queue.
- It takes one parameter, Dequeue (Queue Q). Always element in the front (i.e) element pointed by Q -> next is deleted always.
- Element to be deleted is made "temp".
- If the Queue is Empty, then deletion is not possible.
- If the Queue has only one element, then the element is deleted and Front and Rear pointer is made NULL to represent Empty Queue.
- Otherwise, Front element is deleted and the Front pointer is made to point to next node in the list.
- The free ( ) function informs the compiler that the address that temp is pointing to, is unchanged but the data present in that address is now undefined.

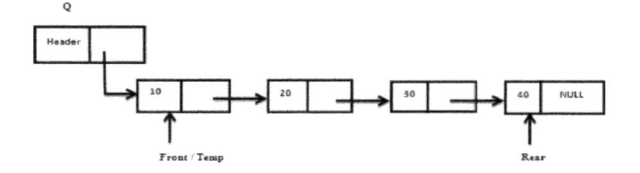

```
         Q
    ┌────────┐
    │ Header │
    └────┬───┘
         │
         ▼
    ┌──┬──┐    ┌──┬──┐    ┌──┬──────┐
    │20│ ─┼──▶ │30│ ─┼──▶ │40│ NULL │
    └──┴──┘    └──┴──┘    └──┴──────┘
      ▲                     ▲
      │                     │
    Front                  Rear
```

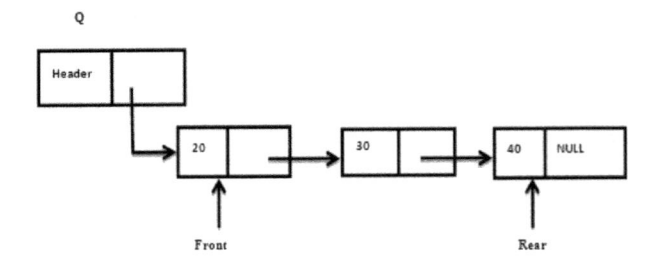

Routine to DeQueue an Element from the Queue

```
void DeQueue ( Queue Q )
{
struct node *temp;
if (Front = = NULL)
Error ("EmptyQueue!!! Deletion not possible." );
    else if (Front = = Rear)
{
        temp = Front;
        Q -> next = NULL;
Front = NULL;
Rear = NULL;
        free ( temp );
}
else
        {
            temp = Front;
            Q -> next = temp -> next;
            Front = Front →Next;
free (temp);
}
}
```

C Program for Linked List Implementation of Queue

```
#include<stdio.h>
#include<conio.h>
void enqueue();
void dequeue();
void display();
typedef struct node *position;
position front=NULL,rear=NULL,newnode,temp,p;
struct node
{
    int data;
    position next;
};
void main()
```

```c
{
int choice;
clrscr();
do
{
printf("1.Enqueue\n2.Dequeue\n3.display\n4.exit\n");
printf("Enter your choice\n\n");
scanf("%d",&choice);
switch(choice)
{
case 1:
        enqueue();
        break;
case 2:
        dequeue();
        break;
case 3:
        display();
        break;
case 4:
        exit(0);
}
}
while(choice<5);
}
void enqueue()
{
newnode=(struct node*)malloc(sizeof(struct node));
printf("\n Enter the data to be enqueued\n");
scanf("%d",&newnode->data);
newnode->next=NULL;
if(rear==NULL)
front=rear=newnode;
else
{
rear->next=newnode;
rear=newnode;
}
  display();
}
 void dequeue()
{
if(front==NULL)
```

```
printf("\nEmpty queue!!!!! Deletion not possible\n");
else if(front==rear)
{
printf("\nFront element %d is deleted from queue!!!! now queue is empty!!!! no more deletion possible!!!!\n",front->data);
front=rear=NULL;
}
else
{
temp=front;
front=front->next;
printf("\nFront element %d is deleted from queue!!!!\n",temp->data);
free(temp);
}
display();
}
void display()
{
p=front;
while(p!=NULL)
{
printf("%d -> ",p->data);
p=p->next;
}
printf("Null\n");
}
```

Output

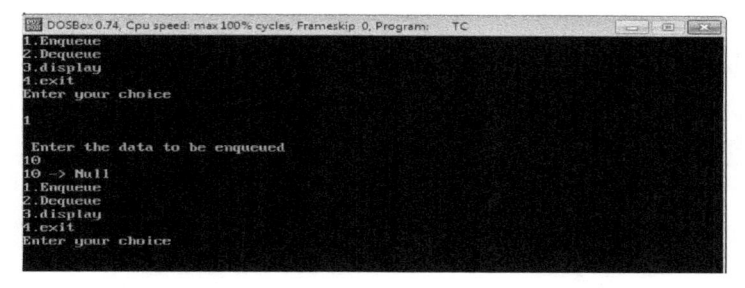

13.5. Applications of Queue

1. Serving requests on a single shared resource, like a printer, CPU task scheduling etc.
2. In real life, Call Center phone systems will use Queues, to hold people calling them in an order, until a service representative is free.

3. Handling of interrupts in real-time systems. The interrupts are handled in the same order as they arrive, First come first served.
4. Batch processing in operating system.
5. Job scheduling Algorithms like Round Robin Algorithm uses Queue.

13.6. Drawbacks of Queue (Linear Queue)

- With the array implementation of Queue, the element can be deleted logically only by moving Front = Front + 1.
- Here the Queue space is not utilized fully.

To overcome the drawback of this linear Queue, we use Circular Queue.

CHAPTER 14

CIRCULAR QUEUE

14.1. Introduction

- A circular queue is an abstract data type that contains a collection of data which allows addition of data at the end of the queue and removal of data at the beginning of the queue.
- It has a fixed size.
- It follows FIFO principle.
- Data items are added at the rear end and deleted from the front end of the circular queue.
- Here the Queue space is utilized fully by inserting the element at the Front end if the rear end is full.

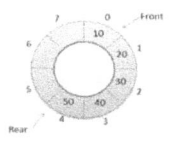

14.2. Operations on Circular Queue

Fundamental operations performed on the Circular Queue are

- Circular Queue Enqueue.
- Circular Queue Dequeue.

Formula to be Used in Circular Queue

For Enqueue   Rear = (Rear + 1) % ArraySize
For Dequeue   Front = (Front + 1) % ArraySize

1. Circular Queue Enqueue Operation

- It is same as Linear Queue EnQueue Operation (i.e) Inserting the element at the Rear end.
- First check for full Queue.
- If the circular queue is full, then insertion is not possible.
- Otherwise check for the rear end.

- If the Rear end is full, the elements start getting inserted from the Front end.

Routine to EnQueue an Element in Circular Queue

```
void Enqueue (int X,CircularQueue CQ)
{
    if(Front== ( Rear+1)% ArraySize)
            Error( "Queue is full!!Insertion not possible");
    else if( Rear == -1)
    {
            Front= Front+1;
            Rear= Rear+1;
            CQ[ Rear]= X;
    }
    else
    {
            Rear=( Rear+1)%Arraysize;
            CQ[ Rear]=X;
    }
}
```

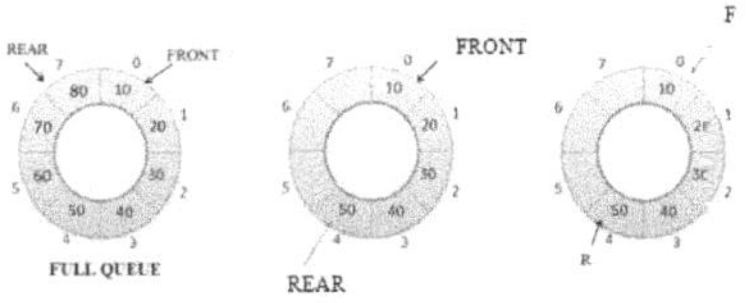

2. Circular Queue DeQueue Operation

- It is same as Linear Queue DeQueue operation (i.e) deleting the front element.
- First check for Empty Queue.
- If the Circular Queue is empty, then deletion is not possible.
- If the Circular Queue has only one element, then the element is deleted and Front and Rear pointer is initialized to - 1 to represent Empty Queue.
- Otherwise, Front element is deleted and the Front pointer is made to point to next element in the Circular Queue.

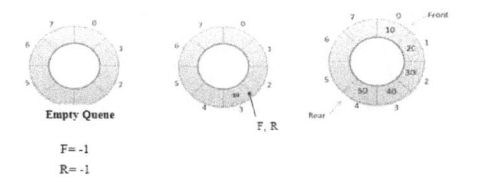

215

Routine to DeQueue an Element in Circular Queue

```
void DeQueue (CircularQueue CQ)
{
if(Front== - 1)
    Empty("Empty Queue!");
else if(Front==rear)
{
X=CQ[Front];
 Front=-1;
 Rear=-1;
}
else
{
X=CQ[Front];
Front=(Front+1)%Arraysize;
}
}
```

C Program for Implementation of Circular Queue

```
#include<stdio.h>
#include<conio.h>
#define max 3
void insert(); void delet(); void display();
int q[10],front=0,rear=-1;
void main()
{
int ch;
clrscr();
printf("\nCircular Queue operations\n"); printf("1.insert\n2.delete\n3.display\n4.exit\n");
while(1)
{
printf("Enter your choice:");
scanf("%d",&ch);
switch(ch)
{
case 1:
        insert();
        break;
case 2:
        delet();
        break;
```

```c
case 3:
        display();
        break;
case 4:
        exit();
default:
        printf("Invalid option\n");
}
}
}
void insert()
{
int x;
if((front==0&&rear==max-1)||(front>0&&rear==front-1))
printf("Queue is overflow\n");
else
{
printf("Enter element to be insert:");
scanf("%d",&x);
if(rear==max-1&&front>0)
{
rear=0;
q[rear]=x;
}
else
{
if((front==0&&rear==-1)||(rear!=front-1))
q[++rear]=x;
}
}
}
void delet()
{
int a;
if((front==0)&&(rear==-1))
printf("Queue is underflow\n");
if(front==rear)
{
a=q[front];
rear=-1;
front=0;
}
else if(front==max-1)
```

```
{
a=q[front];
front=0;
}
else
a=q[front++];
printf("Deleted element is:%d\n",a);
}
void display()
{
int i,j;
if(front==0&&rear==-1)
printf("Queue is underflow\n");
if(front>rear)
{
for(i=0;i<=rear;i++)
printf("\t%d",q[i]);
for(j=front;j<=max-1;j++)
printf("\t%d",q[j]);
printf("\nrear is at %d\n",q[rear]);
printf("\nfront is at %d\n",q[front]);
}
else
{
for(i=front;i<=rear;i++)
printf("\t%d",q[i]);
printf("\nrear is at %d\n",q[rear]);
printf("\nfront is at %d\n",q[front]);
}
printf("\n");
}
```

```
DOSBox 0.74, Cpu speed: max 100% cycles, Frameskip 0, Program: TC
1.insert ( max 3 element)
2.delete
3.display
4.exit
Enter your choice:1
Enter element to be insert:10
Enter your choice:1
Enter element to be insert:20
Enter your choice:1
Enter element to be insert:30
Enter your choice:1
Queue is overflow
Enter your choice:2
Deleted element is:10
Enter your choice:1
Enter element to be insert:40
Enter your choice:1
Queue is overflow
Enter your choice:3
        40      20      30
rear is at 40

front is at 20

Enter your choice:
```

218

CHAPTER 15

DOUBLE-ENDED QUEUE (DEQUE)

15.1. Introduction

- A double-ended queue is an abstract data type similar to an simple queue.
- In DEQUE, insertion and deletion operations are performed at both ends of the Queue.

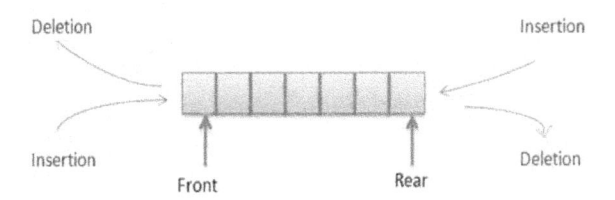

15.2. Exceptional Condition of DEQUE

1. Input Restricted DEQUE

Here insertion is allowed at **one end** and deletion is allowed at **both ends.**

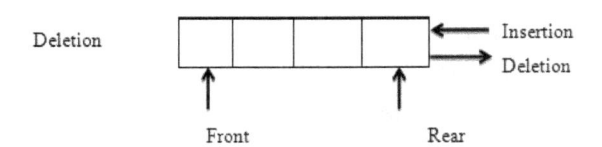

2. Output Restricted DEQUE

Here insertion is allowed at **both ends** and deletion is allowed at **one end.**

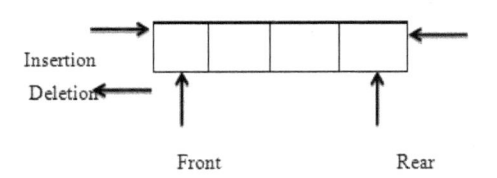

15.3. Operations on DEQUE

Four Cases for Inserting and Deleting the Elements in DEQUE are

- Insertion At Rear End [same as Linear Queue]
- Insertion At Front End
- Deletion At Front End [same as Linear Queue]
- Deletion At Rear End

```
void Insert_Rear(int X, DEQUE DQ)
{
 if( Rear ==Arraysize-1)
 Error("Full Queue!!!! Insertion not possible");
 else if(Rear == -1)
 {
          Front =Front +1;
          Rear = Rear +1;
          DQ[Rear ] = X;
 }
 else
 {
          Rear =Rear +1;
          DQ[ Rear ]=X;
 }
}
```

Case 1: Routine to Insert an Element at Rear End

- It is the process of inserting a new element at the Rear end of the Queue.
- It takes two parameters, Insert_Rear(X,DEQUE DQ) The elements X to be inserted at the Rear end of the Queue.
- Before inserting a new Element into the Queue, check for Full Queue.
- If the Queue is already Full, Insertion is not possible.
- Otherwise, Increment the Rear pointer by 1 and then insert the element X at the Rear end of the Queue.
- If the Queue is Empty, Increment both Front and Rear pointer by 1 and then insert the element X at the Rear end of the Queue.

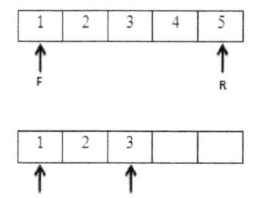

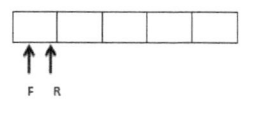

Case 2: Routine to Insert an Element at Front End

- It is the process of inserting a new element at the Front end of the Queue.
- It takes two parameters, Insert_Front(X,DEQUE DQ) The elements X to be inserted at the Front end of the Queue.
- Before inserting a new Element into the Queue, check the Front end of the Queue.
- If an element is present in the Front end then Insertion is not possible.
- Otherwise, decrement the Front pointer by 1 and then insert the element X at the Front end of the Queue.
- If the Queue is Empty, Increment both Front and Rear pointer by 1 and then insert the element X at the Front end of the Queue.

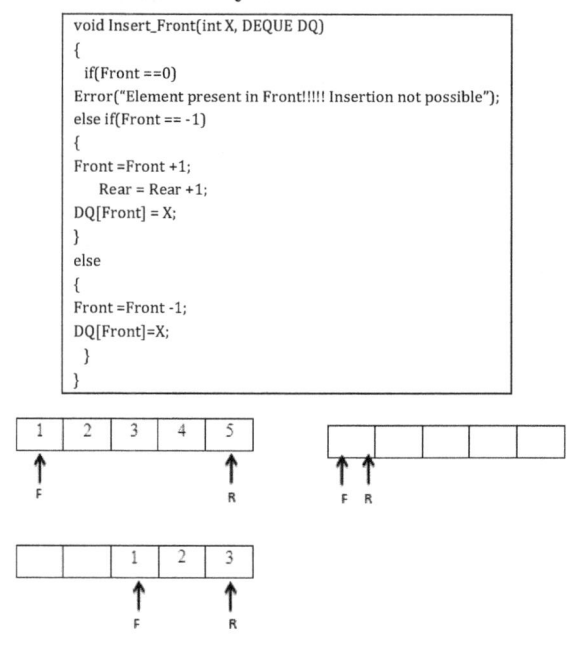

```
void Insert_Front(int X, DEQUE DQ)
{
    if(Front ==0)
    Error("Element present in Front!!!!! Insertion not possible");
    else if(Front == -1)
    {
        Front =Front +1;
        Rear = Rear +1;
        DQ[Front] = X;
    }
    else
    {
        Front =Front -1;
        DQ[Front]=X;
    }
}
```

1	2	3	4	5

↑   ↑
F   R

↑↑
F R

		1	2	3

↑ ↑
F R

Case 3: Routine to Delete an Element from Front End

- It is the process of deleting a element from the Front end of the Queue.
- It takes one parameter, Delete_Front(DEQUE DQ). Always front element in the Queue will be deleted.
- Before deleting an Element from the Queue, check for Empty Queue.

- If the Queue is empty, deletion is not possible.
- If the Queue has only one element, then delete the element and represent the empty queue by updating Front = - 1 and Rear = - 1.
- If the Queue has many Elements, then delete the element in the Front and move the Front pointer to next element in the queue by incrementing Front pointer by 1.

```
void Delete_Front(DEQUE DQ)
{
if(Front = = - 1)
Error("Empty queue!!!! Deletion not possible");
  else if( Front = = Rear )
  {
    X = DQ[ Front];
    Front = - 1;
    Rear = - 1;
  }
  else
  {
    X = DQ [ Front ];
    Front = Front + 1;
  }
}
```

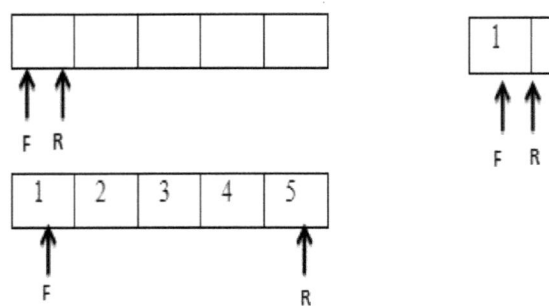

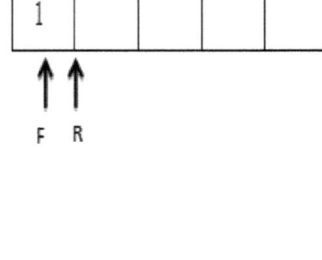

Case 4: Routine to Delete an Element from Rear End

- It is the process of deleting a element from the Rear end of the Queue.
- It takes one parameter, Delete_Rear(DEQUE DQ). Element in the Rear end of the Queue will be deleted.

- Before deleting an Element from the Queue, check for Empty Queue.
- If the Queue is empty, deletion is not possible.
- If the Queue has only one element, then delete the element and represent the empty queue by updating Front = - 1 and Rear = - 1.
- If the Queue has many Elements, then delete the element in the Rear end and move the Rear pointer to previous element in the queue by decrementing Rear pointer by 1.

```
void Delete_Rear(DEQUE DQ)
{
  if( Rear = = - 1)
  Error("Empty queue!!!! Deletion not possible");
  else if( Front = = Rear )
  {
    X = DQ[ Rear ];
    Front = - 1;
    Rear = - 1;
  }
  else
  {
    X = DQ[ Rear ];
    Rear = Rear - 1;
  }
}
```

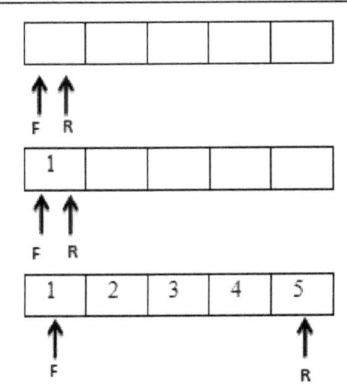

Review Questions with Solution

1. Define Stack and Give Example

A Stack is an ordered collection of items into which new items may be inserted &items may be deleted at one end, called the top of the stack. The other name of stack is Last-in -First-out list. The Insert operation is called **"PUSH"**. Delete operation is called **"POP"**.

Diagram

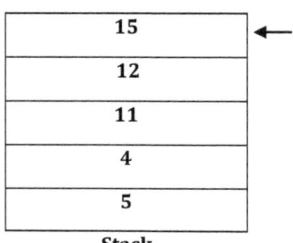

15	←
12	
11	
4	
5	

Stack

2. How do you push and pop elements in a linked stack

The **push** operation adds (stores) an item to the list. The **push** is implemented as an insertion in to the front of a linked list, where the front of the list serves as the **top** of the stack.

The **top** is examined as the element in the first position of the list.

The **pop** operation removes (deletes) an item from the list. The **pop** is implemented by deleting the element at the front of the list.

3. Write the applications of stack

The various applications of Stack are:

- Checking for Balanced Parenthesis in an expression.
- Conversion of expressions from Infix to Postfix.
- Function calls.
- Solving Towers of Hanoi problem.

4. Convert the following infix expression into prefix and postfix notations

a * b - c - d + e * f - g / h

Prefix: -+ - - *abcd*ef/gh

Postfix: ab*c-d-ef*+gh/-

5. Write the role of stack in function call

When a call is made to a new function, all the variables local to the calling routine need to be saved by the system, otherwise the new function overwrites the calling routine's variables. All the important information like register values, return address need to be saved.

This information is stored in the stack for further use. The information saved is called either an **activation record** or **stack frame**.

6. Define queue and give example

A Queue is an ordered collection of items from which items may be deleted at one end called the **front** of the queue and the items may be inserted at the other end called **rear** of the queue. Queue is called as First –in-First-Out(FIFO). Insert operation is called "**ENQUEUE**". Delete operation is called as "**DEQUEUE**".

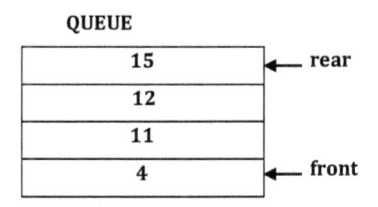

```
         QUEUE
    ┌─────────────┐
    │     15      │ ◄── rear
    ├─────────────┤
    │     12      │
    ├─────────────┤
    │     11      │
    ├─────────────┤
    │      4      │ ◄── front
    └─────────────┘
```

7. How do you test for an empty queue?

Two structure variables front & rear denote the first and last node in the Queue. If front and rear is equal to NULL, then we can say queue is empty.

Program Code:

```
intisempty(queue *front, queue *rear)
{
    if(front==NULL && rear==NULL)
    return 0;
    else
    return 1;
}
```

225

8. Write any two applications of stacks and queues

Applications of Stack

- Balancing symbols.
- Conversion of Infix to Postfix expressions.
- Function calls.
- Evaluation of postfix expression.
- Towers of Hanoi problem.

Applications of Queue

- Waiting lists(print jobs).
- access to shared resources(computer networks).
- Multiprogramming(OS).
- Real-life waiting lines.

9. What is circular queue?

- A circular queue is an abstract data type that contains a collection of data which allows addition of data at the end of the queue and removal of data at the beginning of the queue.
- Circular queues have a fixed size.
- Circular queue follows FIFO principle.
- Queue items are added at the rear end and the items are deleted at front end of the circular queue.
- Here the Queue space is utilized fully by inserting the element at the Front end if the rear end is full.

10. Define Double Ended Queue.(May\Jun2014, Nov\Dec2014)

- A double-ended queue is an abstract data type similar to an simple queue.
- In DEQUE, insertion and deletion operations are performed at both ends of the Queue.

11. List the applications of a Queue.May\Jun2014)

- Waiting lists(print jobs)
- access to shared resources(computer networks)
- Multiprogramming(OS)
- Real-life waiting lines

226

12. Give the applications the Stack.(Nov\Dec2014)

- Balancing symbols.
- Conversion of Infix to Postfix expressions.
- Function calls.
- Evaluation of postfix expression.
- Towers of Hanoi problem.

13. Write the syntax of Calloc() and Realloc() and mention its application in linked list.(Apr\May2015)

Calloc() – Calloc(number,sizeof(int));

Realloc() – realloc(pointer_name, number*sizeof(int));

calloc () initializes the allocated memory to zero.

realloc () function modifies the allocated memory size by malloc () and calloc () functions to new size.

PART V

- Sorting
- Searching
- Hashing
- Review Questions with solution

CHAPTER 16

SORTING

16.1. Introduction

A **sorting algorithm** is an algorithm that puts elements of a list in a certain order.

It refers to ordering data in an increasing or decreasing fashion according to some linear relationship among the data items.

It can be done on names, numbers and records.

For example, it is relatively easy to look up the phone number of a friend from a telephone dictionary because the names in the phone book have been sorted into alphabetical order.

16.2. Types of Sorting

- Internal Sorting
- External Sorting

1. Internal Sorting

Internal Sorting takes place in the main memory of the computer. It is applicable when the number of elements in the list is small.

E.g. Bubble Sort, Inserting Sort, Shell Sort, Quick Sort.

2. External Sorting

External Sorting takes place in the Secondary memory of the computer. It is applicable when the number of elements in the list is large.

E.g. Merge Sort, Multiway Merge Sort.

16.3. Sorting Algorithms

- Insertion sort
- Selection sort
- Shell sort
- Bubble sort
- Quick sort
- Merge sort
- Radix sort

16.3.1. Insertion Sort

- One of the simplest sorting algorithm is the Insertion sort
- For "n" elements, it consist of "n – 1" passes

How Insertion Sort Algorithm Works?

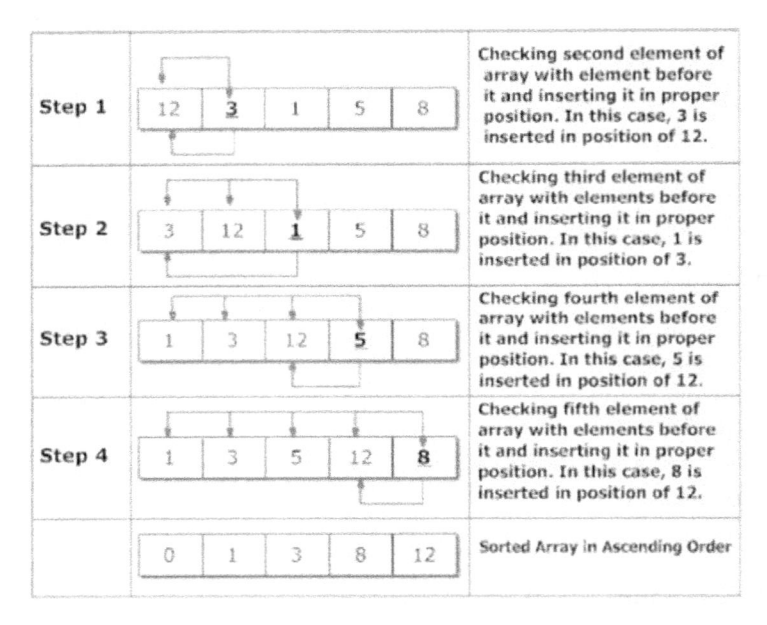

Step 1	12 3 1 5 8	Checking second element of array with element before it and inserting it in proper position. In this case, 3 is inserted in position of 12.
Step 2	3 12 1 5 8	Checking third element of array with elements before it and inserting it in proper position. In this case, 1 is inserted in position of 3.
Step 3	1 3 12 5 8	Checking fourth element of array with elements before it and inserting it in proper position. In this case, 5 is inserted in position of 12.
Step 4	1 3 5 12 8	Checking fifth element of array with elements before it and inserting it in proper position. In this case, 8 is inserted in position of 12.
	0 1 3 8 12	Sorted Array in Ascending Order

Sorting Array in Ascending Order Using Insertion Sort Algorithm

Insertion SORT Routine

```
void Insertion_sort(int a[ ], int n)
{
        int i, j, temp;
        for ( i = 0 ; i < n -1 ; i ++ )
    {
    for ( j = i + 1 ; j > 0  && a [ j -1 ] > a [ j ] ; j -- )
                {
                    temp = a [ j ] ;
                    a[ j ] = a [ j – 1 ] ;
                    a[ j – 1 ] = temp ;
                }
    }
}
```

Program for Insertion Sort

```
#include < stdio.h >
void main( )
{
int n, a[ 25 ], i, j, temp;
printf( "Enter number of elements \n" );
scanf( "%d", &n );
printf( "Enter %d integers \n", n );
for ( i = 0; i < n; i++ )
scanf( "%d", &a[i] );
for ( i = 0 ; i < n - 1; i++ )
{
j = i + 1;
while ( j > 0 && a[ j ] < a[ j-1 ])
{
        temp = a[ j ];
        a[ j ]  = a[ j - 1 ];
        a[ j - 1 ] = temp;
        j --;
}
}
printf( "Sorted list in ascending order: \n ");
for ( i = 0 ; i < n ; i++)
printf ( "%d \n ", a[ i ] );
}
```

Advantage of Insertion Sort

- Simple implementation.
- Efficient for (quite) small data sets.
- Efficient for data sets that are already substantially sorted.

Disadvantages of Insertion Sort

- It is less efficient on list containing more number of elements.
- As the number of elements increases the performance of the program would be slow.
- Insertion sort needs a large number of element shifts.

16.3.2. Selection Sort

Selection sort algorithm starts by comparing first two elements of an array and swapping if necessary, i.e., if you want to sort the elements of array in ascending order and if the first element is greater than second then, you need to swap the elements but, if the first element is smaller than second, leave the elements as it is. Then, again first element and third element are compared and swapped if necessary. This process goes on until first and last element of an array is compared. This completes the first step of selection sort.

If there are n elements to be sorted then, the process mentioned above should be repeated n-1 times to get required result. But, for better performance, in second step, comparison starts from second element because after first step, the required number is automatically placed at the first (i.e., In case of sorting in ascending order, smallest element will be at first and in case of sorting in descending order, largest element will be at first.). Similarly, in third step, comparison starts from third element and so on.

Selection Sort Routine

```
void Selection_sort( int a[ ], int n )
{
int i , j , temp , position ;
        for ( i = 0 ; i < n - 1 ;  i ++ )
        {
                position = i ;
                for ( j = i + 1 ; j < n ; j ++ )
                {
                        if ( a[ position ] > a[ j ] )
                        position = j;
                }
                temp = a[ i ];
                a[ i ] = a[ position ];
                a[ position ] = temp;
        }
}
```

- For "n" elements, (n-1) passes are required.
- At the end of the ith iteration, the ith smallest element will be placed in its correct position.

How Selection Sort Algorithm Works?

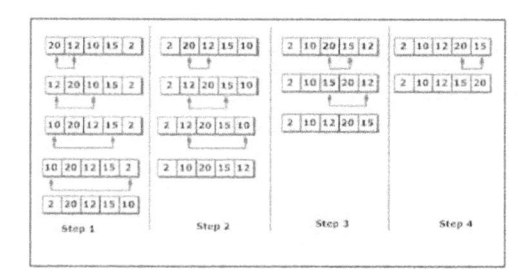

Selection Sort

Program for Selection Sort

```
#include <stdio.h>
void main( )
{
        int a [ 100 ] , n , i , j , position , temp ;
        printf ( "Enter number of elements \n" ) ;
        scanf ( "%d", &n ) ;
        printf ( " Enter %d integers \n ", n ) ;
for ( i = 0 ; i < n ; i ++ )
        scanf ( "%d", & a[ i ] ) ;
for ( i = 0 ; i < ( n - 1 ) ; i ++ )
{
        position = i ;
for ( j = i + 1 ; j < n ; j ++ )
{
        if ( a [ position ] > a [ j ] )
        position = j ;
}
if ( position != i )
{
        temp = a [ i ] ;
        a [ i ] = a [ position ] ;
        a [ position ] = temp ;
}
}
        printf ( "Sorted list in ascending order: \n ") ;
for ( i = 0 ; i < n ; i ++ )
        printf ( " %d \n ", a[ i ] ) ;
}
```

Advantages of Selection Sort

- Memory required is small.
- Selection sort is useful when you have limited memory available.
- Relatively efficient for small arrays.

Disadvantage of Selection Sort

- Poor efficiency when dealing with a huge list of items.
- The selection sort requires n-squared number of steps for sorting n elements.
- The selection sort is only suitable for a list of few elements that are in random order.

16.3.3. Shell Sort

Shell sort works by comparing elements that are distant rather than adjacent elements in an array or list where adjacent elements are compared. Shell sort uses an increment sequence. The increment size is reduced after each pass until the increment size is 1. With an increment size of 1, the sort is a basic insertion sort, but by this time the data is guaranteed to be almost sorted, which is insertion sort's "best case". The distance between comparisons decreases as the sorting algorithm runs until the last phase in which adjacent elements are compared hence, it is also known as diminishing increment sort.

Consider a list has nine items. If we use an increment of three, there are three sublist, each of which can be sorted by an insertion sort. After completing these sorts, we get the list shown below. Although this list is not completely sorted, something very interesting has happened. By sorting the sublist, we have moved the items closer to where they actually belong.

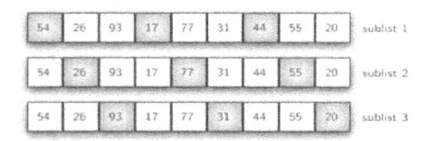

A Shell Sort with Increments of Three

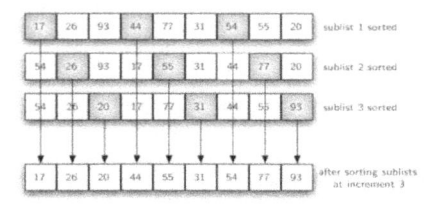

A Shell Sort After Sorting Each Sublist

Note that by performing the earlier sublist sorts, we have now reduced the total number of shifting operations necessary to put the list in its final order. For this case, we need only four more shifts to complete the process.

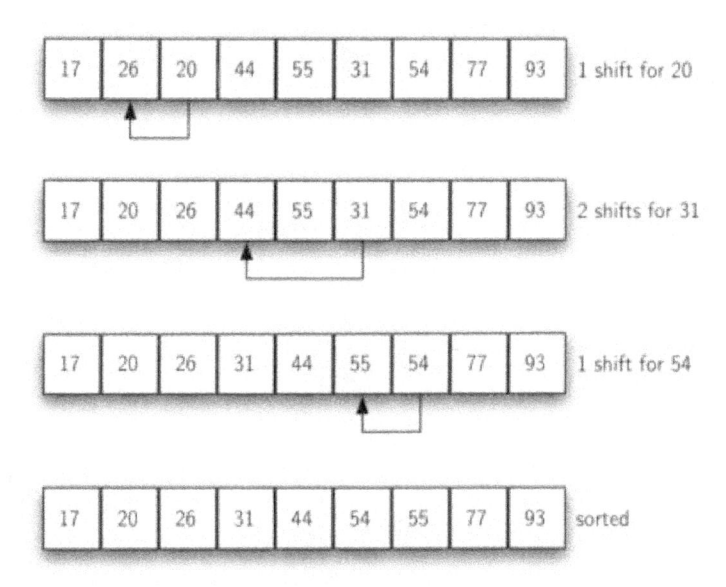

| 17 | 26 | 20 | 44 | 55 | 31 | 54 | 77 | 93 | 1 shift for 20

| 17 | 20 | 26 | 44 | 55 | 31 | 54 | 77 | 93 | 2 shifts for 31

| 17 | 20 | 26 | 31 | 44 | 55 | 54 | 77 | 93 | 1 shift for 54

| 17 | 20 | 26 | 31 | 44 | 54 | 55 | 77 | 93 | sorted

Shell Sort: A Final Insertion Sort with Increment of 1

Shell Sort Routine

```
void Shell_sort ( int a[ ], int n )
{
int i, j, k, temp;
for ( k = n / 2 ; k > 0 ;  k = k / 2 )
for ( i = k ; i < n ; i + + )
{
temp = a [ i ] ;
for ( j = i ; j > = k && a [ j - k ] > temp ; j  =  j - k )
{
a [ j ] = a [ j - k ] ;
}
a [ j ] = temp ;
}
}
```

235

Program for Shell Sort

```
#include < stdio.h >
void main( )
{
int a [ 5 ] = { 4, 5, 2, 3, 6 }, i = 0 ;
ShellSort ( a, 5 ) ;
printf( " After Sorting :" ) ;
for ( i = 0 ; i < 5 ; i ++ )
printf ( " %d ", a[ i ] ) ;
}
void ShellSort (int a [ 5 ] , int n )
{
int i , j , k , temp ;
for ( k = n / 2 ; k > 0 ; k / = 2)
{
for ( i = k ; i < n ; i ++ )
{
  temp = a [ i ] ;
  for ( j = i ; j > = k && a [ j - k ] > temp ; j = j - k )
  {
  a [ j ] = a [ j - k ] ;
  }
  a [ j ] = temp ;
}
}
}
```

Advantages of Shell Sort

- Efficient for medium-size lists.

Disadvantages of Shell Sort

- Complex algorithm, not nearly as efficient as the merge, heap and quick sorts.

16.3.4. Bubble Sort

This algorithm starts by comparing the first two elements of an array and swapping if necessary, i.e., if you want to sort the elements of array in ascending order and if the first element is greater than second then, you need to swap the elements but, if the first element is smaller than second, you mustn't swap the element. Then, again second and third elements are compared and swapped if it is necessary and this process go on until last and second last element is compared and swapped. This completes the first step of bubble sort.

If there are *n* elements to be sorted then, the process mentioned above should be repeated *n-1* times to get required result. But, for better performance, in second step, last and second last elements are not compared because; the proper element is automatically placed at last after first step. Similarly, in third step, last and second last and second last and third last elements are not compared and so on.

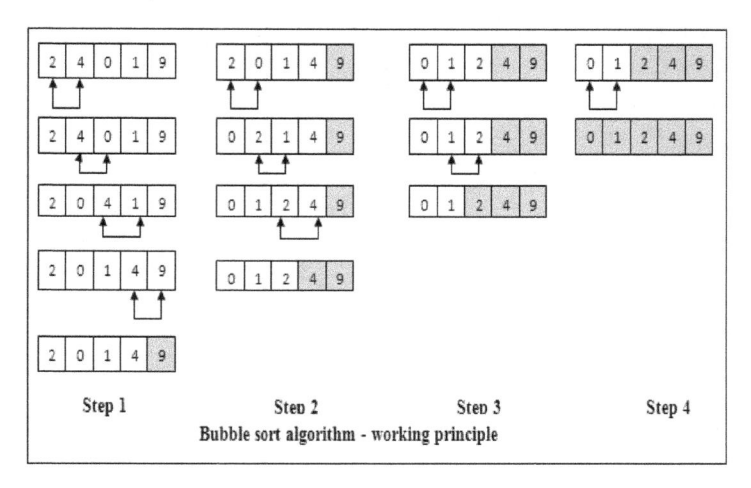

```
  2 4 0 1 9          2 0 1 4 9          0 1 2 4 9          0 1 2 4 9
    ↑_↑                ↑_↑                  ↑_↑                ↑_↑

  2 4 0 1 9          0 2 1 4 9          0 1 2 4 9          0 1 2 4 9
    ↑_↑                  ↑_↑                  ↑_↑

  2 0 4 1 9          0 1 2 4 9          0 1 2 4 9
      ↑_↑                  ↑_↑

  2 0 1 4 9          0 1 2 4 9
        ↑_↑

  2 0 1 4 9

    Step 1             Step 2             Step 3             Step 4
              Bubble sort algorithm - working principle
```

Bubble Sort Routine

```
void Bubble_sort (int a [ ], int n )
{
int i, j, temp;
for( i = 0; i < n - 1;  i++ )
{
for( j = 0; j < n – i - 1; j++ )
{
if( a[ j ] > a [ j + 1 ] )
{
temp = a [ j ];
a[ j ] = a[ j + 1 ];
a[ j + 1 ] = temp;
}
}
}
}
```

- For "n" elements, (n-1) passes are required.
- At the end of ith pass, the ith largest element will be placed in its correct position.

Program for Bubble Sort

```c
#include < stdio.h >
#include < conio.h >
void main( )
{
        int a [ 20 ], i, j, temp, n ;
        printf ( "\n Enter the number of elements \t " );
        scanf ( " %d ", &n );
        printf ( " \n Enter %d numbers \n ", n );
        for ( i = 0 ; i < n ; i++ )
        scanf ( " %d ", & a [ i ] );
        printf (" \n  Elements \t " );
        for ( i = 0 ; i < n ; i++ )
        printf ( " %d \t ", a [ i ] );
        for ( i = 0 ; i < n - 1 ; i++ )
        {
        for ( j = 0 ; j < n – i – 1 ; j++ )
        {
        if ( a [ j ] > a [ j + 1 ] )
        {
        temp = a [ j ] ;
        a [ j ] = a [ j + 1 ] ;
        a [ j+ 1 ] = temp;
        }   }
}
        printf("\nSorted array\t");
        for(i=0;i<n;i++)
        printf("%d\t",a[i]);
}
```

Advantage of Bubble Sort

- It is simple to write
- Easy to understand
- it only takes a few lines of code.

Disadvantage of Bubble Sort

- The major drawback is the amount of time it takes to sort.
- The average time increases almost exponentially as the number of table elements increase.

16.3.5. Quick Sort

Quick sort algorithm is based on divide and conquer strategy. In a quick sort we take one element called as pivot, then we list all the smaller elements than pivot, and greater than pivot. After partitioning we have pivot in the final position. After recursively sorting the partition array, we get the sorted elements.

The basic steps to partition an array are:

1. Find a "pivot" item in the array. This item is the basis for comparison for a single round.
2. Start a pointer (the left pointer) at the first item in the array.
3. Start a pointer (the right pointer) at the last item in the array.
4. While the value at the left pointer in the array is less than the pivot value, move the left pointer to the right (add 1). Continue until the value at the left pointer is greater than or equal to the pivot value.
5. While the value at the right pointer in the array is greater than the pivot value, move the right pointer to the left (subtract 1). Continue until the value at the right pointer is less than or equal to the pivot value.
6. If the left pointer is less than or equal to the right pointer, then swap the values at these locations in the array.
7. Move the left pointer to the right by one and the right pointer to the left by one.
8. If the left pointer and right pointer don't meet, go to step 1.

Below figure shows that 54 will serve as our first pivot value. Since we have looked at this example a few times already, we know that 54 will eventually end up in the position currently holding 31. The **partition** process will happen next. It will find the split point and at the same time move other items to the appropriate side of the list, either less than or greater than the pivot value.

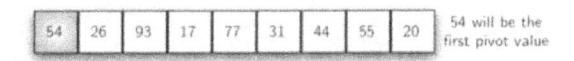

| 54 | 26 | 93 | 17 | 77 | 31 | 44 | 55 | 20 | 54 will be the first pivot value |

The First Pivot Value for a Quick Sort

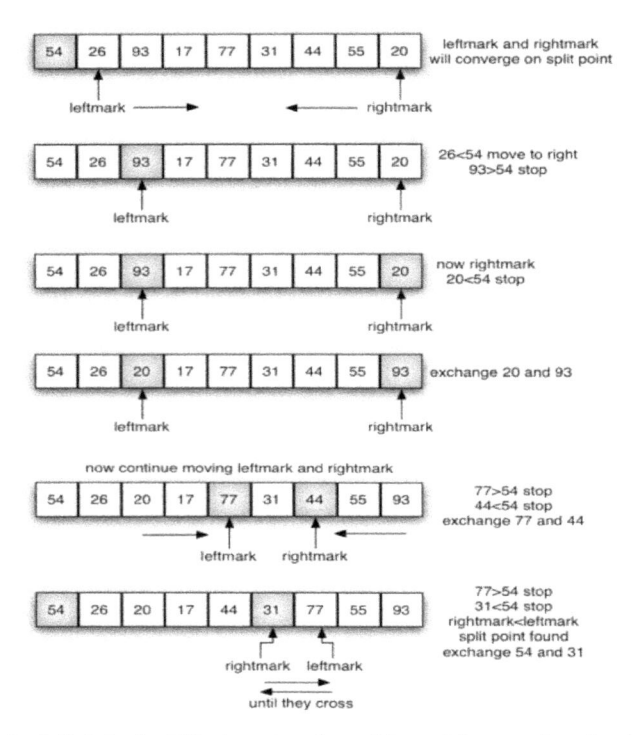

Finding the Split Point for 54 At the point where rightmark becomes less than leftmark, we stop. The position of rightmark is now the split point. The pivot value can be exchanged with the contents of the split point and the pivot value is now in place. In addition, all the items to the left of the split point are less than the pivot value, and all the items to the right of the split point are greater than the pivot value. The list can now be divided at the split point and the quick sort can be invoked recursively on the two halves.

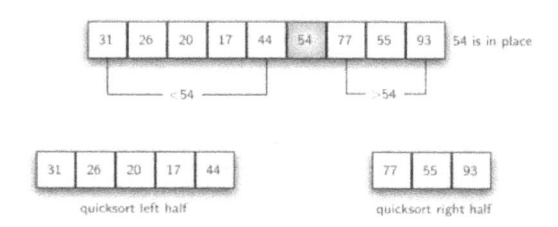

Completing the Partition Process to Find the Split Point for 54

Quick Sort Routine

```
void Quicksort ( int a [ ], int left, int right )
{
int i, j, p, temp;
if ( left < right )
{
p = left;
i = left + 1;
j = right;
while ( i < j )
{
while ( a [ i ] < = a [ p ] )
i = i + 1;
while ( a [ j ] > a [ p ] )
j = j - 1;
if ( i < j )
{
temp = a [ i ];
a [ i ] = a [ j ];
a [ j ] = temp;
}
}
temp = a [ p ];
a [ p ] = a [ j ];
a [ j ] = temp;
quicksort ( a, left, j - 1 );
quicksort ( a, j + 1, right );
}
}
```

Program for Quick Sort

```
#include < stdio.h >
void quicksort ( int [ 10 ], int, int ) ;
void main( )
{
    int a [ 20 ], n, i ;
    printf ( " Enter size of the array: " );
    scanf ( " %d ", & n );
    printf( " Enter % d elements : ", n );
    for ( i = 0 ; i < n ; i ++ )
        scanf ( " %d ", & a [ i ]);
    quicksort ( a , 0 , n – 1 );
    printf ( " Sorted elements: " );
    for ( i = 0 ; i < n ; i ++ )
        printf ( " %d \ t ", a [ i ] );
}
void quicksort ( int  a [ 10 ], int left, int right )
{
```

```
int p, j, temp, i ;
if ( left < right )
{
        p = left ;
        i = left ;
        j = right ;
while ( i < j )
{
        while ( a [ i ] < = a [ p ] && i < right )
        i ++ ;
        while ( a [ j ] > a [ p ] )
        j - - ;
if ( i < j )
{
        temp = a [ i ] ;
        a [ i ] = a [ j ] ;
        a[ j ] = temp ;
}
}
        temp = a [ p ] ;
        a [ p ] = a [ j ] ;
        a [ j ] =temp ;
quicksort ( a , left , j - 1 ) ;
quicksort ( a , j + 1 , right ) ;
}
}
```

Advantages of Quick Sort

- Fast and efficient as it deals well with a huge list of items.
- No additional storage is required.

Disadvantages of Quick Sort

- The difficulty of implementing the partitioning algorithm.

16.3.6. Merge Sort

Merge sort is a recursive algorithm that continually splits a list in half. If the list has more than one item, we split the list and recursively invoke a merge sort on both halves. Once the two halves are sorted, the fundamental operation, called a **merge**, is performed. Merging is the process of taking two smaller sorted lists and combining them together into a single, sorted, new list. Below figure shows our familiar example list as it is being split by mergeSort. Below figure shows the simple lists, now sorted, as they are merged back together.

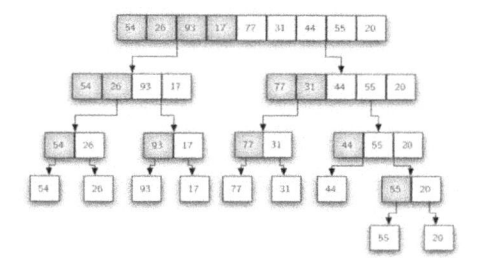

Splitting the List in a Merge Sort

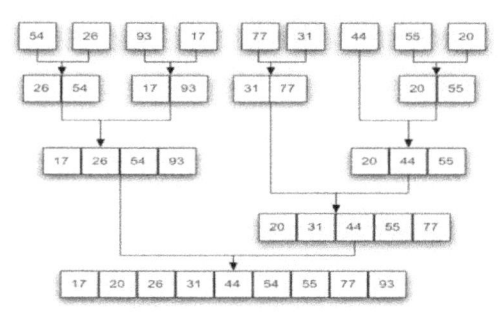

List, as they are Merged Together

Merge Sort Routine

```
void Merge_sort (int a [ ], int temp [ ], int n )
{
    msort ( a , temp , 0 , n - 1 ) ;
}
```

```
void msort ( int a[ ] , int temp [ ] , int left , int right )
{
    int center ;
    if( left < right )
    {
        center = ( left + right ) / 2 ;
        msort ( a , left , center ) ;
        msort ( a , temp , center + 1 , right ) ;
        merge ( a , temp , n , left , center , right ) ;
    }
}
```

```
void merge ( int a [ ] , int temp [ ] , int n , int left , int center , int right )
{
        int i = 0 , j , left_end = center , center = center + 1 ;
        while( ( left < = left_end ) && ( center < = right ) )
        {
                if( a [ left ] < = a [ center ] )
                {
                        temp [ i ] = a [ left ] ;
                        i + + ;
                        left + + ;
                }
                else
                {
                        temp [ i ] = a [ center ] ;
                        i + + ;
                        center + + ;
                }
        }
        while( left <= left_end )
        {
                temp [ I ] = a [ left ] ;
                left + + ;
                i + + ;
        }
        while( center < = right )
        {
                temp [ i ] = a [ center ] ;
                center + + ;
                i + + ;
        }
        for ( i = 0 ; i < n ; i + + )
                print temp [ i ] ;
}
```

Program for Merge Sort

```
#include<stdio.h>
void mergesort(int a[],int i,int j);
void merge(int a[],int i1,int j1,int i2,int j2);
int main()
{
        int a[30],n,i;
        printf("Enter no of elements:");
        scanf("%d",&n);
        printf("Enter array elements:");
        for(i=0;i<n;i++)
                scanf("%d",&a[i]);
```

```c
        mergesort(a,0,n-1);
        printf("\nSorted array is :");
        for(i=0;i<n;i++)
                printf("%d ",a[i]);
        return 0;
}
void mergesort(int a[],int i,int j)
{
        int mid;
        if(i<j)
        {
                mid=(i+j)/2;
                mergesort(a,i,mid);        //left recursion
                mergesort(a,mid+1,j);    //right recursion
                merge(a,i,mid,mid+1,j);   //merging of two sorted sub-arrays
        }
}
void merge(int a[],int i1,int j1,int i2,int j2)
{
        int temp[50];    //array used for merging
        int i,j,k;
        i=i1;    //beginning of the first list
        j=i2;    //beginning of the second list
        k=0;
while(i<=j1 && j<=j2)   //while elements in both lists
{
        if(a[i]<a[j])
                temp[k++]=a[i++];
        else
                temp[k++]=a[j++];
}
        while(i<=j1)   //copy remaining elements of the first list
                temp[k++]=a[i++];
        while(j<=j2)   //copy remaining elements of the second list
                temp[k++]=a[j++];
        //Transfer elements from temp[] back to a[]
        for(i=i1,j=0;i<=j2;i++,j++)
        a[i]=temp[j];
}
```

Advantages of Merge Sort

- Mergesort is well-suited for sorting really huge amounts of data that does not fit into memory.
- It is fast and stable algorithm.

Disadvantages of Merge Sort

- Merge sort uses a lot of memory.
- It uses extra space proportional to number of element n.
- This can slow it down when attempting to sort very large data.

16.3.7. Radix Sort

Radix sort is an unusual sorting algorithm.

All the sorting algorithms discussed so far compare the elements being sorted to each other. The radix sort doesn't. A radix sort uses one or more keys to sort values.

On a radix sort pass, a list of items to be sorted is processed from beginning to end. One at a time, the items in the list are placed at the end of a list of items with the same key value. After all items have been processed, the lists of key values are reassembled smallest key to largest key.

Radix sort passes should be performed from the last character to the first character. The first pass will use the Nth character, the second pass will use the (N - 1)th character, ..., the Nth pass will use the first Character.

Algorithm for Radix sort

Steps 1: Consider 10 buckets (1 for each digit 0 to 9)

Step 2: Consider the LSB (Least Significant Bit) of each number (numbers in the one's Place.... E.g., in 43 LSB = 3)

Step 3: place the elements in their respective buckets according to the LSB of each number

Step 4: write the numbers from the bucket (0 to 9) bottom to top.

Step 5: repeat the same process with the digits in the 10's place (e.g. In 43 MSB =4)

Step 6: repeat the same step till all the digits of the given number are consider.

Consider the Following Numbers to be Sorted Using Radix Sort

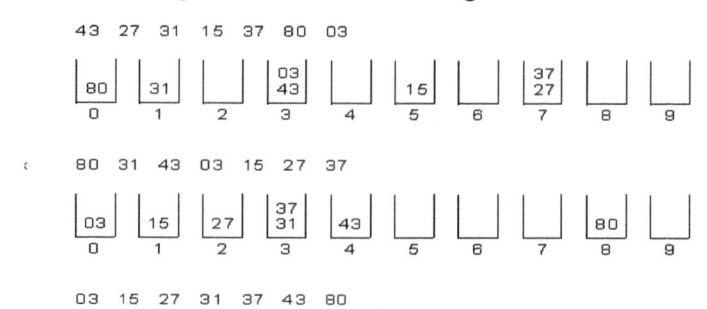

43 27 31 15 37 80 03

80	31		03 43		15		37 27		
0	1	2	3	4	5	6	7	8	9

80 31 43 03 15 27 37

03	15	27	37 31	43				80	
0	1	2	3	4	5	6	7	8	9

03 15 27 31 37 43 80

Sorted list of array : 3 15 27 31 37 43 80

```
void Radix_sort ( int a [ ] ,int n )
{
        int bucket [ 10 ] [ 5 ] , buck [ 10 ] , b [ 10 ] ;
        int i , j , k , l , num , div , large , passes ;
        div = 1 ;
        num = 0 ;
        large = a [ 0 ] ;
        for ( i = 0 ; i < n ; i ++ )
        {
                if ( a[ I ]> large )
                {
                        large = a [ i ] ;
                }
                while ( large >0 )
                {
                        num ++ ;
                        large = large / 10 ;
                }
                for ( passes = 0 ; passes < num ; passes ++ )
                {
                        for ( k = 0 ; k <10 ; k ++ )
                        {
                                buck [ k ]=0 ;
                        }
                        for ( i = 0 ; i < n ; i ++ )
                        {
                                l =( ( a [i] / div ) % 10 ) ;
                                bucket [ l ] [ buck [ l ] ++ ]= a [ i ] ;
                        }
                        i = 0 ;
                        for ( k = 0 ; k <10 ; k ++ )
                        {
                                for ( j = 0 ; j < buck [ k ] ; j ++ )
                                {
                                        a [ i ++ ]= bucket [ k ] [ j ] ;
                                }
                        }
                        div * = 10 ;
                }
        }
}
```

Advantages of Radix Sort

- Fast and complexity does not depend on the number of data.
- Radix Sort is very simple.

Disadvantages of Radix Sort

- It takes more space than other sorting algorithms, since in addition to the array that will be sorted, you need to have a sub list for each of the possible digits or letters.
- Since it depends on the digits or letters, Radix Sort is also much less flexible than other sorts.

CHAPTER 17

SEARCHING

17.1. Introduction

Searching is an algorithmto check whether a particular element is present in the list.

17.2. Types of Searching

- Linear search.
- Binary Search.

17.2.1 Linear Search

Linear search or sequential search is a method for finding a particular value in a list, that consists of checking every one of its elements, one at a time and in sequence, until the desired one is found.

Linear search is the simplest search algorithm. For a list with n items, the best case is when the value is equal to the first element of the list, in which case only one comparison is needed. The worst case is when the value is not in the list (or occurs only once at the end of the list), in which case n comparisons are needed. The worst case performance scenario for a linear search is that it has to loop through the entire collection, either because the item is the last one, or because the item is not found.

Linear Search Routine

```
void Linear_search ( int a[ ] , int n )
{
int search , count = 0 ;
for ( i = 0 ; i < n ; I ++ )
{
if ( a [ i ] = = search )
{
count ++ ;
}
}
if ( count = = 0 )
print "Element not Present" ;
else
print "Element is Present in list" ;
}
```

Program for Linear Search

```
#include < stdio.h >
void main( )
{
int a [ 10 ] , n , i , search, count = 0 ;
printf ( " Enter the number of elements \ t " ) ;
scanf ( " %d " , & n ) ;
printf ( " \n Enter %d  numbers \n " , n ) ;
for ( i = 0 ;  i < n ; i ++ )
        scanf ( " %d " , & a [ i ] ) ;
printf ( " \n Array Elements \n " ) ;
for ( i = 0 ; i < n ; i ++ )
        printf ( " %d \t " , a [ i ] ) ;
printf ( " \ n \ n Enter the Element to be searched: \ t " ) ;
scanf ( " % d " , & search ) ;
for ( i =0 ; i < n; i ++ )
{
if ( search = = a [ i ] )
        count ++ ;
}
if ( count = = 0 )
        printf( " \n Element %d is not present in the array " , search ) ;
else
        printf ( " \n Element %d is present %d times in the array \n " , search , count ) ;
}
```

Advantages of Linear Search

- It is simple, very easy to understand and implement.
- It does not require the data in the array to be stored in any particular order.

Disadvantages of Linear Search

- Slower than many other search algorithms.
- It has a very poor efficiency.

17.2.2 Binary Search

It is possible to take greater advantage of the ordered list .Instead of searching the list in sequence, a binary search will start by examining the middle item. If that item is the one we are searching for, we are done. If it is not the correct item, we can use the ordered nature of the list to eliminate half of the remaining items. If the item we are searching for is greater than the middle item, we know that the entire lower half of the list as well as the middle item can be eliminated from further consideration. The item, if it is in the list, must be in the upper half.

We can then repeat the process with the upper half. Start at the middle item and compare it against what we are looking for. Again, we either find it or split the list in half, therefore eliminating another large part of our possible search space.

17.3. Working Principle

Algorithm is quite simple. It can be done either recursively or iteratively:

1. Get the middle element.
2. If the middle element equals to the searched value, the algorithm stops.
3. Otherwise, two cases are possible.
   - Search value is less than the middle element. In this case, go to the step 1 for the part of the array, before middle element.
   - Searched value is greater, than the middle element. In this case, go to the step 1 for the part of the array, after middle element.

First case is when search element is found. Second one is when subarray has no elements. In this case the search value is not present in the array.

Binary Search Routine

```
void Binary_search ( int a[ ] , int n , int search )
{
        int first, last, mid ;
        first = 0 ;
        last = n-1 ;
        mid = ( first + last ) / 2 ;
        while ( first < = last )
        {
        if ( Search > a [ mid ] )
        first = mid + 1 ;
        else if ( Search = = a [ mid ] )
        {
        print "Element is present in the list" ;
        break ;
        }
        else
        last = mid - 1 ;
        mid = ( first + last ) / 2 ;
        }
        if( first > last )
        print "Element Not Found" ;
}
```

Example 1

Find 6 in {-1, 5, 6, 18, 19, 25, 46, 78, 102, 114}.

Step 1 (middle element is 19 > 6):   -1 5 6 18 19 25 46 78 102 114

Step 2 (middle element is 5 < 6):   -1 5 6 18 19 25 46 78 102 114

Step 3 (middle element is 6 == 6):   -1 5 6 18 19 25 46 78 102 114

Advantages of Binary Search

- In Linear search, the search element is compared with all the elements in the array. Whereas in Binary search, the search element is compared based on the middle element present in the array.

Disadvantages of Binary Search

- It employs recursive approach and this approach requires more stack space.
- It requires the data in the array to be stored in sorted order.
- It involves additional complexity in computing the middle element of the array.

CHAPTER 18

HASHING

18.1. Introduction

Hashing is a technique that is used to store, retrieve and find data in the data structure called Hash Table. It is used to overcome the drawback of Linear Search (Comparison) & Binary Search (Sorted order list). It involves two important concepts-

- Hash Table.
- Hash Function.

Hash Table

- A hash table is a data structure that is used to store and retrieve data elements (keys) very quickly.
- It is an array of some fixed size, containing the keys.
- Hash table run from 0 to Tablesize – 1.
- Each key is mapped into some number in the range 0 to Tablesize – 1.
- This mapping is called Hash function.
- Insertion of the data in the hash table is based on the key value obtained from the hash function.
- Using same hash key value, the data can be retrieved from the hash table by few or more Hash key comparison.
- The load factor of a hash table is calculated using the formula:

    (Number of data elements in the hash table) / (Size of the hash table)

Factors Affecting Hash Table Design

- Hash function.
- Table size.
- Collision handling scheme.

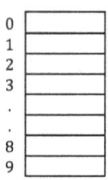

```
0
1
2
3
.
.
8
9
```

Simple Hash table with table size = 10

Hash Function

- It is a function, which distributes the keys evenly among the cells in the Hash Table.
- Using the same hash function we can retrieve data from the hash table.
- Hash function is used to implement hash table.
- The integer value returned by the hash function is called hash key.
- If the input keys are integer, the commonly used hash function is

    H (key) = key % Tablesize

```
typedef unsigned int index;
index Hash ( const char *key , int Tablesize )
{
    unsigned int Hashval = 0 ;
    while ( * key ! = ' \0 ' )
        Hashval + = * key ++ ;
    return ( Hashval % Tablesize ) ;
}
```
A simple hash function

18.2. Types of Hash Functions

1. Division Method.
2. Mid Square Method.
3. Multiplicative Hash Function.
4. Digit Folding.

1. Division Method

- It depends on remainder of division.
- Divisor is Table Size.
- Formula is (H (key) = key % table size)

E.g. consider the following data or record or key (36, 18, 72, 43, 6) table size = 8

Assume a table with 8 slots :

Hash key = key % table size

4	=	36	%	8
2	=	18	%	8
0	=	72	%	8
3	=	43	%	8
6	=	6	%	8

Index	Value
[0]	72
[1]	
[2]	18
[3]	43
[4]	36
[5]	
[6]	6
[7]	

2. Mid Square Method

We first square the item, and then extract some portion of the resulting digits. For example, if the item were 44, we would first compute $44^2=1,936$. Extract the middle two digit 93 from the answer. Store the key 44 in the index 93.

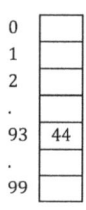

0	
1	
2	
.	
93	44
.	
99	

3. Multiplicative Hash Function

Key is multiplied by some constant value.

Hash function is given by,

H(key)=Floor (P * (key * A))

P = Integer constant [e.g. P=50]

A = Constant real number [A=0.61803398987]

E.g. Key 107

H(107)=Floor(50*(107*0.61803398987))

=Floor(3306.481845)

H(107)=3306

Consider table size is 5000

0	
1	
2	
.	
3306	107
.	
4999	

4. Digit Folding Method

The folding method for constructing hash functions begins by dividing the item into equal-size pieces (the last piece may not be of equal size). These pieces are then added together to give the resulting hash key value. For example, if our item was the phone number 436-555-4601, we would take the digits and divide them into groups of 2 (43, 65, 55, 46, 01). After the addition, 43+65+55+46+01, we get 210. If we assume our hash table has 11 slots, then we need to perform the extra step of dividing by 11 and keeping the remainder. In this case 210 % 11 is 1, so the phone number 436-555-4601 hashes to slot 1.

0	
1	436-555-4601
2	
3	
.	
8	
9	
10	

18.3. Collision

If two keys hashes to the same index, the corresponding records cannot be stored in the same location. So, if it's already occupied, we must find another location to store the new record.

Characteristics of Good Hashing Function

- It should be Simple to compute.
- Number of Collision should be less while placing record in Hash Table.
- Hash function with no collision ➔ Perfect hash function.
- Hash Function should produce keys which are distributed uniformly in hash table.

18.4. Collision Resolution Strategies / Techniques (CRT)

If collision occurs, it should be handled or overcome by applying some technique. Such technique is called CRT.

There are a number of collision resolution techniques, but the most popular are:

- Separate chaining (Open Hashing).
- Open addressing. (Closed Hashing).
  - Linear Probing.
  - Quadratic Probing.
  - Double Hashing.

18.4.1 Separate Chaining (Open Hashing)

- Open hashing technique.
- Implemented using singly linked list concept.

- Pointer (ptr) field is added to each record.
- When collision occurs, a separate chaining is maintained for colliding data.
- Element inserted in front of the list.

H (key) = key % table size

Two operations are there:

- Insert.
- Find.

Structure Definition for Node

```
typedef Struct node *Position;
Struct node
{
        int data;                            defines the nodes
        Position next;
};
```

Structure Definition for Hash Table

```
typedef Position List;
struct Hashtbl
{
        int Tablesize;                       Defines the hash table which contains
        List * theLists;                     array of linked list
};
```

Initialization for Hash Table for Separate Chaining

```
Hashtable initialize(int Tablesize)
{
        HashTable H;
        int i;
        H = malloc (sizeof(struct HashTbl));          ➔ Allocates table
            H ➔ Tablesize = NextPrime(Tablesize);
        H➔the Lists=malloc(sizeof(List) * H➔Tablesize);  ➔ Allocates array of list
        for( i = 0; i < H ➔ Tablesize; i++ )
        {
                H ➔ TheLists[i] = malloc(Sizeof(Struct node));   ➔ Allocates list headers
                H ➔ TheLists[i] ➔ next = NULL;
        }
        return H;
}
```

Insert Routine for Separate Chaining

```
void insert (int Key, Hashtable H)
{
  Position P, newnode;                *[Inserts element in the Front of the list always]*
  List L;
  P = find ( key, H );
  if(P = = NULL)
  {
        newnode = malloc(sizeof(Struct node));
        L = H → TheLists[Hash(key,Tablesize)];
        newnode → nex t= L → next;
        newnode → data = key;
        L → next = newnode;
  }
}
Position find( int key, Hashtable H)
{
  Position P, List L;
  L = H →TheLists[Hash(key,Tablesize)];
  P = L → next;
  while(P != NULL && P → data != key)
      P = P → next;
  return P;
}
```

If two keysmapto samevalue,the elements are chained together.

Initial configuration of the hash table with separate chaining. Here we use SLL(Singly Linked List) concept to chain the elements.

0	NULL
1	NULL
2	NULL
3	NULL
4	NULL
5	NULL
6	NULL
7	NULL
8	NULL
9	NULL

Insert the following four keys 22 84 35 62 into hash table of size 10 using separate chaining.

The hash function is

H(key) = key % 10

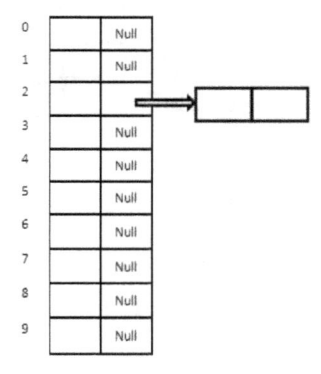

1. H(22) = 22 % 10

    = 2

```
0  | Null
1  | Null
2  | ─→ □ □
3  | Null
4  | Null
5  | Null
6  | Null
7  | Null
8  | Null
9  | Null
```

Insert the following four keys 22 84 35 62 into hash table of size 10 using separate chaining

The hash function is key % 10

84 %10 =4

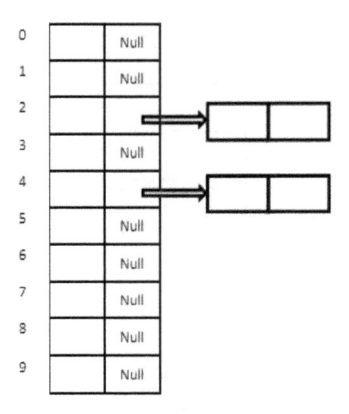

```
0  | Null
1  | Null
2  | ─→ □ □
3  | Null
4  | ─→ □ □
5  | Null
6  | Null
7  | Null
8  | Null
9  | Null
```

Insert the following four keys 22 84 35 62 into hash table of size 10 using separate chaining

The hash function is key % 10

35 %10 =5

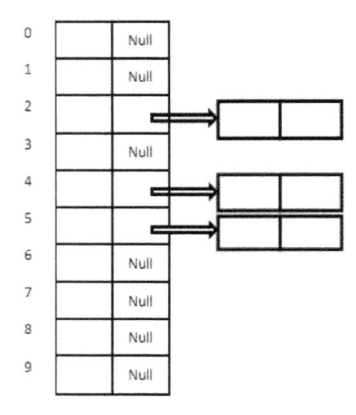

0		Null
1		Null
2		→ [22	]
3		Null
4		→ [84	]
5		→ [35	]
6		Null
7		Null
8		Null
9		Null

Insert the following four keys 22 84 35 62 into hash table of size 10 using separate chaining

The hash function is key % 10

62 %10 =2

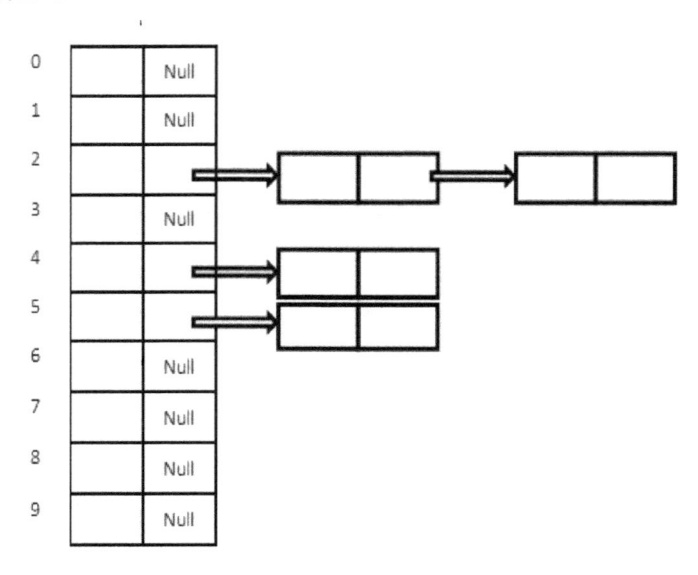

0		Null
1		Null
2		→ [22	] → [62	]
3		Null
4		→ [84	]
5		→ [35	]
6		Null
7		Null
8		Null
9		Null

Advantage

- More number of elements can be inserted using array of Link List.

Disadvantage

- It requires more pointers, which occupies more memory space.
- Search takes time. Since it takes time to evaluate Hash Function and also to traverse the List.

18.4.2 Open Addressing

- Closed Hashing.
- Collision resolution technique.
- When collision occurs, alternative cells are tried until empty cells are found.
- Types:
    - Linear Probing.
    - Quadratic Probing.
    - Double Hashing.
- Hash function
    - H(key) = key % table size.
- Insert Operation
    - To insert a key; Use the hash function to identify the list to which the element should be inserted.
    - Then traverse the list to check whether the element is already present.
    - If exists, increment the count.
    - Else the new element is placed at the front of the list.

18.4.3 Linear Probing

Easiest method to handle collision.

Apply the hash function H (key) = key % table size

How to Probing

- first probe – given a key k, hash to H(key).
- second probe – if H(key)+f(1) is occupied, try H(key)+f(2).
- And so forth.

Probing Properties

- we force f(0)=0.

261

- The ith probe is to (H (key) +f (i)) %table size.
- If I reach size-1, the probe has failed.
- Depending on f (), the probe may fail sooner.
- Long sequences of probe are costly.

Probe Sequence is

- H (key) % table size.
- H (key)+1 % Table size.
- H (Key)+2 % Table size.

1. **H(Key)=Key mod Tablesize**

    This is the common formula that you should apply for any hashing.
    If collocation occurs use Formula 2.

2. **H(Key)=(H(key)+i) Tablesize**

    Where i=1, 2, 3, ... etc

    Example: - 89 18 49 58 69; Tablesize=10

    1. H(89) =89%10

        =9

    2. H(18) =18%10

        =8

    3. H(49) =49%10

        =9 ((coloids with 89.So try for next free cell using formula 2))

        $\boxed{i=1}$ h1(49) = (H(49)+1)%10

        = (9+1)%10

        =10%10

        =0

    4. H(58) =58%10

        =8 ((colloids with 18))

        $\boxed{i=1}$ h1(58) = (H(58) +1)%10

        = (8+1) %10

        =9%10

        =9 =>Again collision

        $\boxed{i=2}$ h2(58) =(H(58)+2)%10

        =(8+2)%10

        =10%10 =0 =>Again collision

	EMPTY	89	18	49	58	69
0				49	49	49
1					58	58
2						69
3						
4						
5						
6						
7						
8				18	18	18
9		89	89	89	89	

Linear Probing

18.4.4 Quadratic Probing

insert(76)	Insert(93)	Insert(40)	Insert(47)	Insert(10)	Insert(55)
76%7=6	93%7=2	40%7=5	47%7=5	10%7=3	55%7=6

#							
0		0		0		0	47	0	47	0	47
1		1		1		1		1		1	55
2		2	93	2	93	2	93	2	93	2	93
3		3		3		3		3	10	3	10
4		4		4		4		4		4	
5		5		5	40	5	40	5	40	5	40
6	76	6	76	6	76	6	76	6	76	6	76
	1		1		1		3		1		1

263

To resolve the primary clustering problem, quadratic probing can be used. With quadratic probing, rather than always moving one spot, move i2 spots from the point of collision, where i is the number of attempts to resolve the collision.

- Another collision resolution method which distributes items more evenly.
- From the original index H, if the slot is filled, try cells H+12, H+22, H+32,.., H + i2 with wrap-around.

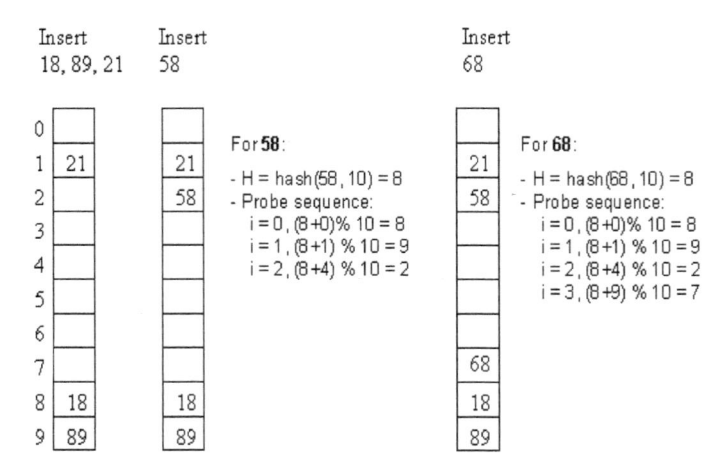

Insert
18, 89, 21

Insert
58

Insert
68

Index	Table 1	Table 2	For 58	Table 3	For 68
0			- H = hash(58, 10) = 8		- H = hash(68, 10) = 8
1	21	21	- Probe sequence:	21	- Probe sequence:
2		58	i = 0, (8+0)% 10 = 8	58	i = 0, (8+0)% 10 = 8
3			i = 1, (8+1) % 10 = 9		i = 1, (8+1) % 10 = 9
4			i = 2, (8+4) % 10 = 2		i = 2, (8+4) % 10 = 2
5					i = 3, (8+9) % 10 = 7
6					
7				68	
8	18	18		18	
9	89	89		89	

Limitation: at most half of the table can be used as alternative locations to resolve collisions. This means that once the table is more than half full, it's difficult to find an empty spot. This new problem is known as secondary clustering because elements that hash to the same hash key will always probe the same alternative cells.

18.4.5 Double Hashing

Double hashing uses the idea of applying a second hash function to the key when a collision occurs. The result of the second hash function will be the number of positions forms the point of collision to insert.

There are a couple of requirements for the second function:

It must never evaluate to 0 must make sure that all cells can be probed

A popular second hash function is:

Hash2 (key) = R - (key % R) where R is a prime number that is smaller than the size of the table.

Table Size = 10 elements
Hash$_1$(key) = key % 10
Hash$_2$(key) = 7 − (k % 7)

Insert keys: 89, 18, 49, 58, 69

Hash(89) = 89 % 10 = 9

Hash(18) = 18 % 10 = 8

Hash(49) = 49 % 10 = 9 a collision!
        = 7 − (49 % 7)
        = 7 positions from [9]

Hash(58) = 58 % 10 = 8
        = 7 − (58 % 7)
        = 5 positions from [8]

Hash(69) = 69 % 10 = 9
        = 7 − (69 % 7)
        = 1 position from [9]

Index	Value
[0]	49
[1]	
[2]	
[3]	69
[4]	
[5]	
[6]	
[7]	58
[8]	18
[9]	89

18.5. Rehashing

Once the hash table gets too full, the running time for operations will start to take too long and may fail. To solve this problem, a table at least twice the size of the original will be built and the elements will be transferred to the new table.

Advantage

- A programmer doesn't worry about table system.
- Simple to implement.
- Can be used in other data structure as well.

The New Size of the Hash Table

- Should also be prime.
- Will be used to calculate the new insertion spot (hence the name rehashing).
- This is a very expensive operation! O(N) since there are N elements to rehash and the table size is roughly 2N. This is ok though since it doesn't happen that often.

The Question Becomes When Should the Rehashing be Applied?

Some possible answers:

- once the table becomes half full.
- once an insertion fails.
- once a specific load factor has been reached, where load factor is the ratio of the number of elements in the hash table to the table size.

18.6. Extendible Hashing

Extendible Hashing is a mechanism for altering the size of the hash table to accommodate new entries when buckets overflow.

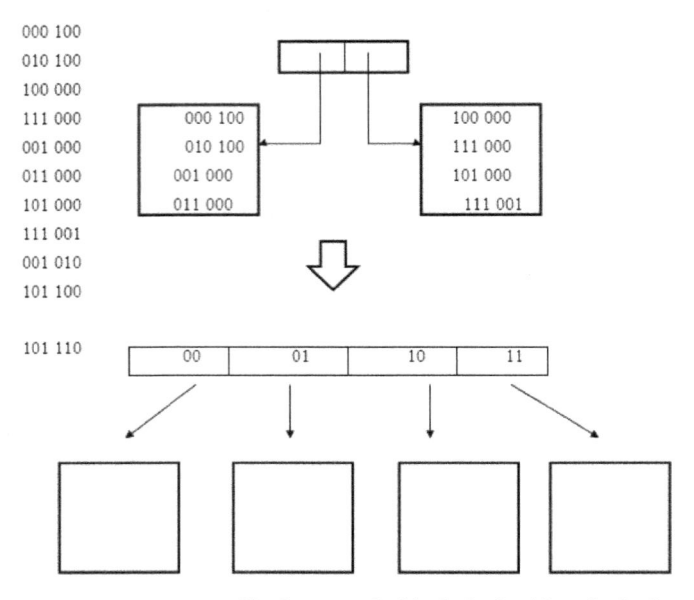

```
000 100
010 100
100 000
111 000        000 100              100 000
001 000        010 100              111 000
011 000        001 000              101 000
101 000        011 000              111 001
111 001
001 010
101 100

101 110     00    01    10    11
```

- Common strategy in internal hashing is to double the hash table and rehash each entry. However, this technique is slow, because writing all pages to disk is too expensive.
- Therefore, instead of doubling the whole hash table, we use a directory of pointers to buckets, and double the number of buckets by doubling the directory, splitting just the bucket that overflows.
- Since the directory is much smaller than the file, doubling it is much cheaper. Only one page of keys and pointers is split.

18.7. Applications of Hashing

- Construct a message authentication code (MAC).
- Digital signature.
- Make commitments, but reveal message later.
- Timestamping.
- Key updating: key is hashed at specific intervals resulting in new key.

Review Questions with Solution

1. What is meant by Sorting and searching?

Sorting and searching are fundamentals operations in computer science. Sorting refers tothe operation of arranging datain some given order it refers to the operation of searching the particular record from the existing information.

2. What are the types of sorting available inC?
   - Insertion sort.
   - Merge Sort.
   - Quick Sort.
   - Radix Sort.
   - Heap Sort.
   - Selection sort.
   - Bubble.

3. Define Bubble sort.

Bubble sort is the oneof the easiest sorting method.In this method each data item is compared with its neighbor and if it is an descending sorting , then the bigger number is moved to the top of all. The smaller numbers are slowly moved to the bottom position, hence it is also called as the exchange sort.

4. Mention the various types of searching techniques inC
   - Linear search.
   - Binary search.

5. What is linear search?

In Linear Search the list is searched sequentially and the position is returned if the keyelement to be searched is available in the list, otherwise-1 is returned.

The search in Linear Search starts at the beginning of an array and move to the end, testing for a match at each item.

6. What is binary search?
   - Binary search is simple rand faster than linear search. Here the array to be searched is divided into two parts, one of which is ignored as it will not contain there quired element.
   - One essential condition for the binary search is that the array which is to be searched, should be arranged in order.

7. Define mergesort?

Mergesort is based on divide and conquer method. It takes the list to bestored and divide itin half to create two unsorted lists. The two unsorted lists are then sorted and merged to get a sorted list.

8. What is the time complexity of binary search?(May/Jun 2014)

The complexity of an algorithm is the amount of a resource, such astime, that the algorithm requires. It is a measure of how 'good' the algorithm is at solving the problem. The complexity of a problem is defined as the best algorithm that solves a problem. Time complexity of binary search is O (log2n).

9. List the sorting algorithm which uses logarithmatic time complexity.(May/Jun 2014)

Algorithm	Time Complexity	
	Best	Average
Quicksort	O(n log(n))	O(n log(n))
Mergesort	O(n log(n))	O(n log(n))

10. Define Extendible hashing.(Nov\Dec 2014)

- Extendible Hashing is a mechanism for altering the size of the hash table to accommodate new entries when buckets overflow.
- Common strategy in internal hashing is to double the hash table and rehash each entry. However, this technique is slow, because writing all pages to disk is too expensive.
- Therefore, instead of doubling the whole hash table, we use a directory of pointers to buckets, and double the number of buckets by doubling the directory, splitting just the bucket that overflows.

11. Differentiate internal and external sorting.(Nov\Dec 2014)

Internal sorting takes place in the main memory of a computer. The internal sorting methods are applied to small collection of data. It means that, the entire collection of data to be sorted in small enough that the sorting can take place with in main memory. The External sorting methods are applied only when the number of data elements to be sorted is too large. These methods involve as much external processing as processing in the CPU. This sorting requires auxiliary storage.

12. What is meant by internal and external sorting? Give four examples of each type.(Apr\May 2015)

Internal Sorting takes place in the main memory of a computer. The internal sorting methods are applied to small collection of data. It means that, the entire collection of data to be sorted in small enough that the sorting can take place within main memory.

Examples–Bubble sort, Insertion sort, Selection sort, Shell sort.

This sorting methods are applied only when the number of data elements to be sorted is too large. These methods involve as much external processing as processing in the CPU. This sorting requires auxiliary storage Examples-Merge sort, Quick sort, Multi way Merge sort.

13. State the applications of linear and binary search techniques. (Apr\May 2015)

Searching is to find a target in a collection of elements, or determine the target does not exist. Here we consider data in arrays stored in the memory; while in real problems data may be stored in disk files, databases, or even distributed over the Internet.

B.E./B.Tech. Degree Examination, April/May 2015.

Second Semester

Computer Science and Engineering

CS 6202 – Programming and Data Structures – I

(Common to Information Technology)

(Regulation 2013)

Time : Three hours　　　　　　　　　　　　　　　　　　　　　　Maximum : 100 marks

Answer ALL Questions

PART A-(10 × 2 = 20 marks)

1. Give two examples of C preprocessor with syntax.
2. What are function pointers in C ? Explain with example.
3. What is the difference between getc( ) and getchar( ) ? Explain.
4. Explain the syntax as given below:
   Fread(&my_record, sizeof(struct rec),ptr_myfile);
5. Define ADT.
6. What is static linked list ? State any two applications of it.
7. Write the syntax of calloc( ) and realloc( ) and mention its application in linked list.
8. Given the prefix for an expression, write its postfix

   - * - + a b c / e f - g / h i
9. What is meant by internal and external sorting ? Give four example of each type.
10. State the applications of linear and binary search techniques.

PART B-(5 × 16 = 80 marks)

11. (a) (i) Write a function that returns a pointer to the maximum value of an array of double's. If the array is empty, return NULL. Double * maximum (double *a, int size) (8)

    (ii) Write a C program to find all the roots of a quadratic equation. (8)

    (or)

    (b) (i) Write a C program using function to check if the given input number is palindrome or not (8)

    (ii) Explain the C preprocessor operations, each with a neat example that is used to create macros. (8)

    (or)

12. (a) (i) Write a C program that uses functions to perform the following operations using structure:

    1) Reading a complex number.

2) Writing a complex number.
   3) Addition of two complex numbers.
   4) Multiplication of two complex numbers. (12)
   (ii) State the advantage and disadvantage of structures and unions in
   C Programming (4)
 (b) (i) Perform the following to manipulate file handling using C.
   1) Define an input file handle called *input_file*, which is a pointer to a type FILE.
   2) Using *input_file*, open the file *results.dat* for read mode.
   3) Write C statements which tests to see if *input_file* has opened the data file successfully. If not,print and error message and exit the program.
   4) Write C code which will read a line of characters (terminated by a\n)from *input_file* into a character array called buffer. NULL terminate the nuffer upon reading a \n.
   5) Close the file associated with input_file. (12)
   (ii) Using C programming, display the contents of a file on screen. (4)
13. (a) Write a C program to perform addition, subtraction and multiplication operations on polynomial using linked list. (16)

(or)

(b) Write C code for Circular link list with create, insert, delete, display operations using structure pointer. (16)

14. (a) (i) Write C program that checks if experssion is correctly parenthesized using stack (12)
   (ii) Write the function to checkfor state status as Full ( ) or Empty ( ). (4)

(or)

(b) Write C program to implement Queue functions using Arrays and Macros. (16)

15. (a) (i) Sort the given integers and show the intermediate results using shell sort 35, 12, 14, 9, 15, 45, 32, 95, 40, 5 (8)
   (ii) Write C code to sort an integer array using shell sort. (8)

(or)

 (b) (i) Explain a C code to perform binary search. (10)
   (ii) Explain the Rehashing techniques. (6)

B.E./B.Tech. Degree Examination, November/December 2014.

Second Semester

Computer Science and Engineering

CS 6202 – Programming and Data Structures – I

(Common to Information Technology)

(Regulation 2013)

Time : Three hours Maximum : 100 marks

Answer ALL Questions

PART A - (10 X 2 = 20 marks)

1. Define an array. Give an example.
2. Give example on call by reference.
3. What are the statements used for reading a file.
4. Define the need for union in C.
5. What are abstract data type?
6. What is circular linked list?
7. Give the applications of stack.
8. What is double ended queue?
9. Define extendible hashing.
10. Differentiate internal and external sorting.

PART B - (5 X 16 = 80 marks)

11. (a) Explain the various control statements in C language with example in detail. (16)

    (Or)

    (b) Briefly discuss about:
    1. Functions with number of arguments.
    2. Function Pointers. (8 + 8)

12. (a) Explain the difference between structure and union with examples. (16)

    (Or)

    (b) Explain about file manipulations in detail with suitable program. (16)

13. (a) Describe the creation of a doubly linked list and appending the list. Give relevant coding in C. (16)

    (Or)

    (b) Explain the following:
    1. Applications of lists.
    2. Polynomial manipulation. (8 + 8)

14. (a) Discuss about Stack ADT in detail. Explain any one application of stack. (16)

(Or)

(b) Explain about Queue ADT in detail. Explain any one application of queue with suitable example. (16)

15. (a) What are the different types of hashing techniques? Explain them in detail with example. (8 + 8)

(Or)

(b) Write an algorithm to sort a set of 'N' numbers using quick sort. Trace the algorithm for the following set of numbers:

88, 11, 22, 44, 66, 99, 32, 67, 54, 10. (16)

B.E./B.Tech. Degree Examination, May/June 2014.

Second Semester

Computer Science and Engineering

CS 6202 – Programming and Data Structures – I

(Common to Computer and Communication Engineering and Information Technology)

(Regulation 2013)

Time : Three hours　　　　　　　　　　　　　　　　　Maximum : 100 marks

Answer ALL Questions

PART A - (10 X 2 = 20 marks)

1. With the help of the printf function show how C handles functions with variable number of arguments.
2. Define macro with an example.
3. Give applications in which union rather than structures can be used.
4. Will the following declaration work. Justify your answer.

    Struct Student
    {
    　　int rollno = 12;
    　　float marks[] = { 55, 60, 56 };
    　　char gender;
    };

5. Should arrays or linked lists be used for the following types of applications. Justify your answer.
    a) Many search operations in sorted list.
    b) Many search operations in unsorted list.
6. What is advantage of an ADT?
7. Define double ended queue.
8. List the applications of a Queue.
9. What is the time complexity of binary search?
10. List sorting algorithm which uses logarithmatic time complexity.

PART B – (5 X 16 = 80 MARKS)

11. (a) (i) write a c program to find the unique elements in an arrya using a function 'Unique". The function takes the array as a parameter and prints the unique elements　　(10)

    (ii) Write a C program to print Fibonacci numbers.　　(6)

(Or)

(b) Write a C program to multiply two matrices that are represented as pointers. Use a function pointer to the function 'Multiply' which takes the two matrices as parameter and prints the result of the multiplication. (16)

12. (a) (i) Write a C program to read the contents of a file "in.txt" from last to first and write the contents to "out.txt". (8)

    (ii) Write the function prototype and explain how files are manipulated in C. (8)

(Or)

(b) (i) Create a structure to store a complex number and write function (for addition) that handles this new structure. (8)

    (ii) Write a program to perform the following operations for the customers of a bank using the concept of structures. (8)

1. Input the customer details like name, account number and balance.
2. When a withdrawal transaction is made the balance must change to reflect it.
3. When a deposit transaction is made the balance must change to reflect it..

13. (a) Write an algorithm to perform insertion and deletion on a doubly linked list. (16)

(Or)

(b) Consider an array A[1:n]. Given a position, write an algorithm to insert an element in the array. If the position is empty, the element is inserted easily. If the position is already occupied the element should be inserted with the minimum number of shifts. (Note: The elements can shift to the left or right to make the minimum number of moves) (16)

14. (a) Write an algorithm to convert an infix expression to a postfix expression. Trace the algorithm to convert the infix expression "(a+b)*c/d+e/f" to a postfix expression. Explain the need for infix and postfix expressions. (16)

(Or)

(b) Write an algorithm to perform the four operations in a double ended queue that is implemented as an array. (16)

15. (a) Write short notes on hashng and the various collision resolution techniques. (16)

(Or)

(b) Write an algorithm to sort 'n' numbers using quicksort. Show how the following numbers are sorted using quicksort: 45, 28, 90, 1, 46, 39. 33, 87. (16)

A			E		
Accessing Array Elements		54	Escape Sequences		11
Accessing Structure Member		101	Evaluating Arithmetic Expression		187
Application of Data Structure		130	Extendible Hashing		266
Applications of Hashing		266	F		
Applications of Queue		212	File Operations		112
Applications of Stack		186	For Loop		24
Array Implementation of List		132	Function Call		38
Array Implementation of Queue		202	Function Declarations		38
Array Implementation of Stack		174	Function Definition		38
Array of Structure		104	Function Pointer with Argument		86
B			Function Pointer without Argument		85
Balancing the Symbols		198	Function Pointers		84
Basic Structure of C Programming		3	Function Prototypes		41
Binary Search		250	Function with arguments and no return value		44
Break Statement in C		21	Function with Argument and a Return Value		44
Bubble Sort		236	Function with no arguments and no return value		42
C			Function with no arguments but with return value		42
C-Pointer to Pointer		86	Function with variable number of arguments		89
C Tokens		5	G		
Call by Reference		40	goto Statement in C		20
Call by Value		40	I		
Circular Linked List		149	Identifiers		5
Classification of Data Structure		131	if else Statement		17
Collision		256	Implementation of Queue		202
Collision Resolution Strategies/Techniques		256	Implementation of Stack		174
Conditional Statements		16	Initialization of String		68
Continue Statement		22	Insertion Sort		230
D			Introduction		2,16,34,53,68, 77,82,89,101, 112,173,201, 229,249,253
Data Types		5	Introduction to Control Statements		22
Declaration of Strings		68	L		
Defining a Structure		101	Library Functions		34

Linear Probing	261	**S**	
Linear Search	249	Sample Program for Arrays	59
Linked List Implementation of List	139	Sample Programs using structure and union	108
Linked List Implementation of Queue	207	Sample Programs	156
Linked List Implementation of Stack	179	Sample Programs for String Manipulations	71
List ADT	132	Selection Sort	232
M		Self-referential Structure	105
Macro Continuation	79	Separate chaining	256
Merge Sort	242	Shell sort	234
Methods to Implement a List	132	Singly linked list	139
Modifiers	6	Sorting Algorithms	229
N		Stack Model	173
Need for a file	112	Storage Classes	7
Nested if in C	17	String Handling Function	70
NULL Pointers in C	83	String Manipulations Using Library Functions	70
		Stringize	79
O		Structure as function argument	102
Open Addressing	261	Structure and pointer	103
Operations on Circular Queue	214	Switch statement	19
Operations on Queue	201	**T**	
Operations on Stack	173	Text file	112
Operators	12	The defined() Operator	80
P		Token Pasting	79
Parameter Passing Methods	39	Towers of Hanoi	195
Parameterized Macros	80	Type def in C	107
Passing Arrays as Function Arguments in C	56	Types of Array	53
Passing Strings to Functions	69	Types of File	112
Pointer Arithmetic	87	Types of C Functions	34
Predefined Macros	78	Types of Hash Functions	254
Preprocessor Directives in C	77	Types of Searching	249
Preprocessor Operators	78	Types of Sorting	229
Preprocessors Examples	77	**U**	
Q		Union	105
Quadratic Probing	263	User defined function	37
Qualifiers	6	**V**	
Queue Model	201	Variable	7
Quick Sort	239	Variation in pointer declarations	83
R		Void Pointers in C	84
Radix Sort	246	**W**	
Recursion	45	While loop	23
Reference Operator	82	Working of Pointers in C	82
Rehashing	265		